COMMON SENSE GOVERNMENT

COMMON SENSE GOVERNMENT

Works Better and Costs Less

VICE PRESIDENT

AL GORE

RANDOM HOUSE
NEW YORK

Publisher's Note:
On September 7, 1995, Vice President Al Gore
and the National Performance Review
released a report, entitled "Common Sense Government:
Works Better and Costs Less." This edition,
published by Random House, reproduces the text of the
Government Printing Office document.

Published in the United States by Random House, Inc., New York,
and simultaneously in Canada by Random House
of Canada Limited, Toronto.

ISBN 0-679-77132-8

Manufactured in the United States of America

2 4 6 8 9 7 5 3

FIRST EDITION

Foreword by President Bill Clinton

OUR COUNTRY NEEDS a government that is smaller and more responsive—that has lower cost but a higher quality of service—that moves more authority away from the federal government to states and localities, and to entrepreneurs in the private sector—that produces fewer regulations and more incentives—that has more common sense and seeks more common ground.

That kind of change in government is important for three reasons: First, government needs to change along with the people it serves. After all, we have moved through a rapid transition at the end of the Cold War, and at the end of the traditional industrial economy. We've moved into a global economy with new challenges, new conflicts characterized by a high rate of change, rapid movement of money and capital, and a revolution in information technology. In that environment, the model that we have used to deliver government services and fill public needs is simply no longer relevant to the present, let alone the future.

Second, even though we have cut our huge budget deficit in half, we need to eliminate it completely. Yet we still need to invest more money in critical priorities that help people convert from a Cold War economy to the twenty-first century global economy: like educating and training young people and adults, research and development, and new technologies. Our objectives are to build the American economy, to strengthen the American society, and to free up investment so that the American people can live up to the fullest of their potential.

That means that we must balance the budget, but not in a way that will drive us into a prolonged recession. We must not be penny-wise and pound-foolish. We have to cut spending, but use the money that's left in ways that really serve the American people and serve their larger purposes.

Third, we need to cure the anxiety and alienation many people feel toward their government. People will regain confidence in government if we make it work better. We need to make quality management the culture of government so that no future administration can fail to embrace it. It has to become part of the daily lives, the breathing, the working habits of every manager in the government, of every federal employee.

Above all, this is about fundamental values. Go back and read the Declaration of Independence and our Constitution. Americans created our government to do those things that can only be done by government—by all of us working together. Americans created government to be an instrument of the public interest.

We have to keep in mind that there are still public purposes that as far as we know today cannot be fully discharged without the involvement of America's national government—the health care of elderly citizens; the protection of our environment; the safety of our food; the needs of the people who have fought and won wars for us; giving the poor a chance to work their way into the middle class; giving our children, and increasingly our adults, access to the best possible education opportunities. Those are the values and priorities of the people of this country. They must be reflected in the budget and the activities of their government as well.

We in the government have a moral obligation to make government work right—to use the hard-earned money of the American people only in ways that further the public interest. If we can't do that, we can't justify being here and we can't justify taking the money.

So, we have begun the change. Not only to cut the size of government, to cut the number of programs and regulations, but to change the way the government *works*. To invest in education and the future, to develop new partnerships, and to move responsibilities to others who can more properly make the decisions. To provide service to Americans that is second to none.

We have surely not finished, nor succeeded in everything we have tried. But we have been faithful to our commitments. And we have made a great deal of progress.

This report is about the promise and the progress of government reinvention. It is about creating a government that makes sense, one that puts people first and gets results, one that gives Americans their money's worth. Our progress is America's progress, and every American can be proud of it.

Acknowledgments

REINVENTING THE FEDERAL government is no small task. Tens of thousands of federal employees, private citizens, state and local government officials, and business organizations have been involved so far. It is their persistent creativity to which we owe the greatest debt of gratitude. Their continued enthusiasm in this endeavor is our greatest hope.

Chronicling "the quiet revolution" of reinvention is no small task either. This year's report was researched by the staff of the National Performance Review and representatives of more than two dozen major federal agencies. Author and public policy consultant William E. Nothdurft built upon the foundation laid by David Osborne, Kathleen Sylvester, Janet Topolsky, Roger Vaughan, and Larry Haas in 1993, and again by Larry Haas last year.

Finally, for their leadership and plain hard work, I extend my thanks to Elaine Kamarck, Senior Policy Advisor to the Vice President; to Bob Stone, NPR's Project Director; and to John Kamensky, Deputy Project Director.

Contents

Introduction
by Philip K. Howard

On a hot August afternoon in 1991, I found myself talking with an elderly woman who lived in public housing on Manhattan's Lower East Side. Her refrigerator had broken, and she couldn't find anyone in the Housing Authority who could tell her how to get it fixed. As she told the story of being shunted from bureaucrat to bureaucrat, each passing responsibility to someone else, her face twisted in frustration.

That same morning I had been with the chief executive of a large company, and he began describing his ongoing failure to get a response from government on a large project. He then leaned forward to the chair's edge, as if reaching for help, and said "They won't say yes. They won't say no. They just won't respond." And his face twisted in frustration.

On that day, I realized that government had almost completely divorced itself from the citizens it supposedly serves. Rich or poor, conservative or liberal, Americans are united in their frustration at a government that has little interest even in discussing the sensible result.

At about the same time, Bill Clinton began focusing on the notorious inefficiencies of government. Drawing on the influential study by David Osborne and Ted Gaebler, *Reinventing Government,* President Clinton then set up the National Performance Review to begin making government work more effectively. For almost three years this group, under the direction of Al Gore, has been quietly changing the way government works. Clearing customs in Miami used to take days, but now reputable shippers can send goods through in hours.

Over 160,000 jobs have been cut from the federal workforce, saving billions.

The book you hold in your hand today, *Common Sense Government,* chronicles these changes and now announces the National Performance Review's most important reform: a complete U-turn away from the reigning philosophy of government regulation.

For over thirty years, the premise of government regulation has been that law should dictate the answer. Under this defective philosophy, no one—not the bureaucrat, not the private citizen—is allowed to use his own brain to achieve a sensible result. Regulation is supposed to be like an instruction manual, telling us not only what to do, but exactly how to do it. This approach, accepted by both parties, essentially bans common sense from all public decisions.

A dark legal shadow has steadily come across all the important institutions of our lives—schools, hospitals, factories, government itself. The simplest task now seems like moving a mountain, usually a mountain of forms and rules. No one, it seems, has the authority to say yes. Government has brought Americans to the brink where, whenever we encounter it, all our faces twist in frustration.

I hardly need to argue that this way of governing is not working well. Politicians have been apologizing or attacking it, depending on who's in office, for years. But this report, *Common Sense Government,* is the first one to present a plan for radical reorganization of how government works.

Common Sense Government boldly announces a strategy to reverse direction toward a government which, whatever its regulatory goals, will be able to serve American citizens instead of crushing us under rigid and often incomprehensible dictates. By laying aside political bickering, this nonpartisan plan holds the key to alleviating the frustration of Americans of every interest and philosophy. By searching for common sense, it embraces the common good.

FINDING COMMON SENSE

Critics of government usually focus, in my view, on the wrong problem. They think the government lacks common sense because it does too many stupid things, and, as it gets bigger, it just does more stupid things. I confess that ample evidence exists to support this view. Whenever a storm washes away beach houses, for example, the government pays the owners to build them again. Why, a taxpayer might ask, should government pay for the follies of those who build on sand and then are surprised by nature's nerve?

The beach-house subsidy, I was pleased to read in the Vice President's report, is being eliminated, along with a number of other nonsensical programs. Personally, picking up on Newt Gingrich's idea for a "corrections day" to fix bad laws, I think we could use a long period of similar corrections—perhaps we could call it Corrections Decade—to clean out programs that have outlived their actual or political usefulness.

But our frustration isn't caused mainly by unwise programs, but by government's inability to deal sensibly with almost any issue.

Common sense is mainly about *how* government does things. It is one thing for government to establish regulatory goals, wise or not, but it is quite another then to write thousands of rules to tell us exactly how to satisfy the goals.

Cleaning up the environment, for example, is a goal that virtually everyone supports. Disagreement exists on how far to go, but no one wants dirty water or filthy air. Environmental laws can nonetheless drive otherwise sane businessmen and property owners into raving maniacs. The reason is that the laws often force people to do things that are unnecessary and, in many cases, counterproductive.

In one incident, Amoco put a scrubber in the waste pipes at its Yorktown, Virginia, refinery to comply with a detailed rule designed to eliminate benzene, a harmful pollutant. It cost $31 million. This precisely drawn regulation, as it turned out, almost totally missed the pollution. Almost no benzene was going into the waste pipe. The benzene was escaping at the nearby loading dock. But there was no rule for the loading dock. The regulation was almost perfect in its failure: it maximized the cost to Amoco while minimizing the benefit to the public.

But, you might ask, hasn't government always been inept? Well, government never worked great, but it has gotten a lot worse in our lifetimes. Only a few decades ago, for example, public schools maintained order because teachers had some authority and were allowed to use their common sense.

The New Deal, the symbol of big government, actually accomplished much of what it set out to do. The WPA built hundreds of sewage treatment plants in only a few years. How long do you think it would take to get permits for one sewage treatment plant today? Dwight Eisenhower set up the interstate highway system with a short statute of less than thirty pages, and, in a little over a decade, the largest public works project in American history was substantially completed. Forest rangers, as Al Gore pointed out, used to be able to do their job with a pamphlet of guidelines that fit in their shirt pocket. Now they have to consult several volumes of rules.

What happened? Back in the 1960s, the age of Sputnik and moon expeditions, we decided to invent a scientific legal system that would cure, once and for all, the frailty of human judgment. At a time when values were clashing over civil rights and Vietnam, and the Cuyahoga River in Cleveland was so polluted that it caught fire, it was perhaps natural that we wanted to avoid decisions coming out of our existing institutions. In this new way of regulating, no one would have to make decisions. Rules would replace thinking. Process would replace responsibility.

Ironically, both the right and the left agreed on this point. Liberal reformers wanted iron legal manacles on slippery businessmen and authoritarian teachers. Conservatives, fighting a rear-guard action against big government, wanted to make sure power-hungry bureaucrats had no discretion. Bureaucrats and citizens alike were instructed that their job was only to comply with the detailed instructions, not to apply their own judgment in the particular situation.

After three decades of compulsive law writing—addressing each new situation with a new rule—we have ended up with a huge legal edifice, 100 million words of federal law alone, telling us exactly what to do. No one, of course, knows the law. There's too much of it.

Nor did the mutual distrust by conservatives and liberals prove productive. Binding up bureaucrats and citizens in layers of law just meant that neither's goals were accomplished. Telling Amoco to stop the benzene was obviously a sensible goal, but telling Amoco exactly how to catch the benzene was not much different than Soviet central planning. Both Amoco and EPA got a nonsensical result because neither had the authority to sit down and work out a more sensible plan.

Until now.

Common Sense Government promises an approach that liberates regulation from rigid rules.

One new program, "Project XL," encourages companies and regulators to use their common sense, and indeed, tells polluters they do not have to comply with detailed requirements of environmental law. The catch? Only that the company come up with a plan that EPA agrees can protect the environment more effectively. Companies like Amoco know a lot better how their refineries and factories work than any bureaucrat who spends his day hanging out in a government office building.

Since the announcement of Project XL, a line of companies have appeared at EPA's doorstep carrying plans that will significantly cut pollution. Until now, legal rigidity had fostered a "culture of resistance" that virtually precluded any honest dialogue. The simple act of opening the legal blinds has allowed good ideas to come pouring in.

Plenty of debate will still occur over how far environmental regulation should go. But common sense is apolitical. Buoyed by the favorable reaction from all corners, EPA Administrator Carol Browner is looking over seventeen volumes of cast-iron rules: "We're taking all the regulations that relate to the individual industries and putting them on the table."

RUNNING A COMMON SENSE GOVERNMENT

But how will common sense work?

Let's start with the easy part, where government is just managing itself and not enforcing regulatory goals on private citizens.

Many Americans believe that government squanders taxpayer money. They hear about $600 toilet seats and imagine an unruly crowd of lobbyists and second-rate suppliers feeding at the public trough. These nightmares, unfortunately, are basically accurate.

But the reason isn't what most Americans expect. It isn't that bureaucrats are handing out special favors or that they are too stupid to see what is happening (although those things sometimes happen). The reason is that government employees are told, "Don't think. Just follow the procedures."

You may remember Al Gore on *David Letterman* two years ago, donning goggles while he smashed a government ashtray that had been specifically designed to break apart in a certain way. As a result of his efforts, Congress passed legislation that actually allows contracting officials—hold on to your seats—sometimes to shop around for commercially available products. Because of this small concession to common sense, government has realized savings in the order of 50 percent, saving millions of dollars. Duffle bags that cost $6.75 now cost $2.29. Long underwear is now $6.95 instead of $10.22.

Buying goods and services is hardly rocket science, and yet government contracting is still governed by over 5,500 pages of rules. The rules exist only to prevent bureaucrats from making ordinary commercial judgments.

The cost of this rigidity is staggering. The federal government spends $200 billion in outside contracts each year and, knowledgeable observers estimate, it wastes at least 30 percent of it. That's enough to pay for one third of the annual federal deficit. A recent audit of Houston's Veterans Administration research lab showed that it paid, on average, over 40 percent more for the same supplies as Baylor University's nearby lab.

But the seed of common sense is now planted. Al Gore has enlisted the leading critic of government procurement, Professor Steven Kelman of Harvard's Kennedy School of Government. Kelman is working with leaders of both parties and, with the cooperation of Congress, all these rules could be replaced by contracting professionals—mere mortals—who could be allowed to use their common sense to try to save taxpayers money. And, as a side benefit, we'll know who to check up on.

How much improvement, you might ask, can we realistically expect from government? Look at the National Security Agency's travel office. Before these reforms, it took 79 days to process the paperwork for a business trip. Now costs are down 75 percent, the time for paperwork is down 93 percent, and the office is ranked by *Business Travel News* in the top four of all American businesses, alongside Hewlett-Packard, Bankers Trust, and Texas Instruments.

There's no genetic defect in bureaucrats that keeps them from being effective. *Common Sense Government* is loaded with stories that, to those familiar with government, are almost like miracles.

REGULATING WITH COMMON SENSE

But where does common sense fit in when government is telling private citizens what to do? A factory cannot use common sense, after all, to tell it how much it can pollute.

Laying out public goals in the law, like environmental standards, is obviously important. But people must be allowed latitude to meet those goals. As Randall Browning, an Amoco environmental manager, put it: "What is the point of spending

$31 million to solve a problem that wasn't a problem while doing nothing about the real problem? Give us a goal to meet rather than all the regulations." That's what governing by common sense promises.

The exile of common sense from regulation has been most harmful in areas like teaching, nursing care, and worker safety. Success in these activities hinges on human qualities, not anything that can be written in a detailed rule. Jamming the complex shapes of human choices through square legal holes just leaves us bruised and broken, unable to accomplish any goals.

The Occupational Safety and Health Act is a classic example. Enacted in 1970 with the worthy goal of protecting the safety of every worker "to the maximum extent feasible," OSHA has written over 4,000 rules detailing, well, just about everything they could think of—what kind of ladder to buy, how high the railings should be, even a rule on keeping the storage closets neat and tidy. Business has spent tens of billions of dollars complying, but, after every inspection, even the most diligent factory finds itself with thousands of dollars of fines. Last year, a small bakery in Chicago was fined $2,500 for not having the proper warning form for the Clorox under its kitchen sink.

All this regulating has done almost nothing for worker safety, because it doesn't focus on what's important. Lax management and careless attitudes are critical problems. The height of a railing is not. But it is hard to make a rule about careless attitudes, so OSHA has focused on railings.

In *Common Sense Government*, the Clinton administration has announced that OSHA will now redirect its energies from nitpicky violations to actual results. Letting in a little common sense, as found by an OSHA experiment in Maine, has had remarkable results.

As described in *Common Sense Government*, the two hundred largest companies in Maine were told that they would no longer have to dread the safety inspections and inevitable laundry list of violations as long as they sat down with their workers and drew up their own safety program. Within one year, the injury rates in Maine, which previously had the worst safety record in the nation, dropped 35 percent. Companies and their workers began identifying the real hazards and felt free to ignore the numerous minor violations. (Who cares if the closet is messy?) One company reported that the new program also boosted worker morale and, as a result, increased overall productivity by 25 percent.

Regulating with common sense is a process that encourages people to take responsibility and, where there are differences, to look each other in the eye and work it out.

But whose common sense, I am sometimes asked, do I trust? The question misses the point: Common sense isn't some absolute truth. Often the "common sense solution" is the result of a dialogue or an argument between, say, the safety inspector and the foreman, or between the citizen getting a permit and the bureaucrat behind the desk. There are many ways to skin a cat. What I trust is not any particular person's common sense, but the ability of all people to argue for what they think is right. And I have noticed no reluctance in people to complain when things go wrong. Let people on the spot think for themselves.

Allowing common sense gives both sides more control to achieve a fair result. A bureaucrat can bear down on the sleazy businessman who is trying to play fast and loose. A businessman can stand up to an unreasonable inspector and, if necessary, appeal the decision up the ladder. No one has absolute power. Both sides are at risk. And that maximizes the chance for a sensible result, because most of the time people will go back and forth until they come up with a reasonable resolution.

As government wrote rules at the speed of fast-forward for the last thirty years, it forgot that law is not supposed to dictate exactly how to do things. Law is mainly a framework that allows individuals to search for the just and fair answer. Supreme Court Justice Benjamin Cardozo, writing in the 1920s, said that he too was "disheartened" when he realized no "solid land of fixed and settled rules existed." Yet, as he explained, life is too complicated for law to be an instruction manual:

> No doubt the ideal system, if it were attainable, would be a code at once so flexible and so minute, as to supply in advance for every conceivable situation the just and fitting rule. But life is too complex to bring the attainment of this idea within the compass of human power.

I realized how far we had gone in the wrong direction when I recently debated before Congress a lawyer who opposes government contracting reform. He made the following pronouncement: "What America is about," he said, "is rules."

What America is about, of course, is freedom. Individuals must be allowed to think and do as they believe best. That is the only way, outside and inside of government, things get done sensibly.

COMMON SENSE ON THE HORIZON

Waking up tomorrow morning, Americans are unlikely to see a huge difference in their lives. Making sense of thirty years of lawmaking won't be accomplished in one day, or even in several years. Bad habits are still habits, and many will be hard to break.

Right away, however, *Common Sense Government* provides all Americans with something important. It allows us to begin to talk back to rules that don't make sense.

Modern regulation has allowed us to talk only in a binary language: Is it legal or illegal? From now on the main question should be this: What is reasonable? Black and white regulations will begin to take on the tints of gray that reflect life's complexity.

Common Sense Government provides numerous examples of how this will work. The rancher in Arizona will not have to test for pesticides that are only used on Hawaiian pineapple plantations. One Miami company that used to file 700,000 customs forms every year now files one per month. Pension rules will no longer be so complex that they discourage employers from providing their workers with pension-plan benefits. Who knows, with a little help from legislators, maybe teachers will regain the authority to run their classrooms.

Scraping away decades of bureaucratic rules is well under way. This year alone, as *Common Sense Government* reports, the Clinton administration has eliminated over 16,000 pages of rules out of 130,000, and is revising another 30,000, a prodigious start toward a government which allows room for judgment on the spot. With the help of Congress, more rules could be cut, in my view dramatically more, without damaging any regulatory goals. Setting basic regulatory standards doesn't require that much ink. What keeps the rule writers and printing presses running day and night is telling us how to perform every task.

In 1937 a blue ribbon committee made the following point in a report to President Roosevelt:

> Government is a human institution . . . it is human throughout; it rests not only on formal arrangements . . . but even more upon attitudes . . . it is certainly not a machine . . . what we want is not a streamlined, chromium trimmed government that looks well in the advertisement, but one that will actually deliver the goods in practice."

Common Sense Government announces that government will once again aspire to be a human institution. No longer will our leaders bow before rules which promise a perfect system and end up delivering only failure and frustration. From now on, the focus will be on people. This means the rules must be simple enough to be understandable, and flexible enough so that individuals can try to make sense of each situation.

When Americans are released from rigid and mindless rules, as the many stories in Vice President Gore's *Common Sense Government* make clear, we can accomplish things we had almost given up on.

Common Sense Government is an important event for America. I urge all Americans to read it and then demand it in their own dealings with government.

COMMON SENSE GOVERNMENT

Overview

People said it couldn't be done. When President Bill Clinton announced in March 1993 that "the federal government is broken and we intend to fix it," the old hands in Washington, D.C., shook their heads. You'll never fix the federal government, they said. Been there, done that, doesn't work.

When he announced a governmentwide initiative to "reinvent government" called the National Performance Review, the skeptics raised a collective eyebrow.

And six months later, when the National Performance Review's first report—*From Red Tape to Results: Creating a Government that Works Better and Costs Less*, the blueprint for reinvention—was published, they sighed, "Another report for the shelf."

But they didn't count on the experts President Clinton called in to run the show.

CALLING IN THE REAL EXPERTS

If you want to make a real change, you have to engage the people most likely to be affected—the ones who are already involved and who have the most at stake in getting the job done right. You have to seek their advice and give them the power to fix what they—more than anyone else—know needs fixing.

The bigwigs who said the federal government couldn't be reinvented had never talked to the real experts. When they said it couldn't be done, they didn't count on the folks who

REINVENTING GOVERNMENT: A HISTORY

On March 3, 1993, President Bill Clinton asked Vice President Al Gore to lead the National Performance Review, a campaign to reinvent the federal government. Milestones:

- September 7, 1993, Vice President Gore presents 384 recommendations in the report *From Red Tape To Results: Creating a Government That Works Better and Costs Less.*
- September 14, 1994, first year *Status Report* published.
- September 20, 1994, *Putting Customers First: Standards for Serving the American People* published—the government's first-ever customer service standards.
- September 7, 1995, publication of *Common Sense Government: Works Better and Costs Less*, describing the impact of reinvention on the American people and their government and presenting more than 300 *new* recommendations.

had been wanting the chance to do things right for years, the folks who had been trapped between the needs of the American people and the rigidity of the government bureaucracy.

• They didn't count on Bill Freeman, the Occupational Health and Safety Administration's man in Maine. Freeman's inspection team won award after award for finding and fining worker safety violations, yet he knew injury rates weren't improving. So he sat down with the companies with the most injuries, and negotiated agreements that would really work. Now, the companies' own workers are finding and fixing *14 times* as many hazards as Freeman's people could have found. Worker injuries are dropping, and it's costing less.

• They didn't count on Bob Molino, director of procurement for the Defense Logistics Agency. Molino got fed up with 700-page specifications for chocolate chip cookies, massive and costly inventories of unused supplies languishing in government warehouses, and a rigid and senseless system of sealed bids for selecting suppliers. He keelhauled the whole system. Now Defense buys many of its supplies from normal commercial suppliers like everyone else does. And it's using an electronic purchasing system so simple and inexpensive that other agencies are asking Defense to handle their purchases too.

• They didn't count on Neil Jacobs, of the Immigration and Naturalization Service in Dallas. Jacobs decided it was crazy to surround a factory and arrest and deport immigrants with fraudulent papers. This only crippled the business that had unknowingly hired them—and the workers themselves simply returned a few weeks later. Now, Jacobs meets with the business owner, arranges for legal replacement workers at the same wages, and *then* deports the illegal immigrants—protecting the business and filling the vacancies the illegal immigrants might try to come back to claim. At last, business owners feel helped, not harassed.

Don't believe it? Then believe the Ford Foundation and John F. Kennedy School of Government at Harvard, which named these and other federal reinvention initiatives as finalists for the prestigious Innovations in American Government awards this year.

THERE'S A WRONG WAY AND A RIGHT WAY

Sure, people have tried to reform the federal government before—almost a dozen times this century, and almost always unsuccessfully. But most of these earlier attempts went nowhere because they were done backwards: from the top down instead of the bottom up. They didn't ask for ideas from the American public—or from the federal government's own front-line workers, who try to serve the public every day. Most often, the efforts consisted of studies led by outsiders with no real stake in the results.

Doomed from the start, they failed. It could hardly have been otherwise.

As frustration with the federal government has mounted, some people, including many in Congress, have decided that the way to fix government is just to eliminate as much of it as possible. That might help bring the budget into line—or it might do no more than shift around a lot of organizational "boxes." Much of the government would then simply continue operating as it always had.

The main problem with taking an axe to the federal government is that it won't fix what remains. Government would be smaller, but it would still be as inflexible and bureaucratic. Cutting may treat a couple of symptoms, but it won't cure the disease.

RECLAIMING GOVERNMENT "FOR THE PEOPLE"

Americans are frustrated, irritated, confused, even angry about our government—about the cost, and the hassle, and the in-

Reinvention at a Glance

Reinvention Is Well Under Way

- Agencies have completed nearly one-third of NPR's original recommendations; of the remainder, nearly all are well under way.
- More than 200 agencies have published customer service standards.
- Agencies have created nearly 200 "reinvention labs" to test new approaches to business.
- The President has issued 30 directives to implement NPR recommendations.
- Agencies have formed more than 400 labor-management partnerships with their unions.

Government Costs Less

- $58 billion of NPR's $108 billion in savings proposed in 1993 are already locked in.
- $4 billion in NPR-related savings are pending before Congress.
- $46 billion in savings are still to come, based on 1993 proposals.
- Agencies have put in place $10 billion in reinvention savings beyond the recommendations made in the original 1993 report.
- Federal employment has dropped more than 160,000; reductions are nearly a full year ahead of schedule.
- More than 180 new recommendations will result in an additional $70 billion in savings over the next five years.

Government Is Becoming Less Intrusive

- Agencies are sending 16,000 pages of obsolete regulations to the scrap heap, of 86,000 pages of regulations reviewed.
- Agencies are reworking another 31,000 pages of regulations.
- Regulatory and administrative burdens on the public will be reduced by nearly $28 billion.
- Attitudes are changing; in many cases, fines will be waived for honest mistakes.
- Agencies are closing more than 2,000 field offices.

Congress Is Helping

- Congress has enacted 36 NPR-related laws, including the biggest procurement streamlining bill ever, with a second in progress.
- Congress has passed 66 of the 280 NPR items requiring legislation (24 percent).
- Nearly 70 NPR-related bills are currently pending in Congress.
- Congress has held more than 120 hearings on various NPR recommendations.

flexible rules, and the uncooperative attitude. But we're even angrier that our great dream seems to be slipping away—the dream of a government that is "of the people, by the people, and for the people," a government that isn't "them" but "us." And we don't want to give up on that dream. It is what set us apart from the rest of human history nearly 220 years ago, when we

Report at a Glance

A Government That Makes Sense

America was born angry at government nearly 220 years ago, and we're no different today. The less government there is, the more we like it—until disaster strikes, or we lose our job, or need medical care we can't afford. Then we want government to be there for us, and quickly.

For years, Americans had been complaining their government was in their face, not on their side. That was then. This is now: throughout government, front-line workers are asking their customers what they need, instead of telling them. They are beginning to manage the work of the people like the best in business. Federal Agencies are actually getting fan mail. Social Security's "800" number is rated better than L.L. Bean's for customer service.

Along the way, government is getting smaller. As a result of actions taken on recommendations made in 1993, there are more than 160,000 fewer federal workers than when President Clinton and Vice President Gore took office. It is becoming smaller daily. Savings totaling $58 billion are locked in. Another $50 billion are on the way.

Americans have waited a long time for a government that makes more sense. Out of frustration, some have proposed scrapping large portions of it. But this isn't what the people say they want. Polls show Americans are angered less by what government does than by how it goes about its business. We want it better managed. We want it to use common sense.

Getting Results

People want to do the right thing. Problem is, the government makes it almost impossible to figure out what the right thing is. So President Clinton challenged federal agencies earlier this year to overhaul in 100 days the way the government regulates people and businesses—by focusing on results, not red tape.

He asked agencies to assume people are honest, not dishonest, and intelligent, not stupid. He asked that rules be written in plain language and that obsolete rules be dropped. He asked that agencies get out of Washington, create partnerships with those being regulated, and negotiate, not dictate. As a result, of the 86,000 pages of federal regulations reviewed so far, 16,000 pages of obsolete regulations are headed for the scrap heap. Another 31,000 are being reworked. Agencies held more than 300 meetings around the country and identified 40 instances where negotiating made sense. Agencies are beginning to evaluate their employees' performance based on results, like reduced worker injuries, and not on the number of fines or penalties assessed. In the process, they are reducing regulatory and administrative burdens on the public by nearly $28 billion.

Putting Customers First

Last year, in many cases for the first time, federal agencies asked their customers what they wanted and how they defined good service. They used these results to develop customer service standards. Then more than 200 agencies did something most businesses don't do—they published their standards and distributed them to their customers. Just recently, agencies surveyed their customers to find out how well the government is living up to those standards, and they will use the responses to improve service even more. In addition, several agencies are comparing their operations to the best in business—and increasingly are beating them.

Getting Our Money's Worth

Obsolete government programs and waste drive Americans crazy—after all, it's their money. Since the reinventing government initiative began in 1993, the Clinton Administration has proposed eliminating more than 400 obsolete programs and is in the process of closing more than 2,000 unnecessary field offices.

But that wasn't enough. President Clinton asked Vice President Gore to launch a new effort to identify additional programs that could be reinvented, terminated, privatized, or sold. He identified nearly $70 billion in new savings. The Energy Department will sell the Naval Petroleum and Oil Shale Reserves. The Office of Personnel Management has privatized its training operations. The Department of Housing and Urban Development will consolidate its 60 programs into four, Congress willing. The Department of Transportation plans to shrink its 10 agencies into three. And more.

In addition, to better manage its business, the government is beginning to measure what matters. Government must be accountable every day, not just every four years at the election booth. As a result, the President is signing performance agreements with his major agency heads. All agencies are developing measures of performance. And by 1998, the federal government will have its first financial statement. Americans will soon know for the first time whether they are getting what they pay for.

Conclusion

At the turn of the century, the phrase "good enough for government work" meant the best. Now it is a term of derision—much like the phrase "made in Japan" meant cheap and shoddy just two decades ago. Now "made in Japan" is a sign of the best there is in many product categories. With the hard work of federal employees, the phrase "good enough for government work" will mean the same. Already in many instances, government isn't just fixed, it's the best. Social Security's toll-free number is the best. The Air Combat Command's pharmacy is the best. The Consumer Product Safety Commission's hotline is the best. *Business Week, Newsweek,* the *New York Times,* and *Financial World* have noticed. For the first time, the Ford Foundation and the Kennedy School of Government will make prestigious awards to several federal agencies for their innovations.

If you haven't felt a difference yet, you will. This year. Many of the initiatives begun this past year are being expanded nationwide. The federal government will regain the faith of the American people, says President Clinton, "one customer at a time."

declared independence from England, and it's what we stand for throughout the world today.

And while the great debate continues over what government should do, we know what basics we expect to get: protection from enemies here and abroad, clean air and water, food that's safe to eat and toys that are safe for our kids to play with, help in emergencies, safe workplaces, and so on. We don't want to get rid of government; we want it to work better and cost less. We want it to *make sense*.

And we're pretty clear about what common-sense government means:

• It means a government that focuses on results, that moves heaven and earth to make it easy for all of us—citizens, businesses, and state and local governments—to meet the nation's common goals, instead of burying us in rules and punishing us when we can't figure out how to comply.

• It means a government that recognizes that we are its customers, works with us to understand our needs, and puts us first, not last.

• And it means getting our money's worth—a government that works better, faster, and cheaper than in the past, one that operates as well as, or better than, the best private businesses.

DELIVERING THE GOODS AT LAST

For two years, quietly but persistently, thousands of ordinary Americans—Americans who happen to work for the federal government—have been striving to change dramatically what the government does and how it does it. And folks who keep tabs on things—*Business Week*, *Newsweek*, *The New York Times*, and others—have been taking notice.

The *New York Times* calls it the "quiet revolution." It's pick-and-shovel work—hard, often tedious, but crucial. The plain fact is that if you want to change something big in a big way, you can't get by with a little light landscaping and a coat of paint. You have to excavate and renovate. And you can't do it overnight.

And progress is everywhere around us. In 1993, the Administration announced a goal to save $108 billion and cut 252,000 government jobs—especially administrative jobs that don't serve people directly—in five years. (Congress and the President later raised this last goal to 272,900.) Both tasks are ahead of schedule: savings locked into place total $58 billion (53 percent of the goal), and job reductions total more than 160,000 (60 percent of the goal). Of the 1,250 recommendations in the 1993 blueprint, 379 (30 percent) have been implemented, 214 (17 percent) require legislative action, and 657 (53 percent) are still in the pipeline. The Administration recently developed more than 180 additional recommendations that, when implemented, will result in $70 billion in new savings over the next five years. These savings have already been incorporated in President Clinton's balanced budget proposal.

In addition, President Clinton has issued 30 reinvention directives on customer service, agency streamlining, procurement reform, labor-management relations, cooperation and partnerships with state and local governments, paperwork reduction, and regulatory reform, among others. And Congress has passed 36 laws to implement reinvention recommendations.

This report, *Common Sense Government: Works Better and Costs Less*, is a report to the American people on the progress of the "quiet revolution" to reinvent the federal government—what it is, how it's going, and what it means for ordinary folks.

IT'S NEVER FINISHED

They said it couldn't be done ... and it isn't. Reinventing the federal government isn't an event. It isn't an Act of Congress or a Presidential Executive Order. Nor is it something you can accomplish with a swing of the budget axe.

Reinvention Rolls On!

In 1995 NPR worked with agencies to develop more than 180 new recommendations for improving agency programs and serving customers better. Some highlights of the recommendations include:

Consolidate Operations

- Consolidate servicing of USDA's $30 billion single-family housing loan portfolio and close some county offices to save $250 million.
- Realign Small Business Administration operations to save $122 million and improve service by increasing public-private partnerships.
- Eliminate a layer of management in the Department of Health and Human Services by combining the Office of the Assistant Secretary for Health with the Office of the Secretary.
- Merge the Agency for Toxic Substances and Disease Registry with the Centers for Disease Control and Prevention.

Give Customers a Choice

- Shift HUD public housing funding directly to tenants, who can determine where they want live.
- Pay Department of Labor job training grants directly to workers rather than passing funds through states or private contractors.

Increase Local Control

- Increase the State role in the Superfund Program and decrease EPA's role, saving $283 million.

• Shift control of transportation-related spending from the Department of Transportation to the states.

Cancellations / Terminations

• Eliminate Commerce's National Oceanic and Atmospheric Administration Corps, saving $35 million.

• Shave $1.2 billion over five years from Energy's applied research programs, ending the Clean Coal Technology Program.

• Eliminate Interior's Office of Territorial and International Affairs, saving $5 million.

• Abolish the Interstate Commerce Commission, saving $129 million.

Adminstrative Changes

• Target Medicare Program abusers in five key states and develop a health care fraud fund to pay for investigations and prosecutions.

• Allow employees at large companies to file for Social Security benefits through their company's personnel office, to save $289 million.

• Improve debt collection practices at Treasury, Labor, and Education to increase revenues by more than $1 billion.

Privatization

• Convert Connie Lee from a government corporation to a fully privatized entity.

• Shift NASA's space craft communications to private sources to save $200 million.

• Convert Sallie Mae from a government corporation to a fully privatized entity.

This effort to reinvent government, part of the ongoing National Performance Review, is becoming a way of life for employees in agencies and the customers they serve across the nation. It's like the job of painting the Golden Gate Bridge in San Francisco. The story goes that the task is so huge that by the time the painters get to the far end of the bridge, it's time to go back to the beginning and start again. It never stops. It's never "finished."

The world has become more complex, and so has our government. Yet even as the government has become more complicated, it has been slow to adapt to real changes in the world —particularly those changes driven by advances in technology and communication. Along the way, the government has become distant from the people it is supposed to serve and, occasionally, lost touch with what it was created to do nearly 220 years ago. Our nation began with a solemn covenant: that the government that we were establishing would be the people's servant—not their master.

We need to renew that covenant for the next century. That's what reinventing government is all about.

YOU ARE OUR CUSTOMER.

If you've felt a difference, let us know. If you haven't, let us know that, too.

Write to: Vice President Al Gore
Reinventing Government
Washington, DC 20501

I

A Government That Makes Sense

In framing a government . . . you must first enable [it] to control the governed; and in the next place oblige it to control itself.

JAMES MADISON
The Federalist, *No. 40 (1787)*

AMERICA WAS BORN angry at government. We were so sick of the English Crown treating us like, well, *colonies*, that we did what no career counselor today would recommend: we quit colonialism before we had something else lined up. We weren't entirely sure what we wanted—indeed, we argued among ourselves about it at length—but we knew what we didn't want, and that was to be jerked around by a distant and insensitive government.

We're no different today.

And today, once again, we feel our government has become distant and insensitive—not to mention too big, too meddlesome, and too costly. We don't much care whether it's a problem of politicians, issues, or government agencies—or even if it's federal, state, or local. It's just a problem. A big one.

Distrust of government is buried deep in America's genetic code. For more than two centuries, wave after wave of people who have been harassed or abused by their governments have seen this country as a last refuge, a haven: persecuted French Huguenots and Cambodians, Irish famine survivors and Salvadoran refugees, people fleeing Nazi Germany and Somalia. Our ancestors' distrust of authority is deeply ingrained in our national character. Take a close look at your birth certificate.

Down in the fine print—after "Citizen: U.S.; Birthplace: Peoria; Eyes: brown; Blood type: B positive"—it says, "Attitude: Distrusts government." If it's not there, it should be: it's who we are.

The less government there is, the more we like it...

Until the earth cracks open in California and people's lives crack with it. Until the rains keep raining in the heartland and people's achievements and memories disappear in a swirl of angry brown water. Until a river becomes so polluted that it catches fire. Until a child dies from a contaminated hamburger. Or until we lose a job, need help feeding our family, grow old and can't afford medical care for our infirmities, or become victimized on our own neighborhood streets. Then we want that government to be there for us, and quickly.

THE REAL BUSINESS OF GOVERNMENT

The call came in to the Washington, D.C., headquarters of the Federal Emergency Management Agency (FEMA) at 9:30 a.m. on Wednesday, April 19, 1995. Twenty-eight minutes earlier, at 9:02 a.m., a bomb had exploded in front of the Alfred P. Murrah Federal Building in Oklahoma City, killing scores of government workers and the citizens they serve, and injuring hundreds more. Now Tom Feuerborne, director of the state's Civil Emergency Management Department, was on the line asking for help.

A couple of years earlier he would have been told that his governor needed to file a written request for federal emergency assistance and mail it to Washington. No longer. Four and a half hours after Feuerborne's call, at 2:05 p.m., FEMA's advance team got there, complete with damage assessors. At

8:10 p.m., James Lee Witt, FEMA's director, arrived to personally coordinate the federal response. Witt had been a state emergency services director himself and he knew the drill. By 2:30 a.m., FEMA's own search and rescue teams were on the scene to help the city's fire department.[1]

Can the federal government meet the needs of the American people? Without question, yes. It takes a radical rethinking of what government should do and how.

Meanwhile, the federal agencies whose Oklahoma offices were shut down were working furiously to restore services for their customers throughout the region. Within hours of the blast, the Social Security Administration had arranged for its Dallas office to provide services to the citizens the Oklahoma City office served. GSA was setting up temporary office locations all over the city so federal agencies could restore their services to the public. By the next day, the Department of Labor was issuing apprenticeship certifications out of an employee's home, so that construction workers' pay would be uninterrupted. The U.S. Marine Corps Recruitment office was keeping appointments in a new location. The Federal Highway Administration was operating out of the Federal Aviation Administration's offices elsewhere in the city. The Department of Agriculture was issuing health certificates for animals awaiting export to Canada, Japan, and Taiwan so customers did not lose expensive reserved air cargo space.

Oklahoma City reminded America that "the government" isn't something separate. It is ourselves—our neighbors and friends trying to do their jobs. The bomb turned these simple acts of service into heroic acts. Yet helping people is what people in the federal government do every day.

At the same time, the event taught us that when it needs to, the government can untangle itself from its own red tape and take care of people's needs. Quickly. Efficiently. And well.

Can the federal government meet the needs of the American people? Without question, yes. Does it take a disaster for it to work right? No, it does not.

Rather, it takes a radical rethinking of what government *should* do, and *how*. The world has changed, and so have people's needs and expectations. For years, we Americans complained that the government hadn't kept up. Not only wasn't our government serving us, we said, it was hindering us—it had become so bogged down in process that it had forgotten about its purpose. But the government hadn't gotten the message.

Now, it has. Throughout the federal government, people are taking their cue from the business world and asking customers what their needs are, instead of telling them. They're eliminating programs that are obsolete and reforming activities and agencies whose purposes are still relevant. They're streamlining and simplifying regulations. And they're managing the work of the people's government like the best in private business.

Not surprisingly, government is getting smaller. As mentioned earlier, there are more than 160,000 fewer federal workers today than there were in 1993, when President Clinton took office, and more than 2,000 offices are being closed. And that's just the beginning.

Along the way, government is also getting better. Federal agencies are actually getting fan mail. The Post Office is guaranteeing counter service within five minutes in many places around the country. The Customs Service is clearing passengers and cargo even before planes land and ships dock.

AMERICANS WANT A GOVERNMENT THAT WORKS BETTER, COSTS LESS

Americans have waited a long time for a government that makes more sense. Out of frustration, some—including some Members of Congress—have proposed scrapping large pieces of the system. That would be dramatic, if nothing else.

But it turns out that isn't what people want at all:

- A 1993 poll asked people whether they would prefer a candidate who would "cut the federal bureaucracy by 20 percent" or one who would "change the way government does things—cut bureaucracy, make government more efficient, and give ordinary people better service and more choices." People overwhelmingly chose the latter—no matter whether they had voted for Bill Clinton, Ross Perot, or George Bush in the 1992 elections.[2]
- In a 1994 poll, after the mid-term elections, voters were asked whether it was most important to make government "smaller so it will cost and do less" or "more efficient so it delivers more services for less money," among other choices. Only 25 percent chose the first option; 51 percent chose the second.[3]
- Half of the respondents in a January 1995 Business Week/Harris poll said the federal government "mainly needs fine-tuning to make it more flexible, accountable, and user-friendly." And 44 percent said it "needs to undergo the same

kind of dramatic restructuring and downsizing that is taking place in the private sector."[4]

• Based on a survey they conducted together in March 1995, Democrat pollster Peter Hart and Republican pollster Robert Teeter concluded that a strong majority of Americans want more effective government and believe this can be accomplished through better management.[5]

In other words, Americans don't want the guillotine for our government. We want intensive care. Says David Osborne, co-author of the best-seller *Reinventing Government*:

> Voters want smaller government, yes, but they also want government that works. They want a government that narrows the deficit, creates economic growth, improves the schools, reduces crime, protects the environment, and helps them find the opportunities they need to succeed. They want a more efficient government, but they are desperate for a more effective government.[6]

The bipartisan Hart/Teeter poll found that Americans still want the federal government to have primary responsibility for things like controlling immigration, helping the needy, improving education, reducing crime, and preventing air and water pollution. Surprisingly, we even think the government, not private industry, should have primary responsibility for improving jobs and the economy.[7]

At the same time, Americans also think this work should be shared with others. We think that state governments would be better than the federal government at running some of these programs, though we expect the federal government to set standards and follow up. We think individuals and community leaders bear important responsibilities in meeting our national goals. And we think the business community should be consulted more.

In short, Americans don't like big government much, and we want less of it wherever possible. Yet we also expect much from our government and have high aspirations for it. And when something personal or threatening—or both—hits home, we want our government there for us.

WHY WE HAVE A FEDERAL GOVENMENT

It is January 1991. On your way to work at Eastern Airlines' headquarters in Miami you pick up the Miami Herald and discover that your job's gone—Eastern has just gone belly-up. This comes as no surprise to you; you've worked for Eastern most of your adult life, and everybody's known the company's been drowning in red ink for years. Bankruptcy has been in the air for months. The surprise comes a few days later, when you discover that your pension's gone belly-up too.

When both Eastern Airlines and Pan American World Airways folded in 1991, the pensions of tens of thousands of people who had worked for these companies evaporated overnight. Luckily for them, a small government organization called the Pension Benefit Guaranty Corporation stepped in to rescue them. Unluckily for the American taxpayer, however, the rescue cost more than a billion dollars, and the agency—like any other creditor—was able to retrieve from the bankrupt companies only pennies on the dollar. This wasn't an isolated incident, either. The pension agency now administers more than 2,000 terminated pension plans for more than 450,000 people.

Frustrated with their inability to head off such disasters before they happened, and under pressure from Congress because of the growing cost of these terminations, the folks at the pension agency decided there had to be a better way. They created an "Early Warning Program" that permitted them to monitor the 400 largest and most troubled pension programs and negotiate with the companies involved, so that pensioners' interests were protected *before* a company took any action that might terminate the pension fund.

Americans don't like big government much, and we want less of it wherever possible. But we also expect much from our government and have high aspirations for it.

Corporations responded. In the last two years, the pension agency has negotiated agreements covering more than 1 million American workers and retirees and providing more than $13 billion in pension protection. The new approach is working better and costing less—much less. And it's helped to change the relationship between the government and industry from adversarial to cooperative. When the General Motors Corporation, whose pension program was underfunded, proposed to sell off its highly profitable Electronic Data Services subsidiary, it didn't wait for the pension agency to call; it called first. The company agreed to set aside $10 billion in cash and stock to help protect the pensions of more than 600,000 workers and retirees—in advance.

You've probably never heard of the Pension Benefit Guaranty Corporation. With any luck at all, you'll never need to. But if the company you work for starts playing fast and loose with your pension fund, you'll be glad it's on top of the case. It's what you *expect* from your government, after all: to protect you when you can't protect yourself.

When the United States was first created, the federal government didn't have much to do. The framers of the Constitution planned for the national government to take care of national defense and foreign relations, define citizenship and protect the borders, regulate interstate commerce, create a postal service, and safeguard individual rights. Everything else would be handled by the states. In 1800, there were only a handful of federal departments. They were run by a secretary and a few clerks and, in one or two instances, a small field structure. There were no bureaus, no middle managers, few specialists.[8] The country was small; things were simple.

But time, experience, and our own changing expectations gradually broadened the scope of the government's responsibilities. When the people needed protection from the abuses of monopolies in the late 1800s, they turned to the federal government. When the nation needed help out of the Great Depression in the 1930s, the federal government shouldered the task, creating programs to stabilize and strengthen the economy and help people in need. The international imperatives of World War II, the Cold War, and global leadership gave the federal government much broader responsibilities in national defense, trade, and foreign affairs than the Constitutional Convention could ever have contemplated. And a wide array of issues—pollution, poverty, and racial injustice, to name a few—became federal responsibilities because they could not be solved by states acting on their own. And so, with each passing year, the federal government did more and more of the people's work.

For a long while, Americans liked what they got from the federal government. They trusted it to do the right thing and to do it well. In 1963, more than three-quarters of all Americans said they believed the federal government did the right thing most of the time.

But today that figure has dropped to less than 20 percent.[9] Many of us don't respect our government anymore; we resent it. We don't feel protected by our government; we feel hassled by it. We don't feel served by our government; we feel suffocated by it. A government that was supposed to preserve our liberties seems bent on proscribing them at every turn. And, to add insult to injury, the whole thing costs way too much.

HOW THINGS GOT OUT OF HAND

It's said that the road to hell is paved with good intentions. There may be no better illustration than the U.S. federal government.

For example, to ensure that politicians don't abuse the public trust and pack government agencies with their cronies, or that federal bureaucrats don't treat government workers unfairly, the government has created 100,000 pages of laws, executive orders, rules and regulations, and agency directives to cover every conceivable personnel decision.[10] These were "summarized" in a 10,000-page Federal Personnel Manual, finally abandoned last year. If you wanted to hire people for federal jobs, you'd have been wise to choose young applicants; they'd mature while they waited for you to go through all the required steps.

To ensure that private businesses don't rip off the taxpayer when the government hires them to do the people's work, the government has created procurement rules—thousands of pages of them—so stupifyingly difficult, time-consuming, and costly to follow that many good companies won't even bother to bid. Do you work for the federal government and need a computer to do your job? Chances are that by the time you get the model you requested, the technology will be out of date—*and* you'll still pay the full retail price.

And to ensure that state and local governments don't subvert the will of Congress and use federal dollars the way *they* think best, the government tied up the funds and programs with restrictions. The knots are so tight that state and local officials often have no flexibility to meet federal goals in ways that make sense locally.

All in all, the Code of Federal Regulations—the government's rulebook—is enormous. If you want a copy for your library, you'll need a shelf *21 feet long*.

The reasons for this overgrowth of rules are remarkably simple.[11] As a matter of political philosophy, we moved away from limited government toward an activist government that we expected to serve as both a national "nanny" and a national police officer. As a matter of governmental practice, we wanted to protect against corruption, treat everyone fairly, and safeguard the common interests of the people. So we created rules to make sure the government makes no mistakes, takes no risks, tolerates no uncertainty. The result was galloping bureaucracy and stifling regulation.

We made these decisions. Not some faceless bureaucrat or power-hungry politician, but we the people, through our elected officials—presidents, senators, and congressional representatives, Republicans and Democrats alike. And while the

A Vacuum-Tube Government in a Microchip World

Twenty years ago, "Pong" was the latest thing in video games. In fact, it was the only thing. Eight-track tapes were the latest thing in music. Fax modems and cellular phones didn't exist. Airline travel was a luxury, and the Boeing 707 was the workhorse of the air.

Today, we've gone from 707s to 777s that are so technologically advanced that they can take off, fly, and land virtually on their own. And though they're bigger than ever, they're also cleaner and quieter than ever.

Yet while a single aircraft now carries computer systems that rival all the computers that existed in the world a few decades ago, our air traffic control system—the system that controls all those airplanes—still relies on the technological equivalent of Pong.

In many of the nation's busiest air traffic control centers, controllers peer at green radar screens that haven't changed much since World War II. Technicians nurse along ancient mainframe computers that take up an entire room but have only a fraction of the power of a modern laptop. Parts of the system run on vacuum tubes, a technology that was obsolete 30 years ago. And it breaks down—a dozen times this year alone. All told, the system's inefficiency costs billions of dollars each year in wasted aircraft fuel, delays, missed connections, and labor—some $3 billion in imposed costs, according to the airline industry. That's more than the industry has ever made in profit in a year.

Why aren't these relics in a museum, instead of controlling the flights of half a billion passengers a year? Because the Federal Aviation Administration, which runs the air traffic control system, faces a unique and virtually impossible task.

Despite the fact that the FAA literally controls the minute-by-minute activities of one of the country's flagship industries, it has none of the tools that have made U.S. companies in that industry the world's best. While the FAA needs to be able to plan for demand a decade or more away, it doesn't even know what its budget will be the next year. Although it has an annual revenue stream of more than $5 billion, it can't leverage one dime, and must pay for all of its equipment in cash and up front. And even with money in hand, the agency faces procurement rules so cumbersome that "new" systems are usually already obsolete by the time they're brought on-line.

Even so, thanks to the efforts of the Federal Aviation Administration's dedicated controllers, technicians and managers, our air traffic control system is still the safest in the world. However, growing demand, aging equipment, and shrinking budgets threaten FAA's ability to keep it that way.

When President Clinton took office, he quickly recognized that the status quo wouldn't fly. Under the leadership of Transportation Secretary Federico Peña and Administrator David Hinson, the FAA overhauled its massive air traffic control modernization program, ensuring that some new equipment will be delivered before the end of this decade and saving taxpayers an estimated $1.5 billion. In the interim, the agency is taking extraordinary steps to maintain the current equipment until the new systems are in place.

Improving hardware and software is still a stopgap measure, however. The real solution would be to fix the underlying cause of the problems. The FAA should be given the same tools to provide air traffic control services that those who use the system already rely on. That's exactly what the federal government's reinvention team has proposed—to create a businesslike government-owned corporation, funded by user fees and working outside of traditional governmental constraints.

Vice President Gore and Secretary Peña displayed the FAA's vacuum tubes over a year ago to dramatize the need for change. The Speaker of the House echoed that call. There is now growing consensus in Congress on the need for personnel and procurement reform; any serious attempt at reform, though, must also address the financial future of the FAA. In the meantime, the airlines and the flying public are stuck in a holding pattern, waiting for the government to catch up.

world around us changed, our government stuck steadfastly to the rules—whether they made sense anymore or not.

FAILING TO CHANGE WITH A CHANGING WORLD

In fact, the proliferation of rules is really only a symptom of the government's trouble, not its cause. The basic problem is that the government has plodded along single-mindedly, answering each new question with yet another rule, but failing to recognize that the world around it had gone in a different direction.

The middle of this century—when we formed much of our vision of what government should do and how—was the pinnacle of the Industrial Age. Not surprisingly, the model we chose to follow was the great American corporation, where policy was decided by top executives, interpreted by mid-level managers in carefully segmented corporate divisions, and carried out by workers divided into narrow specialties, following detailed work specifications and mass-producing identical products of reliable, if unexceptional, quality.

It was said that "What's good for General Motors is good for the nation." And indeed, that system carried us to almost unimaginable levels of productivity and prosperity.

But by the 1970s, what was once good for General Motors wasn't even good for General Motors anymore. The world had changed. People weren't willing to accept "good enough" any more; we wanted the best. We wanted variety, choice, quality, convenience, and service. And with information on almost anything immediately accessible to almost anyone, we knew what the best was. Almost overnight, America had gone from a *producer* economy to a *consumer* economy—we had moved from the Industrial Age to the Information Age.

Almost overnight, America had gone from a producer economy to a consumer economy—we had moved from the Industrial Age to the Information Age.

A lot of major corporations, General Motors included, were slow to respond and struggled to stay in business. Others—companies that were more flexible and moved more quickly to meet rapid changes in consumer demands—thrived. Eventually though, even the Big Three automakers turned around. In 1958, for example, you could buy 21 makes of cars from ten car makers; by the 1990s, you could choose from more than 570 car, van, and truck models.[12] What's more, you could review their features, get information on their safety, and even do price comparisons by personal computer in the comfort of your own home. The consumer insisted on being in the driver's seat, and corporations changed accordingly.

But the federal government was still operating on the producer model, not the consumer model. Decisions were still made at the top, interpreted into rules and regulations by mid-level bureaucrats distant from customers and from each other, and carried out by public employees in narrow line agencies and field offices—whether they made sense or not. Change, if it came at all, came very slowly indeed.

GOING BY THE BOOK

The federal government has done things the way it has in the past for generally good reasons. On the taxpayers' behalf, it wanted to prevent abuse—unfairness, arbitrariness, corruption, willful bias—by its own employees, by companies it hires, and by other governments. It went by the book and demanded that everyone else did too.

But the price was high. Certainty was achieved, but in a rapidly changing world, "certainty" became inflexibility. Fairness was achieved by treating everyone equally, but in a world full of compelling individual situations, "fairness" became unresponsiveness. Bias was avoided by making sure local officials and front-line federal employees couldn't make discretionary decisions—even though they knew best what needed to be done—and by punishing them when they did. The result was a system that hobbled users and abusers alike, treated adults like children, and made everyone a suspect.

It also put the government's customers—which is to say, all of us—at the bottom of the priority list. The first priority was the rules; the second was those who checked whether the rules were being followed (such as auditors and inspectors general); the third was those who made the rules in the first place (such as Congress and interest groups). Customers came last, if at all. It was a sort of "iron triangle"—special interests told Congress what "the people" wanted; Congress passed laws, and then told the agencies what to do about them.

Perhaps the most compelling challenge we face as the next century dawns is how to redeem the promise of self-government—how to make our government make sense again.

Citizens, understandably, do not like being low in the pecking order—or worse, being ignored altogether. And honest people—whether public employees or the people they serve—don't like being treated like potential criminals. The perverse effect of "rule by rules" is that instead of reducing arbitrariness it appears to increase it; instead of fostering cooperation it destroys it; instead of solving problems it worsens them, creating bitterness and resentment along the way.

And the costs are enormous. Fragmentation, duplication of effort, and complexity run up the cost of everything government does—and everything anyone else does that is regulated by the government. It turns out that fully one-third of the entire non-postal federal workforce simply checks on, audits, and controls other federal workers.[13]

Perhaps even worse, bright and committed people who chose to be public servants find they are not permitted to serve the public. Dedicated folks struggle to operate within an antiquated system that they know needs changing, and then have to take the heat when it breaks down.

This might all have been tolerable if the government were effective at doing what it does. But there's the rub; despite the red tape, the irritations, the wasted time, and the incredible cost, the federal government wasn't getting the job done. Often it seemed like it didn't even remember what the job was in the first place. As Philip K. Howard, author of *The Death of Common Sense,* put it, "We seem to have achieved the worst of both worlds: a system of regulation that goes too far while it also does too little."[14] He could easily have said the same of the government as a whole, not just regulation.

Over the years, gradually but relentlessly, the distance between the people and the government has grown—when the whole idea in the first place was that the people and the government should be one and the same thing. As former Supreme Court Justice William Brennan once pointed out, "The characteristic complaint of our time seems to be not that government provides no reasons, but that its reasons often seem remote from human beings who must live with the consequences."[15]

Perhaps the most compelling challenge we face as a nation as the next century dawns is how to redeem the promise of self-government—how to make our government make sense again.

RE-CREATING COMMON SENSE GOVERNMENT

Let's say you're out driving one day and your car suddenly stops. You check the obvious things—the gas gauge, the temperature gauge—but that doesn't help. If you want to get to the bottom of the problem, you're going to have to look under the hood.

Then, you have three options. You can close it again and hope the problem will go away. This will keep your hands clean, but it won't get you anywhere. Or you can start yanking out pieces of equipment. This will make the car lighter and easier to push, but the chances are it won't make it run. Or you can try fixing what's broken—maybe several things. The only way to find out which things, however, is to examine the engine closely. Maybe consult an expert or two. Do a diagnosis. Experiment a bit. The disadvantage of this option, of course, is that it takes longer than simply ripping out equipment. The advantage is that it *will* get you where you want to go.

Just like any business, any government function that has been around a few decades needs to be re-thought.

Some things are obvious. Some government programs are obsolete, or just plain silly, and can be eliminated. Over the years we've been pretty good at creating programs to solve new problems, but lousy at eliminating old ones.

In addition, some workforces are bloated and can be cut. Some field offices are no longer needed and can be closed. You can slim down the government "from the get-go." That's where the federal government's reinvention drive began: with the obvious—and there are more obvious things yet to do.

But "downsizing," as they call it in the business world, isn't enough. Just like any business, any government function that has been around a few decades needs to be re-thought. If it isn't, it loses touch with its original purpose—and with the needs of the times. It also becomes uncontrollable. As President Clinton has noted:

> We know we have to go beyond cutting, even beyond restructuring, to completely reevaluate what the federal government is doing. Are we doing it well? Should we be doing it at all? Should someone else be doing it? Are we being as innovative and flexible as the most creative private organizations in the country?[16]

There is a point at which program and budget cuts fly just as much in the face of common sense as business as usual. As debate rages in Congress over which agencies or programs to cut to reduce the size and influence of the federal government, it's worth noting that when a patient has a systemic disease—say, a debilitating infection—a good doctor doesn't lop off the patient's arms and legs. For one thing, all that does is weaken the patient further. More importantly, it does absolutely nothing to cure the disease.

The federal government is ailing and needs a cure. It needs to be treated systemically, not amputated or—less drastic, but no more effective—dabbed with some dubious topical salve. Even if the wholesale elimination of federal agencies and programs was what Americans wanted—and it is not—that approach would do nothing to improve what is left.

Americans are quite clear about what common sense government means. It means a government that focuses on results, that moves heaven and earth to make it easy for citizens, businesses, and state and local governments to meet the nation's common goals. It means a government that recognizes who its real customers are, works with them to understand their needs, and puts them first, not last. And it means giving taxpayers their money's worth—a government that works better, faster, and cheaper than in the past, one that operates as well as, or better than, the best private businesses.

It means a government that works *for* us, not *against* us. It means a government that is in our corner, not in our face. Real cures tend to be a lot less dramatic than lopping limbs or ripping out machinery. They take time. Progress can be uneven. But in the case of reinventing the federal government, there is progress, and it's real.

Let's face it, this is the way things should have been all along. If you're a citizen, you ought to be able to expect good service from your government. If you run a business, you ought to be able to expect reasonable treatment by regulators—treatment that meets legitimate public needs without crushing yours. And as a taxpayer, you ought to be able to expect that the government, acting as your trustee, is managing your tax dollars wisely. And the federal government shouldn't expect applause when it finally straightens things out to give the American people this kind of treatment.

But the point is, this has never happened before. Despite 11 major exercises in government reform this century, there's been little lasting change.

Until now.

2

Getting Results

It is common sense to take a method and try it;
if it fails, admit it frankly and try another.
But above all, try something.

FRANKLIN D. ROOSEVELT[1]

IT IS AUGUST 1, 1995, and Skowhegan, Maine, is baking in heat seldom experienced that far north. In a huge white tent set up a few miles out of town at the S.D. Warren Company paper plant, 600 people—workers and managers from firms across the state—swelter in their seats, listening to the featured speaker. He is Bill Freeman, area director of what has been, for industry at least, perhaps the most thoroughly disliked of all federal agencies: the Occupational Safety and Health Administration, or OSHA.

As Freeman concludes his remarks, all 600 rise to their feet in a single motion. They do not boo him. They do not stone him. They cheer loudly, applaud enthusiastically.

Freeman has not always received this sort of greeting from the companies he inspects. A few years ago, Bill Freeman and his team of two dozen inspectors were OSHA's "gold medal" winners. They got the agency's top honors for detecting the most safety violations, issuing the most citations, and levying the most fines—sort of the triple jump in the OSHA Olympics.

But Freeman didn't think he and his team were winning at all. OSHA's gold medal notwithstanding, he was convinced they were losing—losing, that is, in the serious business of reducing the number of work-related injuries in Maine.

OVERHAULING FEDERAL REGULATIONS

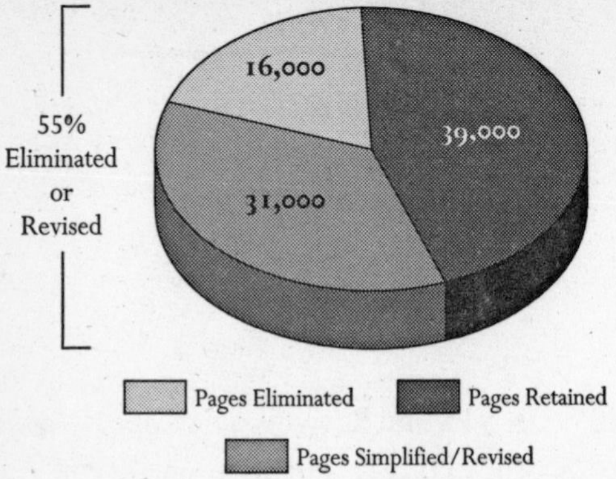

Maine had the worst record in the nation before Freeman's team got its medal, and it still had the worst record afterward. The fact was that, given the limited resources he had and the complexity of OSHA's inspection regulations, his chances of actually improving Maine's injury rate were virtually nil under existing rules.

Following those rules, Freeman's inspectors would move into a company, spend three months on-site, another three months preparing reports, and then anywhere from six months to two years in court. And when all was said and done, they'd find themselves telling the company to do the same things they'd told them years before after an earlier inspection. The process was so cumbersome that it got in its own way, not just the companies' way; in seven years, Freeman's team had been able to inspect only five mills. Indeed, nationwide OSHA has only 2,000 inspectors to monitor the nation's 6.2 million workplaces—more than 3,000 per inspector.[2]

Fed up with getting nowhere, Freeman went to the 200 companies that had the highest injury rates in the state and offered them a deal: you and your workers draw up a safety program that meets the law's objectives, and we'll stop playing "Gotcha!" No more months-long "wall-to-wall" inspections, no more "ignorance is no excuse" enforcement, no more by-the-book fines. We'll stop being cops. We'll be partners instead—you, your workers, and OSHA. And any time you need help, we'll be there.

Employer/worker safety teams are identifying—and fixing—14 times more hazards than OSHA's inspectors ever could have found.

Industry's response was immediate and positive. All but two of the 200 signed up. Employer/worker safety teams in the participating firms are identifying—and fixing—*14 times* more hazards than OSHA's inspectors ever could have found, including hazards for which the agency didn't even have regulations. After all, who knows where the problems are better than the workers themselves?

The new program is working so well that in two years, the group's injury rates dropped 35 percent.[3] Says S.D. Warren's Carl Turner, "There is a direct connection between the 200 Program and the drop in the accident rate; we spent 18 years under the old OSHA program and nothing happened."

More remarkably, Warren's production is up 25 percent, and Warren executives believe it's because their employees feel valued now. "This makes a big difference in how employees feel about the company," says one union official. "Repairing safety items would take forever, if you were lucky; now when I write a repair order it's done in less than 24 hours. We should have done this ten years ago."

The initiative has brought unions and management together as well. Says an official at Georgia Pacific, "We have joint communications and meet together; I never thought I'd see the day." And the effect goes beyond the factory floor. Ed Warren at Boise Cascade says employees are "using safety glasses and earplugs when they use a chain saw at home."

In another time, Bill Freeman probably would have been fired. He broke the rules. He didn't "go by the book." In another time, if you did something different, stepped out of bounds, bent the rules, or acted on the basis of simple common sense, you'd be punished, not rewarded. In short, if you stuck your neck out, you'd get your head cut off. Not surprisingly, people learned not to stick their necks out. Not exactly a way to motivate folks. And a lousy way to run anything, especially a government.

Unless you've ever seen one of those huge metal stamping machines come down on a piece of sheet metal, you can't imagine what it was like to think about the days when people had to put their hands under those machines with no guards, knowing one mistake would mean the hand would be gone forever. Unless you've actually seen things like that, it is hard to visualize what is at stake here.

PRESIDENT CLINTON

May 16, 1995

But Freeman seized on the federal initiative to reinvent government and pushed it hard. Result?—not another empty "gold medal," but an award for the agency from the Vice President, a substantial financial award from the Ford Foundation/

John F. Kennedy School of Government Innovations in American Government program, an announcement by President Clinton that "Maine 200" will henceforth be OSHA's policy nationwide—and injury rates in Maine that are already down by more than a third.

Freeman and his team are real winners at last.

RESULTS, NOT RULES

Franklin D. Roosevelt's message to the government was, in effect: do something; if that doesn't work, do something else. Over the years, however, the message to front-line federal workers—and, for that matter, to the people and companies they regulated—mutated so profoundly it reversed upon itself. It became, "Do it this way. If that doesn't work, do it this way *anyway*. Don't get any bright ideas."

Our own government had become a mine field—for employees and their customers alike. Even if we picked our way through it carefully, following the map we were given, there was always a chance—often a good chance—we'd stumble upon a new mine. They seemed to grow of their own accord. Good, honest, hard-working people ended up sideways with their government, often not so much because they were off track but because there was no way to know which way was the right way. Each time they thought they'd figured it out, the map would change.

People want to do the right thing. Problem is, the government often makes it almost impossible to figure out what the right thing is and, once you've figured it out, impossible to actually do it. Think of it this way: most folks understand why there is a speed limit, respect it, and try to obey. But what if the speed limit wasn't posted or, if it was, it changed so often you never knew whether you were obeying it, and troopers were forever pulling you over and giving you tickets for violating this ever-changing, often mysterious speed limit? And then, just to keep you on your toes, they'd give you a ticket for your car being dirty, leaving you wondering what that had to do with highway safety. Not only would you be pretty steamed but, chances are, the highways would be in chaos. That's what life with the federal government's been like for years, especially for America's businesses.

In February 1995, President Clinton put the challenge facing the federal government simply. The issue, he said, was "How do we do our part to protect the legitimate interests of the American people, without literally taking leave of our senses and doing things that drive people up the wall but don't make them safer?"[4] And then he provided the answer: completely overhaul the way the federal government regulates people, businesses, and state and local governments—*focus on results, not rules*.

WHAT AMERICANS WANT: FEWER RULES, MORE SENSE

There's an old saying that describes how our government works: "The President proposes, the Congress disposes." To that, the American people might add, "and the agency *imposes*." It is those myriad everyday bureaucratic impositions Americans want fixed. And that's what the regulatory overhaul begun by the National Performance Review is designed to do. President Clinton's message to federal agencies was simple: "We are not asking people to spend their time, their money, and their resources fooling around with us if they don't have to and there is no public purpose served by it."[5]

In what has become a hallmark of the reinvention initiative, this year's efforts at regulatory reform began with asking and listening to the people who know most what needs to be done: the government's customers and the front-line workers who serve them. Agencies held more than 300 meetings around the country. Plus, there were hundreds more local meetings as part of the 1995 White House Conference on Small Business. Here's what people said.

Do we need more common sense and fairness in our regulations? You bet we do.

PRESIDENT CLINTON

January 24, 1995

It's Not So Much the "What" as the "How"

We all want clean air and water. We all want safe food and toys our children won't be hurt playing with. We want workplaces that don't injure us. We want our savings protected. And much more. That's why we have laws. And while we may have our disagreements about some laws, the real problem is what happens *after* the laws are passed.

Actually, there are four problems. First, Congress passes laws, but seldom repeals them—whether or not they're relevant anymore, whether or not they work. So an awful lot of laws remain on the books after they are no longer useful. Second, after laws are passed the agencies responsible for carrying them out are required to produce regulations describing how they will achieve what Congress passed the law to do. But between Congress's vagueness and agencies' mania for covering every eventuality, the result has been regulatory overflow:

at last count, the total number of pages in the Code of Federal Regulations—the encyclopedia of federal laws and rules—was more than 130,000 pages. Its 202 volumes take up 21 feet of shelf space. Third, even after the regulations are approved, there are legions of lawyers and others who seek out and find loopholes in them, and legions more of agency regulators who seek to fill those holes with—you guessed it—more regulations. Fourth, agency employees are duty-bound to enforce regulations once they're approved. That's their job. Common sense interpretation is expressly forbidden.

Americans acknowledge that many laws and regulations have made things better. The environment is dramatically cleaner now than it was 25 years ago. Highways and cars are safer. So are kids' toys. Even though the number of people working has grown substantially, the rate of work-related fatalities declined more than 50 percent since OSHA was created in 1970.

But Americans also say that many regulations have created more problems than they solved and even frustrated the very goals they set out to achieve. They say the regulations are often incomprehensible and sometimes simply nonsensical. And even when their purposes make sense, the enforcement procedures are often inflexible and costly. Sometimes the rules miss the point altogether, like requiring a refinery to install $31 million worth of equipment in waste pipes to control benzene when, in fact, its benzene emissions came from its barge-loading dock.[6]

In addition, the punishments for violations sometimes far exceed the violations themselves, not to mention common sense, like fining a company thousands of dollars for failing to require workers to don hard hats as they rushed to save a coworker from a collapsed trench.[7] And complex and costly regulations are causing employers to shy away from doing things they want to do, like employing the disabled or providing health and pension benefits—things the laws are supposed to be promoting.

What we end up with, as President Clinton has pointed out, is a government that is obsessed with procedures but often seems oblivious to results. What's more, all this regulation is immensely expensive—hundreds of billions of dollars, so expensive that no one really knows the figure. It's costly to taxpayers to pay for the system that creates and enforces all these rules; it's costly to employers, state and local governments, and ordinary citizens to comply with them; and it increases the costs of products and services.

Decision making must be transferred from words on a page to people on the spot.

PHILIP K. HOWARD

The Death of Common Sense

And then there is the matter of human judgment. After all, regulations don't think. In the pursuit of equal treatment of everyone, we have created a system that demands that one size fit all, and in the pursuit of certainty we have created a system that attempts to cover every eventuality, spelling everything out in excruciating detail. We have given neither the regulators nor the regulated any leeway. In the words of Philip Howard, we have "exiled human judgment."[8] But the world is neither all one size nor all that certain. Things change constantly, conditions vary, and human judgment is crucial to making things work. Or, as Howard puts it, "Decision making must be transferred from words on a page to people on the spot."[9]

And that's exactly what Americans want—reasonable rules, reasonably applied by people close to the action. The new OSHA is proof that the "how" of government regulation can be changed dramatically for the better. But it isn't the only example. Throughout government, regulators have begun work on programs to cooperate with the industries they regulate.

Americans deserve a government that works. They're starting to get one.

Get Rid of Bad Rules and Make Good Ones Easier to Understand

Some years ago, someone in the federal government decided doctors should be required to fill out and sign an "attestation form"—sort of a truth oath—attesting to the accuracy of the information they provided to the hospital when they discharged a Medicare patient. It didn't add anything to patient care—in fact, it detracted, since filling it out took time away from patients. And it didn't improve medical records; the doctors were already providing all the information required for discharging patients, generally quite accurately. What it did do was create more than 11 million forms, take up 200,000 hours of physician time, and add $22,500 in administrative costs for every hospital in the country.

And now, thanks to President Clinton's reinvention initiative, it's gone. It's one of literally thousands of senseless regulations that people, businesses, and state and local governments don't have to follow anymore now that the federal government is focusing on results rather than rules. Are silly regulations all gone? Hardly. Is all that costly paperwork a thing of the past? Not yet. But agencies are killing bad regulations faster than at any other time in recent history—thousands of pages of them this year alone. And they're working hard to make good regulations better, easier to understand, and easier to observe.

But in the meantime, how do businesses find out which regulations apply to them? And how do they make sense of them? In the past they usually found out when it was too late: after being hit with some violation.

Now there's the U.S. Business Advisor—a one-stop Internet shop for information on regulations and compliance for businesses. A reinvention project of 15 major federal agencies, the Business Advisor is a World Wide Web site (http://www.business.gov), housed at the Department of Commerce, through which businesses can find out what regulations apply to their situation and how to get help complying with them. Lawrence Livermore National Laboratory and the University of Massachusetts developed a technology that is remarkably user-friendly. All you do is tell the system what your question is and it culls the answers you're looking for from thousands of pages of regulations—in seconds. And that's just the beginning; soon the Business Advisor will make it possible for businesses to get not just regulatory information but also information on trade, labor, finance, and selling to the government. Eventually, you may be able not only to retrieve information, but also find out about best practices, send comments, and file documents with the government electronically. But these are just the government's ideas. The final design will be based upon input and ideas from businesspeople. President Clinton has created a task force to get these ideas and report back with a design by the end of 1995.

Better access to the right information will make it easier for businesses and others to do the right thing, but only if the information they receive is written in plain language. And let's face it; most of the time it isn't. Between the vagueness of the original laws and the legalese used by rule-writers trying to cover every eventuality, reading regulations is like wading through a jungle without a machete. Now, however, the government itself is clearing the path, gradually making regulations user-friendly: Interior Department staff, for example, reasoned that if they wrote clearer regulations, people would waste less time trying to figure out what the government wanted, would be less likely to make mistakes, and would be more likely to comply. Now, all regulation-writers at Interior use plain language.

The Forest Service has gone one step better: to help make the government's lands and resources more accessible to Americans with disabilities, it has scrapped detailed and convoluted design and engineering regulations in favor of an award-winning guidebook, "Universal Access to Outdoor Recreation."

Not every effort to make things clear is that easy, however. Take the Securities and Exchange Commission. When it comes to covering every eventuality, perhaps no agency has worked harder than the SEC, created in the 1930s to protect investors from fraud in the financial world. SEC's strategy has been simple: the more people know about what they're buying, the better they'll be able to judge the risks involved. So disclosure is crucial. The result of this simple strategy, however, has been anything *but* simple. As the mutual fund industry has evolved and investment strategies have changed, mutual fund prospectuses have grown too, as SEC requires more and more information to be disclosed. The result? The more information you get, the less you know. The average prospectus runs to 25 dense pages of legalistic prose that almost nobody understands.

Now that's changed. SEC Chairman Arthur Levitt, Jr., decided to have mutual fund prospectuses "speak a new language: the English language."[10] Working with the SEC, eight of the largest mutual fund companies crafted brief, plain English summary documents to help people know what they're buying. They are testing what they did to make sure it works. If it does, all mutual funds will use summary documents and investors will know what they are buying.

Make It Easier for Us to Do What Needs to Be Done

If you want someone to do something, it's generally wise to make it easy for them. At least that's the message Americans have been trying to send to the government. The truth is that most businesspeople, like most other people, are more than willing to work to find ways of achieving the public purposes laws are meant to achieve, if they can find a way to do it easily. What they hate is being required to fill out hundreds of forms—especially when they know nobody reads them. What they hate even more is being pounced on by their own government.

New regulations are created every year. Businesses, big and small, are expected to know all the regulations that pertain to them. As far as the law is concerned, ignorance is no excuse. But for years, instead of helping, the government not only made it difficult to understand the rules, it made it difficult for companies to comply with them (by making them complex, obscure, or simply impractical). Then it pounced, levying fines on any who didn't comply. Sort of a "Catch-22." Lawyers and consultants have made fortunes advising businesses about these rules; they're probably the principal beneficiaries of government regulation.

In February 1995, President Clinton told the agencies to end the Catch-22s. In March, he gave all regulatory agencies permission to waive up to 100 percent of punitive fines so a businessperson who acts in good faith can fix the problem, not fight with the enforcer. The focus is on the objective, not the fines.

Let's return to OSHA. For decades, the old OSHA's inspectors would sweep into your company and start writing up violations of regulations—big ones, little ones, important ones, petty ones—often for things the employers had never heard of (and sometimes for things that didn't seem to have too much bearing on actual worker safety). Then they'd sweep out again, leaving behind the bill. You'd think they were there to make money, not to preserve safety. Not surprisingly, businesses—especially small businesses—were furious.

Now, however, OSHA has increased its emphasis on providing employers confidential consulting services to help them improve working conditions for their employees. Instead of playing "gotcha," they'll help you evaluate your workplace (and encourage you to involve your workers in the process). They'll help you draw up a safety plan. They'll listen to your side of the story—being student as well as teacher—so they can understand your needs and conditions better. They'll provide training for your employees—on site. And when everything's said and done, you may be exempt from inspections for a year. No hassles. And the consulting services are free.

Even the inspections are changing. It used to be that any employer who didn't have an OSHA compliance poster on the wall immediately got slapped with a $400 fine; now inspectors carry posters with them when they visit and help employers put them up.

In fact, the whole issue of fines is changing. A month after President Clinton released *From Red Tape to Results: Creating a Government that Works Better and Costs Less*—the first "reinventing government" report—in 1993, the OSHA office in Parsippany, New Jersey, saw it as an opportunity to change how it handled fines for safety violations. The way the old process worked, if a safety problem was identified the employer had no incentive to fix it until months later, after the reports were completed and the litigation was over. The folks in Parsippany thought that was pointless, so they made a deal with employers: fix the problem now, and we'll reduce the fines by an amount equal to the cost of the safety repair. Since then, immediate abatements of violations have risen by nearly a third and the cost of OSHA follow-ups has dropped. On July 1, 1995, OSHA made this "Quick Fix" initiative its policy nationwide. The point is to make it easy to improve the workplace—and also to make government work better and cost less.

Other federal agencies are making it easier too. For example, both the Coast Guard and the National Oceanic and Atmospheric Administration have shifted to issuing warnings rather than fines for boaters, fishing vessels, and others cited for minor violations of regulations. In addition, the Coast Guard now has a "pollution ticket" program that offers significantly lower penalties for first- and second-time violations of pollution standards. The Federal Highway Administration now imposes penalties only as a last resort, and scales what penalties it does levy to the company's ability to pay. The Environmental Protection Agency will give small businesses a six-month grace period to correct pollution violations.

Assume We're Honest, Not Dishonest; Intelligent, Not Stupid

Sometimes, federal regulations and the way they're enforced give you the impression the government thinks everyone's crooked. Or that we're stupid—that unless the government spells out how to go about doing something we'll never figure out how to do it on our own.

We shouldn't feel bad. For years, government has treated its own employees the same way—assuming, for example, that the people responsible for the national defense cannot be trusted to buy paper clips without defrauding the United States, or detailing exactly how employees should handle every situation, as if they couldn't work it out themselves. If you think you have to fill out a lot of forms, you should see what the government makes its own employees go through for even the most insignificant purchase or action. This lack of trust in its own employees is one reason why doing almost anything in the government has always required a couple of dozen signatures: to be sure no one was cheating the taxpayer. Of course the process sometimes cost more than what was protected, but at least no one could be blamed if something went wrong.

But people—in government or out—are, for the most part, neither crooked nor stupid. Most people want to do the right thing, so long as the right thing makes sense. Perhaps the most important thing about the reinvention initiative, and its regulatory reform work in particular, is that it is based on a new assumption: that people are honest and that if you tell people what needs to be done, and let them get on with doing it, the chances are it will be done better—and more cheaply—than if you tell them how. Moreover, it values them as human beings.

What Americans—individuals, businesspeople, officials from state and local government—told the federal government when they were asked how the burden of regulation could be lifted was remarkable. They did not say, "Get rid of regulations." Their answer was sophisticated and practical at the same time. It was: "Get rid of obsolete or silly regulations, and then *work with us* to improve those regulations that must remain. Trust us. Treat us like partners, not enemies."

For several years now, the Environmental Protection Agency has been doing precisely that, in a program that demonstrates the value of making your objective clear and trusting people to do it right. EPA identified 17 high-priority chemicals and told industry that it wanted their release into the environment reduced by 33 percent by 1992 and 50 percent by the end of this year. Then it stood aside, asking only for a simple letter from industries involved explaining how they would reach those goals. Even the choice of chemicals was sensible; they were chemicals heavily used by industry, that posed significant environmental concerns, and that had a reasonably high likelihood of being reduced through industry action.

Individual companies have responded with remarkable enthusiasm—and not just major corporations. AB&I Pipe Coating in Oakland, California, for example, spent three years developing a plan that will actually eliminate completely its release of chlorinated solvents by this year, along with some 90 percent of emissions of the other volatile organic compounds it uses in its business. Nationwide, the results have exceeded the most optimistic projections. Some 1,200 companies are participating. They reduced emissions more than 100 million pounds *beyond* the 1992 target, and the 1995 goal appears to have been achieved at least a year ago (the data are still being analyzed). And the spirit of the initiative has been infectious; EPA now has several other voluntary partnership programs underway and even more planned. The formula is simple: focus on results. Less "gotcha" enforcement, plus more trust, minus mountains of paperwork, equals a lot less pollution.

THE RESULTS: WORKING BETTER AND COSTING LESS

Harley is a potbellied pig. Pigs happen to be very good at sniffing out drugs. In fact, the police in Portland, Oregon, thought Harley could be even better than a dog in tracking down narcotics on the city's streets. And he sure was a great mascot for anti-drug programs aimed at school kids. The kids loved Harley.

Harley had been such a success that the Portland police wanted to buy some more potbellies, and to train them to detect guns as well as drugs. The whole project would cost about $25,000. But they couldn't find any federal anti-drug money available for training pigs. Dogs, yes. Pigs, no. Never mind that Harley got the right results—that he found the drugs and charmed the kids.

When the White House found out that Harley was denied training funds because he was a pig, it acted swiftly—and designated Harley an honorary dog. It was a comical response to a ludicrous problem—the kind of problem Americans can expect to be fixed, and fixed for good, as the government strips away layers of regulations and mountains of useless paperwork.

The Code of Federal Regulations, the government's rulebook, is a lot like your uncle's garage: crammed to the rafters with all sorts of stuff that's been there for who knows how long. There's stuff of great value in there. There's stuff you don't need anymore. And there's stuff you can't imagine *ever* having needed. On February 21, 1995, President Clinton sent the federal regulatory agencies in to clean up Uncle Sam's garage. By June 1, they had come up with 16,000 pages of regulations to haul out to the curb.

Then they went back in to find more. So far, they've rummaged around in more than 86,000 pages of regulations. Besides the 16,000 they are trashing, they are cleaning up another 31,000 more pages—stuff that's still valuable but needed to be refurbished. And there's still more, further back in the shadows, that they haven't gotten to yet. It's a very big garage.

President Clinton's instructions to the clean-up crew were simple:

1. *Cut obsolete regulations and fix the rest.* Conduct a page-by-page review; eliminate what's outdated and reform what's still needed. Figure out how the goals can be achieved in more efficient, less intrusive ways, and while you're at it, look for ways to push authority down to where it will be used best, like in state and local governments.
2. *Reward results, not red tape.* Change how you measure performance so that you focus on results, not process and punishment. Say what you want to achieve clearly and re-engineer your organizations so that people and programs are evaluated on the basis of outcomes.
3. *Get out of Washington.* Talk to your front-line employees and your customers about how best to achieve your goals; form partnerships.
4. *Negotiate, don't dictate.* Tell people what you want to accomplish and engage them in working out how to get there. Seek consensus at the very start.

The agencies didn't do it alone. In the month and a half after President Clinton's order, they held hundreds of meetings with businesses, individuals, and state and local government officials all over the country to ask them what needed to be eliminated or fixed. As you might expect, people had plenty of ideas; they'd just been waiting for someone to ask.

Progress Report:
Cutting Obsolete Regulations, Pointless Paperwork

It's almost impossible to remember the world before automatic teller machines came along. If you needed cash, you either had to get to the bank before it closed—in the middle of the afternoon—or go to the supermarket, buy something, and ask for cash back. Now you can get money from your account virtually anytime, anywhere. You can even get it overseas. It's incredibly convenient.

The government, however, didn't make it very convenient for banks to set up ATMs. Until this year, the Comptroller of the Currency, which oversees banking operations, required banks to go through a complicated, lengthy, and ultimately costly 35-step application process before they could open up an ATM. Why? Because it treated ATMs as if they were separate bank branches, not as extensions of existing ones. Maybe it made sense in the early days, but it certainly doesn't anymore. Now, the 35 steps are on their way out.

That's just one, very small example of how much simpler life can be with a little common sense. Throughout 1995, the major federal regulatory agencies have been cutting obsolete regulations and eliminating pointless paperwork on a wholesale basis:

- The Environmental Protection Agency is eliminating 1,400 pages of obsolete regulations and is revising 9,400 more; that means cuts or changes to 85 percent of EPA's rules in the Code of Federal Regulations. In the process, it's also cut paperwork requirements by 25 percent—a savings for industry of some 20 million hours of labor a year.
- The Department of Education eliminated 30 percent of its regulations.

• The Department of Housing and Urban Development is cutting 2,800 pages—65 percent of all its regulations.

• The U.S. Department of Agriculture dropped 3 million pages of government forms that America's farmers filled out each year.

• The Small Business Administration will have eliminated 50 percent of its regulations by the end of the year and will have revised the rest.

What does this mean on the street? Here's just one example: 15 years ago, when Mamma Jo's and Zeno's Pizza opened in Wichita Falls, Texas, the owners used an SBA loan to get started. They were grateful for the help, but it didn't come easy; it took them four weeks, with the help of a bank officer, to fill out a stack of forms, gather all the necessary documentation, and wait for the government's answer. Last year, when they needed another loan to expand, they learned that they qualified for an SBA program, designed by Rodney Martin in SBA, San Antonio office, that provides a fast-track application procedure for loans up to $100,000. The whole process took three days, start to finish—and required only a simple one-page form. That's quite a change from the earlier 78-page application and 90-day review. Multiply that improvement by all the rest of SBA's small-loan applications, apply the same math to many of the procedures the other federal agencies engage in every day, and you begin to get an idea how much can be saved simply by cutting obsolete regulations and pointless paperwork.

Of course, regulatory reform means more than just cutting. It also means making sure the remaining rules are user-friendly. It means making it easier for businesses, or state and local governments, or individual citizens to do things the federal government needs them to do. It means throwing away the hoops people have had to jump through when they wanted service from their government. And above all, it means keeping the government's eye on the ball—the objectives the laws were designed to accomplish.

It's happening. Consider the Environmental Protection Agency, the nation's biggest regulator. Sixteen separate laws spell out the agency's monumental task—to clean up pollution and figure out what needs to be done to protect people and the environment in the future. EPA has been enormously successful: the air is cleaner and healthier; you can swim in rivers that once caught fire and in lakes that once were dead; you can drink water and be sure it's safe; you can find out whether there are hazards in your neighborhood that may harm you or your children. But the costs have also been enormous—to the taxpayer and to industry and small businesses.

The EPA listened to the rising chorus of customer complaints and responded. The agency is rapidly changing the way it regulates, moving from mandatory, punitive compliance approaches to voluntary, consensual approaches. In short, instead of telling businesses what to do to prevent pollution and how to do it, down to the very last detail, EPA now invites businesses to describe how they think they can meet the goal and then lets them get on with it. Already, the agency has created more than two dozen such voluntary programs in a wide range of industry sectors. Says EPA Administrator Carol Browner, "Our new philosophy at EPA is tough standards to protect our air, our water, and the health of our people, but common sense, flexibility, innovation, and creativity in how you meet those standards."[11]

That same philosophy—essentially, the philosophy of reinvention—has taken hold in many other agencies as well. There are hundreds of examples throughout the government.

For example, ever since the Depression, we've been pretty firm about wanting our money protected when we deposit it in the bank. But sometimes the government hasn't made it especially easy for banks to meet that sensible objective. It used to be that when examiners from the Office of the Comptroller of the Currency walked in to examine a small bank, they brought along 1,216 pages of arcane technical procedures. No longer. Now they bring along a user-friendly 30-page booklet.

The rules for creating pension plans are currently so cumbersome and costly to follow that many smaller businesses are unable to afford them for their employees, and some businesses are forced to cut pension programs they already have. This is quite the opposite of what policymakers intended. In June, President Clinton announced an initiative to eliminate and simplify many of the rules governing such programs, along with creating a new, simpler IRA-based plan option called the National Employee Savings Trust, or NEST.

In addition, employers also are required to provide their employees with reports on the financial condition of their pension and welfare benefit plans. So that people reluctant to ask their employers have somewhere else to go, the law also requires employers to provide copies to the Department of Labor. But by the time Labor gets the reports, they're typically seven months old and, therefore, useless. Now, the department proposes to eliminate the requirement, ending a quarter-million filings per year and saving employers 150,000 hours of pointless work and $2.5 million per year in additional costs. If employees want the information, they will be able to call Labor and the department will request it from the plan administrator on the spot. It's just common sense.

Very small companies—those with 10 or fewer employees—make up nearly 80 percent of all American businesses. When asked for their number-one complaint about regulations, small business owners said, "Tax compliance and payroll recordkeeping are too complicated." In response, IRS is building the Simplified Tax and Wage Reporting System. When complete, it will let employers file W-2 data to both federal and state governments, electronically and simultaneously, saving billions of dollars for business every year.

Even as the government is reducing the regulatory burdens on its customers, it's finally also cutting much of its own red tape—the stuff that ties the government itself into knots and runs up the cost of governing. For example, it has entirely eliminated the 10,000-page Federal Personnel Manual—the government's rule book for hiring and firing. Gone, too, is the notoriously complicated Form 171 that anyone seeking to work for the government had to fill out. If American industry will accept your resume, why shouldn't your government?

The government's also getting rid of thousands of pages of lengthy and often ludicrous procurement regulations and product specifications—dozens of pages on how to make French fries or tell whether fish is fresh, dozens more just to describe a camp lantern, and on and on. With the possible exception of late-night talk show hosts who use them from time to time for comic relief, it's unlikely many people will miss procurement regulations either.

Progress Report: Rewarding Results, Not Red Tape

The old OSHA wasn't the only agency in the federal government that was measuring its performance the wrong way. Most agencies did. In fact, when the National Performance Review examined how agencies measure their workers' performance, it found that fully 30 percent of the measures tracked punitive acts, like levying fines. Another 50 percent measured were administrative functions, like filling out forms correctly. Only 20 percent of worker performance was mea-

True Grits

President Clinton, speaking at the White House Conference on Small Business on June 12, 1995:

I hate to tell you this, folks, but we're about to lose the regulation that tells us how to test grits. I want you to ask yourself if you can do without this:

> *Grits, corn grits, hominy grits is the food prepared by so grinding and sifting clean, white corn, with removal of corn bran and germ, that on a moisture-free basis, its crude fiber content is not more than 1.2 percent and its fat content is not more than 2.25 percent and when tested by the method prescribed in Paragraph (b)(2) of this section, not less than 95 percent passes through a #10 sieve, but not more than 20 percent through a #25 sieve . . .*

Now here's the really interesting part; they tell how:

> *Attach bottom pan to a #25 sieve. Fit the #10 sieve into the #25 sieve. Pour 100 grams of sample into the #10 sieve, attach cover, and hold assembly in a slightly inclined position, shake the sieves by striking the sides against one hand with an upward stroke, at the rate of about 150 times per minute. Turn the sieve about one-sixth of a revolution, each time in the same direction, after each 25 strokes. . . . The percent of sample passing through a #10 sieve shall be determined by subtracting from 100 percent the percent remaining in the #10 sieve. The percent of material in the pan shall be considered as the percent passing through the #25 sieve.**

I don't know if we can do without that. There is some real sacrifice here; I am personally going to miss the 2,700-word specifications for french fries.

*21 CFR Sec. 137.230.

sured in terms of how well individual employees actually worked with others—and almost none of *that* was about working with customers.[12]

The study concluded agencies were measuring the wrong things. They were measuring *inputs*, not *outcomes*. In some cases, that was because agency or program missions were fuzzy to begin with. More often, however, the problem was that agencies had gotten so caught up in measuring inputs, they forgot what they were in business to accomplish in the first place.

Take the U.S. Coast Guard. The Coast Guard is responsible for, among other things, promoting safety on the high seas. For years it focused on inspecting the condition of vessels and levying fines whenever it found things weren't shipshape. The more fines, the better it was doing. The problem is, however, that faulty ships don't usually cause accidents—people do.

Today, the Coast Guard has shifted its attention from finding rust spots to reducing injuries and fatalities. It's also reexamined its assumptions. The Coast Guard had determined that its highest priority should be commercial fishing, an industry long known for its high injury rate. But when it actually looked at the entire industry, it found that the injury and fatality rate in the area of commercial towing—tugs and barges—was equally high and needed attention. By focusing on its mission and consulting with the industry itself, the agency achieved dramatic results: fatality rates declined from 91 per 100,000 industry employees in 1990 to only 36 per 100,000 last year—nearly a two-thirds reduction. When you're measuring what matters, nothing matters more than lives.

As President Clinton has noted, "If the government rewards writing citations and levying fines more than safety, then there's a good chance that what you get is more citations, more fines, and no more safety."[13] And if what you measure is red tape, you get more red tape. The combination of the reinvention initiative's emphasis on results and the passage of the Government Performance and Results Act of 1993 is turning scores of federal agencies away from procedure and toward performance—serving people better and, at the same time, reducing the cost of government.

If the government rewards writing citations and levying fines more than safety, then there's a good chance that what you get is more citations, more fines, and no more safety.

PRESIDENT CLINTON

January 24, 1995

This new law ordered agencies to spell out their performance goals clearly and succinctly, make specific commitments for meeting them, and establish formal outcome measurement systems to demonstrate their progress. The law also called for the immediate creation of at least ten "pilot projects." To everyone's astonishment, 27 agencies volunteered, including the Defense Logistics Agency, the Coast Guard, the U.S. Mint, SBA, the National Highway Traffic Safety Administration, USDA's Farmers Home Administration, major programs in the Department of Energy, and the Department of Housing and Urban Development. These agencies, and many others, created more than 70 pilot projects, which are now in the vanguard of reinvention.

One of the first pilots was the Internal Revenue Service, an agency that made a comprehensive commitment to performance improvement. The vast majority of Americans are willing to pay our fair share of taxes, so long as the process of meeting our obligation is as painless as possible. To make it so, the agency has established a strategic plan with measurable, customer-driven outcomes that, as of this year, are directly linked to the performance evaluations of executives and managers throughout the organization. The concept is simple: if employees are measured by how well they serve their customers, their customers will be well-served.

The Agriculture Department, the SBA, Social Security, and HUD, among other agencies, also have begun evaluating employee performance on the basis of explicit, customer-driven outcomes. The Department of Education's new performance appraisal system even has a mechanism for incorporating customer feedback into employee evaluations—a process that has the blessings of the agency's labor-management council.

Progress Report: Getting Out of Washington, Creating Partnerships

Joy Lucas came home to Oregon from Germany last year with two small children, a divorce from her soldier husband, and ambition.[14] But with no work experience and no job skills, her options would have been limited—had it not been for the "Oregon Option," a performance-based partnership contract between federal and state agencies that does something states have been craving for years. It consolidates narrow, inflexible federal funding programs and waives the rules that govern them so they can be merged with state funds and turned into real services for real people in real need.

Joy Lucas has never heard of the Oregon Option. Nor has she heard of Oregon Benchmarks, that state's landmark effort to set goals for government services and hold agencies accountable for achieving them—perhaps the main reason the federal government agreed to the Oregon Option. She doesn't need to know about either one; that's the point. They're invisible to her and should stay that way. Instead of having to navigate the unmapped territory of federal and state categorical programs herself, filling out form after form in agency after agency, she can simply get what she needs—in this case, the training to become a 911 emergency dispatcher and the interim support she needs for herself and her children until she lands the job.

The Oregon Option is just one example of the benefits of "getting out of Washington"—that is, of sitting down with customers and developing partnership agreements for reaching common goals quickly and less expensively. In the last year or two, other examples have developed throughout the federal government. Many involve partnerships between Washington and the states designed to consolidate funding streams, eliminate overlapping authorities, create incentives for achieving concrete results, and reduce the innovation-sapping micromanagement that has so often characterized federal grant programs in the past.

In his 1996 budget, President Clinton has proposed that 271 separate programs be consolidated into 27. In the welfare program, 34 states have been granted waivers from federal micromanagement because their programs address the job of reducing welfare dependency more effectively, more flexibly, and in some cases more innovatively than uniform federal rules would have allowed. In addition, ten states have been granted Medicaid waivers. And, under the education flexibility partnerships, Oregon and several other states are receiving waivers from federal statutory and regulatory rules in education.

In a similar vein, the Community Empowerment Board, comprising 15 federal agencies, has helped the agencies provide waivers of federal job training, community development, and various "safety net" rules for 95 Enterprise Communities and nine Empowerment Zones—created last year to enable communities to custom-craft programs that meet their particular needs. The difference between such waivers and simple block grants is that the waivers require the development of comprehensive community plans and results-based measurement systems; they also ensure accountability for taxpayers' money.

The EPA has undertaken several new partnerships with state and local governments. For instance, many communities have hesitated to redevelop inner-city sites and put them to safe, productive use again, for fear they will be held liable under Superfund legislation for past industrial contamination. The new "brownfields" initiative lifts the threat of liability; that program has awarded five pilot projects, and 50 more are planned. EPA has also limited the liability of the operators of municipal solid waste landfills and removed 25,000 sites that had been tracked by Superfund but that either had no contamination or were being fully addressed by state clean-up programs. Developers wouldn't touch those sites as long as they were still on the tracking list.

Government is creating performance partnerships not only with state and local governments, but also with industry.

Pretend for a moment you're a factory owner in Texas. Plenty of your workers are Mexican citizens. They are here legally—they've got papers. Then one afternoon Immigration and Naturalization Service agents surround the building, burst in the door, inform you that the papers for half your workforce are fraudulent, then arrest them and haul them away. And you're left stranded. No workers, no work. No work, no income. You're in deep trouble.

That happens all the time in the Southwest—or at least it did, until Neil Jacobs, INS assistant district director in Dallas, decided he was getting nowhere. The workers just showed up someplace else a few days later, with more fake papers. Meanwhile, he was hurting the people the area needed most: its employers. Working in partnership with employers, local enforcement officials, and employment services, Jacobs created "Operation Jobs." Now INS meets quietly with employers and connects them with documented workers (at the same wage levels) *before* they remove the undocumented workers. Not only does this change eliminate the disruption of the old approach, it ensures there are no empty slots for the undocumented workers to re-occupy later. And it creates a solid market for legal workers—more than 2,500 of them in north Texas alone, and thousands more now that Jacobs' project has expanded to neighboring states.

On a larger scale, EPA's doing the same kind of thing: developing working partnerships with industry and others to achieve environmental goals. Here are just four of the several dozen EPA initiatives already underway:

- "Green Lights," through which more than 1,500 companies have put in energy-saving lighting throughout their installations (American Express in New York is saving more than a quarter-million dollars annually in energy costs and has received nearly a half-million dollars in rebates from Commonwealth Edison);
- "Waste Wise," which has encouraged more than 400 major industries to generate less solid waste (NYNEX, the northeast telecommunications giant, is saving $6 million a year);

• "Climate Wise," a joint EPA-Department of Energy effort, which helps industry decrease energy use, prevent pollution, and reduce greenhouse gases—while increasing profits (DuPont, for example, aims at reducing greenhouse gases by 40 percent by 2000, for a savings of $31 million annually); and

• The "Pesticide Environmental Stewardship Program," in which EPA, the Department of Agriculture, and the Food and Drug Administration join nearly two dozen industry and commodity production organizations to develop methods for reducing pesticide use and risk.

Another intriguing EPA partnership experiment is "Project XL," by which the agency, working with states, enables individual companies to develop their own ways to improve the environment. Partners will be allowed to replace current requirements with alternative, company-developed controls so long as they perform better than current laws and regulations, permit citizens to examine assumptions and track progress, ensure worker safety and environmental justice, are supported by the community, and are enforceable.

Government-industry partnerships like these continue to grow. For example, the Customs Service has involved business in its own efforts to reinvent itself.

Customs was established in 1789, by the second act of the new Congress, to collect revenue for the new nation—a nation that, even then, had a substantial debt. Customs paid for the Revolutionary War. It paid for the Louisiana Purchase. In fact, it was the major source of revenue for the U.S. Treasury until the early 1900s, when income taxes were created. Customs officials met every incoming ship, supervised unloading, inspected cargo, established duties, and established

SOME COST SAVINGS TO THE PRIVATE SECTOR FROM REGULATORY REINVENTIONS

Private businesses, taxpayers, and consumers will save nearly $28 billion as a result of hundreds of changes to regulatory and administrative activities that will reduce burden or allow alternative approaches to achieving national goals. For example, agencies will:

- Eliminate the Physician Attestation Form. Savings: 200,000 burden hours on doctors and $22,500 per hospital from no longer filing 11 million of these forms.
- Implement effluent trading on a national scale as a cost-effective approach for reducing water pollution. Savings: at least $1.2 billion, and possibly as much as $15 billion a year.
- Reduce existing monitoring, recordkeeping, and reporting burdens by at least 25 percent. Savings: 20 million burden hours for employers.
- Revise PCB disposal regulations to allow less expensive disposal methods. Savings: $4 billion a year.
- Streamline the Resource Conservation and Recovery Act's corrective action procedures. Savings: $4 billion a year.
- Streamline the alien labor certification process by decentralizing authority to state employment agencies and automating form processing. Savings: $223.8 million over five years.
- Simplify pension computation procedures by relying on employer calculations and simplifying methods of dealing with complex plan provisions. Savings: $6.3 million over five years.
- Streamline affirmative action plans for federal contractors. Savings: 4.8 million hours of contractor time annually.

• Relieve duplicate filing burden on employers. Three federal agencies—IRS, Labor, and Social Security—have agreed to work together to eliminate duplicate tax data filing requirements on businesses and taxpayers. Savings: $1 billion a year in time spent by employers.

• Expand federal-state tax partnerships to eliminate duplicative tax requirements and allow a single filing. Savings: $1.5 billion in reduced burden on taxpayers.

a written record of every transaction. More than two centuries later, they still did.

In the meantime, both the traffic and the shipping-related problems (drugs, contraband, firearms, diseases) skyrocketed. And so did the paperwork. Forms got longer and longer, inspections more and more complex, and delays reached intolerable levels. Combine this with a measurement system that cared more about how many shipments were detained than about how many were cleared, and you have a recipe for chaos, frustration, anger. Finally, Customs itself got fed up. The result was the Customs Modernization and Informed Compliance Act, signed just months after President Clinton announced the reinvention initiative.

Customs met with shippers all over the country and designed a new automated system for handling shipments—a system so simple that most cargo is now cleared before it is even unloaded. Information is collected monthly instead of transaction-by-transaction, and companies have just one Customs account, rather than one for every port through which their shipments pass. (One Miami company used to file some 700,000 forms every year; now it files one per month.[15]) In the meantime, Customs is in the process of clearing out most of its current regulations and designing new ones, with the help of shippers themselves. Despite the need to completely overhaul their own procedures, businesses are delighted. Time is money; their objective is to move cargo. Now that's Customs' objective too. The bonus is that voluntary compliance with Customs duties and apprehension of violators are increasing as well.

Progress Report: Negotiating, Not Dictating

When government representatives "get out of Washington," meet with customers and front-line employees, and start addressing problems on the ground—not in the rarefied air of the Capital—understanding grows. With understanding comes trust, and a willingness to arrive at agreements jointly, without the intervention of enforcers and lawyers. It's common sense. It's also a world away from the "Decide-Announce-Defend" approach the government has used for years. As Philip Howard explains, "Sensible results come out of discussion and negotiation, not from seizing technicalities and parsing legal language to achieve a victory."[16]

Some agencies have been moving toward regulatory negotiation for a few years. EPA has conducted 16 negotiated rule-setting programs in the last ten years. USDA and the Department of Transportation have also used "reg-negs," as they're called. Agencies like OSHA and the Nuclear Regulatory Commission are using online computer systems to give as wide a range of customers as possible an easy way to comment on proposed rules. This year, as part of President Clinton's 100-day governmentwide regulatory reform initiative, agencies identified more than 40 high-visibility issues that were ripe for negotiated rulemaking.

EPA has gone even farther: its "Common Sense Initiative"—a dramatic departure from its old "command and control" way of operating—has brought together teams of industry representatives, labor, environmental groups, community organizations, and government officials at every level to find ways to change complicated, inconsistent, and costly regulations. Even more unusual, it focuses on six specific industries: auto manufacturing, computers and electronics, iron and steel, metal finishing, petroleum refining, and printing. Under the new initiative, "We're taking all the regulations that relate to the individual industry and putting them on the table," EPA Administrator Carol Browner says. "We're going to seek the best way for that industry to meet environmental standards to ensure clean water and clean air."[17]

Ask industry how it should be regulated? Who else knows the problems, and the potential solutions, better? So long as the government establishes standards that protect the public, why not let the industries and other affected stakeholders help figure out how best to get there? Government, industry, and the public share a common goal—a cleaner environment at less cost to taxpayers and businesses. The stakeholder groups are looking for common sense approaches to regulation, pollution prevention, reporting, compliance, permitting, and technology. The principles of this new partnership are to seek consensus on how to reach the goal, focus on prevention, develop industry-specific solutions rather than trying, as Browner says, to make "one size fit all," and maintain tough standards.

In a way, it's borrowing an idea from the past. As General George S. Patton said, "Never tell people how to do things. Tell them what to do, and they will surprise you with their ingenuity."[18]

THE ROAD AHEAD

As *Newsweek* magazine pointed out this year, in the old federal government the theory was that if you just stipulated every possible regulatory circumstance, a robotic army of inspectors could go out and enforce the rules.[19] The trouble is, circumstances differ, conditions change, life goes on. And the government went on too, but with the same inflexible, red tape-tangled procedures it had always used—in some cases, since the beginning of the Republic.

There's an old saying: "If we keep on doing what we're doing, we're gonna keep on getting what we've got." Americans don't want "what we've got" anymore. We want a government that delivers results, that keeps up with change and actually helps people, businesses, and state and local governments adapt to those changes. We want, in fact, an *enterprising* government, one that moves as quickly as the rest of our society, one that works with us, listens to us, and acts on the things we need in a more efficient, more effective, and less costly manner than it has in the past.

And that's what we're beginning to get. Agencies that treat their customers as partners. That cut rules long out-of-date and make those we still need sensible. That seek to find ways to achieve public goals without damaging the structure of private enterprise that supports us. That remember that the purpose is progress toward those goals, not punishment for those who violate—often unwittingly—rules that are obscure or pointless. And that reward their own employees for doing the right thing, not simply for doing things right according to the rulebook.

As *The New York Times* said, it is a "quiet revolution."[20] But revolutions take time, and no one is suggesting the government's got the problems all licked. There is progress, but there is a great deal that remains to be done—and indeed, it is never finished. New laws get passed. New regulations get written. The government's task is to ensure that those rules are clear about what needs to be accomplished, but flexible about how.

What government reinvention does is reinstate the promise of common sense in self-government. President Clinton has already described the result: "a government that is limited but effective ... that does better what it should do and simply stops doing things it shouldn't be doing in the first place, that protects consumers, workers, and the environment without burdening business, choking innovation, or wasting the money of the American taxpayer."[21]

3

Putting Customers First

Who'd have guessed the Social Security folks give better customer service on the phone than Corporate America's role models?

Business Week, *May 29, 1995*

William Festag will stand behind *Business Week's* assessment of Social Security's new phone service. When his wife died in December 1994, Festag had a lot of calls to make. One of them was to Robert Allen at the Social Security Administration. "Mr. Allen sensed my emotional and mental state at the time of the call and somehow managed to strike the proper balance between being businesslike and sympathetic," Festag wrote later. "His professionalism and skill in performing that job is not only a credit to his ability, but reflects the high standards that your agency must be maintaining."

An isolated example of an exceptional employee in a lumbering bureaucracy? Not according to a major national survey. When researchers from Dalbar Financial Services, North America's biggest financial news publisher, went looking for the best 800-number customer service in their "World-Class Benchmarks" survey this year, they didn't find it at folksy L.L. Bean. They didn't find it at Disney World. Or at Nordstrom, the retail chain so famous for customer service that stores take returns of things they don't even sell. They didn't find it at "When you absolutely, positively have to get it there overnight" Federal Express.

They found it at the Social Security Administration.[1] Dalbar rated the organizations it surveyed for attitude, helpfulness, knowledge, the time it took to answer the phone, and the time it took to reach a personal representative. While SSA lagged considerably behind other organizations in the amount of time callers were on hold, once the agency staff came on the line, they were tops in the nation for being "courteous, knowledgeable, and efficient."[2] The result? Some of these companies are now studying SSA for ideas. Meanwhile, the agency is training 3,300 more people on its own staff to cut that "on-hold" problem.

At a time when government agencies are trying to be as good as private businesses, the way SSA handles its telephone customers isn't as good—it's better. A federal government agency is setting the standard.

This is no fluke. Last year, President Clinton told the federal government to ask its customers what they wanted, listen and respond, and keep checking back with them. And that's exactly what SSA did. It also asked its front-line workers who serve customers every day how they would redesign the system if they had the chance.

The agency got an earful. Folks said that after working hard and paying into Social Security all their lives, they didn't think they ought to have to work just as hard to get their benefits out when they retired. Yet when they called the agency, they said, they got the bureaucratic runaround—plus, they said, they had a hard time getting through at all.

SSA heard these complaints and responded. The agency studied the best in the business of customer telephone service—American Express, Saturn Corporation, AT&T, the GE Answer Center—and then set out to beat them.

It was a tall order. SSA maintains earnings records on almost 140 million Americans and pays out social security insurance and supplemental security income benefits totaling nearly $300 billion to nearly 45 million people every year. The agency receives 64 million calls each year on its toll-free number, sometimes peaking at 1.7 million *in a single day*.[3] For many Americans, Social Security is the difference between a home and homelessness, between food and hunger, between reassurance and worry. A lot of people depend on Social Security. Their number will grow even more as the baby boomers age.

And SSA isn't alone. The Internal Revenue Service gets nearly 96 million calls a year. Until recently, it too had a pretty bleak record. Taxpayers complained constantly about having trouble getting answers from IRS—and even more trouble getting *correct* answers.

IRS got the message. Now, for the first time, the agency has customer service standards with a simple objective: the right answer the first time. It used to be that your chances of getting the wrong answer the first time from IRS were about one in three. Today, you can count on getting the right answer the first time 91 percent of the time—and the agency is working on doing even better. In the meantime, if IRS's representatives make a mistake, you pay no penalty.[4]

THE SERVICE REVOLUTION

We've always had our telephone lines open from 8:00 a.m. to 5:00 p.m., five days a week. Well, guess what? Everybody in this country works during those hours! It was ludicrous.

LARRY WESTFALL, IRS Modernization Program[5]

Just a few decades ago, life was simpler than it is today. There were three TV networks. Four car makers. One phone company. If you wanted to see a movie, you went to a theater. Ours was a mass production economy. You could get pretty good products, though there weren't a lot to choose from. You could get pretty good service, as long as you weren't in too much of a hurry.

Those days are gone. The explosion of information in the last decade or so may have complicated our lives, but it's also given us an explosion of choices—and a lot more power as consumers. So now our expectations are higher. We want quality, value, and variety. We want things customized to our individual needs. And we want convenience and timeliness. Federal Express (now called FedEx—even its name is faster) taught us to take overnight delivery for granted. But even that's old news: with faxes, we want it *now*.

You can't provide this kind of service with an old-fashioned, top-down corporation. So, many large corporations "atomized" into small ones with fewer layers of management. Now, employees—like the folks who work for Southwest Airlines—work in flexible teams and do a little bit of everything. Customers—not executives and engineers—determine what products and services will be offered. Producers and suppliers work together as partners, not adversaries. Companies that may be competitors in one line of business co-operate in others.

In short, companies adapted to consumers' demands for better products and services. The federal government, on the other hand, didn't.

Until reinvention began in 1993, most federal government agencies were like the big corporations of the 1950s: vast, slow-moving, resistant to change, virtually impervious to us lesser folk. But dinosaurs like these can't meet today's needs—either in the private sector or in government.

Government had another complication: many government services are monopolies. If you need a passport, for example, where else are you going to go? With little or no competition, agencies had gotten used to taking their customers for granted—or simply assuming they already knew those customers' needs.

That's changing, and the reason is the agencies are listening now. What Americans are telling them is that when we want service from our government, we ought to get it.

Now, in many places, we can.

WHAT AMERICANS SAY GOOD SERVICE MEANS

The kind of service Americans want from the government is pretty basic—fast, accurate assistance; readily available help; options for where and how to get services; clear advice, letters, publications, and forms; and friendly treatment.

Last year, as mentioned above, federal agencies asked their customers what they wanted, how they defined good service. Here's what they said, and how agencies are responding.

Ask Us What We Want

When you walk into Burger King, the people at the counter don't tell you what you'll have for lunch—you get to choose. And you get to choose from much more than hamburgers—chicken, salads, and more. If you want a hamburger anyway, you get to choose what's on it. The folks at Burger King don't do anything by accident. Each new product o[redacted] vice they introduce is the result of careful analysis of [redacted] tomers' needs and interests. They survey, they test, [redacted] survey again, and then they roll out something new. And [redacted]

President Clinton's Executive Order 12862

"Setting Customer Service Standards"

- Identify customers who are, or should be, served by the agency.
- Survey customers to determine the kind and quality of services they want and their level of satisfaction with existing services.
- Post service standards and measure results against them.
- Benchmark customer service standards against the best in business.
- Survey front-line employees on barriers to, and ideas for, matching the best in business.
- Provide customers with choices in both the sources of service and the means of delivery.
- Make information, services, and complaint systems easily accessible.
- Provide means to address customer complaints.

evaluate how it does. The idea is not so much that "The customer is always right," as "If we're here to serve customers, we'd better know what they want."

In the past, it seemed as though the government rarely gave any thought to what people wanted—or, rather, it *assumed* that it knew. But it's often been wrong. For example, people at the Department of Veterans Affairs often assumed that vets didn't mind sitting around in waiting rooms at VA hospitals because it gave them a chance to swap war stories. But when they finally talked to their customers, they found that vets disliked waiting as much as everyone else does. So VA set out to reduce waiting times.

The Social Security Administration also got a surprise when it made assumptions about what the public would want. SSA already knew that its longstanding policy of mailing everyone's checks on the same day each month caused some problems: it swamped front-line SSA workers and the post office. It created lines at the banks. And it made elderly customers vulnerable to robbery because every petty crook in town knew they'd have their checks that day. The obvious solution, SSA decided, was to spread the mailings for different individuals throughout the month—making sure that the day of payment would be consistent as far as each customer is concerned. But when SSA made this proposal to its customers, it found that people didn't like the "obvious" solution one bit. Even though they weren't pleased with the monthly crunch, most had arranged their lives, and their cash flow, around that beginning-of-the-month Social Security check—and they didn't want their routine to change. So SSA modified its solution. Starting next year, the agency will stagger the payment date for new beneficiaries only; it won't mess with current recipients unless they volunteer to participate.

The federal government is finally getting it right. It's asking us what we want, instead of telling us what we need. It's listening to what we say, and then acting on it quickly and flexibly. It's treating taxpayers like valued customers.

Don't Tell Us "That's Not My Department"

People hate getting the runaround. And the more precious time becomes to busy people, the more they dislike getting bounced from office to office when they call or visit a federal government agency to get something done. There may be no statement in our language more frustrating and less helpful than "Sorry, that's not my department."

And yet, the way the government has been organized for years—with solid brick walls between agencies, and even between divisions inside agencies—that was often the only answer federal government employees could give. Even if they were able to breach those walls (and often they couldn't), they seldom knew much about what was on the other side.

Compare that, for example, to shopping at Nordstrom, the department store chain that prides itself on its customer service. If you buy a dress or a suit at Nordstrom and need several kinds of accessories to complete the outfit, the staff won't send you from department to department. Instead, a cross-trained employee will do the running for you, returning quickly with several choices pulled from several different departments.

Why can't the government have the same attitude? The issues that matter to people don't have nice neat walls; they're complicated and involve lots of players. Americans want these issues—big and small—solved, not frustrated by bureaucratic barriers.

Since the reinvention initiative began in 1993, those barriers have begun to fall—and the first to fall are those that matter most: the ones closest to the customer. Consider Miami International Airport on June 29, 1995—the day, according to Art Torno, managing director for American Airlines in Miami, "that things fell apart in Immigration." Incoming flights swamped the Immigration and Naturalization Service, which is responsible for checking passports and clearing passengers. As the wait approached three hours, fistfights broke out among tired, frustrated travelers in the terminal. Meanwhile, more arriving passengers waited, fuming, in their planes.

Airline and airport officials were ready to complain to Washington—but they didn't have to. The government was already listening. Dan Cadman, the local INS director, and Lynn Gordon, the local Customs Service director, working with their partners in the American Federation of Government Employees and the National Treasury Employees Union, brought together an emergency coalition of customers and officials to solve the problem locally—and fast. In two weeks of brainstorming, the airlines, airport officials, and several government agencies worked out an entirely new passenger handling system.

Two weeks after that, as the vacation travel season peaked, the new system was in place. The three-hour waits were gone. "It's the first time I've seen the airlines and the agencies cheering each other and patting each other on the back," says American's Torno.[6] But now the airlines had a new problem: passengers were clearing Immigration so quickly they were reaching the baggage hall before their bags!

Clearly, if government agencies are freed to respond to customer needs, not just agency directives, they can break down the walls and get things done . . . and quickly.

Treat Us with Courtesy, Respect . . . and Enthusiasm

Federal employees take a lot of heat for what's wrong with government, but the plain truth is that it's the system in which they work, not the workers themselves, that's the main problem. It is so rigid, so rule-bound, so inflexible, so inherently unfriendly that they themselves are frustrated and angry. They want to help customers, to tailor services to their needs, to treat them as individuals—treat them, indeed, as what they are: not only the government's customers, but also its *stockholders.* But too often the system doesn't permit it. Government workers signed on to be public servants, but ended up *program* servants instead. And they don't like it any more than their customers do.

Now that's changing . . . even in the Postal Service. Around the country, customer advocacy councils are suggesting how post offices can best serve local customers. In Houston post offices, for example, officials asked some of their customers to create a sort of "shoppers' checklist" that summed up the kind of service they expected. These volunteers described not only how they wanted to be treated, but also everything from the speed of service to the way postal clerks should dress. Then the post office posted these standards, re-trained its workers, and encouraged the volunteers to act as "mystery shoppers," checking up from time to time.

The employees didn't take this as a new imposition; they saw it as finally being judged on how well they treated their customers, not how well they followed the rules. Not only did physical appearance at the post office change, attitudes changed. Employees were courteous, friendly, prompt. They began to take pride in their job and treat their customers with the respect they deserved. In short, they treated them as they would want to be treated themselves.

Not surprisingly, customer satisfaction soared. An independent company, Opinion Research Corporation, has been measuring customer satisfaction at post offices for years. In 1991, Houston's average customer satisfaction score was 79 out of 100. Today, it's 88.[7]

These kinds of changes are happening not just where services are retailed "over the counter," but throughout the federal government. All it takes is giving workers the freedom to do what needs to be done. "People say I don't act like I work for the federal government because I'm nice to them," says Brenda Oesterheld, an information assistant in the Washington, D.C., Customs office. "But I'm a taxpayer too. I expect the best from the government and I'm going to give the best back."[8]

Make It Easy

Americans have a simple question: if the government works for us and we've already paid for its services, why is it so hard to get anything out of it?

The government has an answer: increasingly, it won't be so difficult to deal with anymore. Agencies are letting people know what help is available and making it accessible through as many means as possible—in person, by phone, by fax, on the Internet. And this is happening throughout the federal government.

For example, to get medical care at a VA hospital, you have to spend an hour with an intake interviewer answering 93 questions to prove you are a veteran and needy. Questions like this: "During the last calendar year, did you have any unmarried children or stepchildren who were under the age of 18 or between the ages of 18 and 23 and attending school or any unmarried children over the age of 17 who became permanently incapable of self-support before reaching the age of 18?" Assuming you understand and answer this and the other 92 questions, the VA then double-checks all your answers with your Social Security records and triple-checks them with your IRS records.

But soon that will be history. In the coming year, there will be only three questions: How much do you make? Do you have any dependents? Would you mind if we checked your IRS records? That's it. All the VA has to do is trust its customers to give honest answers.

Another way to make things easy is to make them convenient. The Forest Service had the right idea: if you want to cut down a Christmas tree in a National Forest, you need a permit. That makes sense; we can't have people chopping down trees willy-nilly. What doesn't make sense is having to make a special trip to some distant Forest Service headquarters to get the permit, or having to do it by mail. One office's solution? Sell the permits where people rent chain saws. Now, that's convenient.

The irony here is that when the federal government responds to what Americans want—a simpler, easier government—it also makes things easier, and cheaper, for itself.

Provide Reliable, Timely Help

Americans are reasonable people. We'd like to have our questions, our applications, our permit requests, and the like answered immediately (and preferably in our favor). But in the event that an answer or a decision may take a little time, we'd like to get what we're used to getting from the best private businesses: an indication when we *will* get an answer, a promise that someone will follow up, and the name and phone number of someone knowledgeable and reliable who we can check with in the future.

It's the waiting that's so annoying. There is no reason—other than sheer bureaucracy—why the government can't be as responsive as the best businesses. When a good business has a defective product, it replaces it immediately and at no cost to the customer. Now the federal government has demonstrated the same kind of service.

STAT-USA, the Commerce Department's one-stop shop for business and economic information, regularly updates the National Trade Data Bank, a CD-ROM database that contains enormous quantities of data vital to exporters. The disks go to some 1,600 subscribers who, in turn, may serve hundreds of others. A few days after it mailed the July 1995 trade data update, STAT-USA started getting calls about a problem with the software. Because STAT-USA's staff knew how time-critical the information was, they didn't wait to go through a complex approval process. As soon as they determined that customers couldn't work around the problem, they immediately shipped replacement disks—despite the fact that, as a self-supported organization, STAT-USA would have to swallow the cost.

The response was dramatic. STAT-USA received scores of calls and letters from customers thanking them for their quick response. Wrote Richard Jurek, an officer at National Trust in Chicago, "STAT-USA is good government: cost-effective, efficient, responsive, and value-adding!"

We have already mentioned the Postal Service—the organization we love to complain about. For years, it seemed like hardly a day went by that there wasn't some postal horror story in the news. But hard as it may be to believe, things are improving. During the first quarter of 1995, the independent American Customer Satisfaction Index surveyed 10,000 customers about the quality of 200 communication, transportation, utility, and service companies they used. Only one showed improvement over the preceding quarter: the U.S. Postal Service. Customer satisfaction with the U.S. mail jumped 13 percent from 1994. Satisfaction with the rest—hotels, long-distance services, and airlines, among others—either declined or remained flat. Postal officials credit the rise to changes such as extended hours, a 24-hour help line in major cities, a five-minute service guarantee at many branches, and a record 85 percent on-time delivery record. Says Claes Fornell, the survey's economist, "You don't see many companies improve an image that quickly."[9]

THE RESULTS: A GOVERNMENT THAT SERVES

Tell your CEO that the federal government may be outclassing your company. . . . For once the federal government is ahead of the private sector.

LAWRENCE MAGID, *Information Week* magazine[10]

Last year, in response to President Clinton's directive, agencies established standards for the service they provide to their customers. The standards address a wide range of customers: the general public, businesses, law enforcement officials, travelers, tourists, outdoor enthusiasts, veterans, state and local governments, natural resource users, and federal employees themselves, among others.

Then the government did something even most businesses don't do. More than 150 agencies published the standards and distributed them to the public. They consist of simple, straightforward statements that spell out, in plain English, exactly what Americans can expect from their government.

Since then, 50 more agencies have added their own standards. (For a comprehensive list of these standards, see the report *Putting Customers First '95: Standards for Serving the American People.*[11])

Finally, this year, the government set about the task of surveying its customers as the first step in measuring how well the agencies were actually living up to those service standards. This is the way the best businesses are run, but in government it was virtually unheard-of.

Just as America's corporations realized they had to change their corporate cultures in order to compete in a globalized economy where the consumer was the boss, rather than a domestic economy where the producer was the boss, so too must the government shift from a *restrictive culture* to a *responsive culture*. It doesn't happen overnight, and it certainly doesn't happen just because you've published some service standards. Still, there is steady progress on every front.

Progress Report: Asking and Listening

It seems simple, asking the customer—but it's not. For one thing, sometimes customers don't know what to ask for. They know what they need, but they don't know the solution or where to find it. For another, not all federal government programs know who their customers are, how to reach them, or what to ask them.

For example, for years the Department of Housing and Urban Development has seen local public housing authorities as its principal customers. That approach has frequently failed to deliver decent housing for low-income people. Now, HUD proposes to make residents their customers, and to provide these people with vouchers for government payments so they can make their own choices about where to live. "Who are we to say...people ought to have to live in those God-awful conditions?" says HUD Secretary Henry Cisneros. "We're putting power with the people to make those choices."[12]

Often, however, the government's customers are easy to identify. They let the government know who they are and what they need. The difference today is that the government is listening.

State and local government officials complained that the process of applying for federal government grants was so time-consuming and costly that it diminished, rather than enhanced, their ability to meet the needs of their jurisdictions. In response, agencies throughout the federal government are consolidating grantmaking programs. For example—with support from Alice Rivlin, Director of the Office of Management and Budget—the Department of Health and Human Services is consolidating 107 health service grants into six performance partnerships and 11 consolidated grants, and giving its state and local government partners more flexibility in the bargain. Part of the motivation is overall governmentwide streamlining, of course, but it is driven by a new awareness of and responsiveness to customers. "The reinventing government effort has been a special opportunity to bring about changes that make sense, and to try new approaches," says HHS Secretary Donna Shalala.

Businesses complained that while they knew there was government help available for small businesses, there was no easy way to get access to it. Time is money, they said, and it's just too time-consuming to figure out what help is available, where to get it, and how to use it. What was needed was a way not just of making more information accessible in user-friendly ways, but of eliminating the artificial (and, for customers at least, irrelevant) distinctions about which agency produced what information.

The result is the U.S. General Store, opened as a test project in Houston on July 6, 1995. Prompted by the reinvention movement to do whatever best served their customers, some 14 federal agencies created a one-stop business assistance center. You go to (or call) one place, and you deal with one person cross-trained in the information, services, and regulations of all the participating agencies. That person can provide loan information, assist with tax problems, help you comply with regulations (a request that came up often in discussions with businesspeople), explain federal contract bidding procedures, and more. The store plans to have all the agencies' databases merged and accessible in one place. Parking is free. It's open some evenings and weekends. Better yet, it required no new funding; it was simply a matter of making what was already available easier to use. "Our goal is 100 percent customer satisfaction, and we ask each customer if they are satisfied with service they received. We hear great things from customers everyday," says store manager Sandra Ellison.

"Starting a business is like walking into a forest of redwoods," says Houston business owner Alan Bergeron. "You don't know what direction to go.... It's great to be able to be able to knock on one door and get a whole library of answers." Next step?—if customers approve, the General Store will become a national chain. Call it "Gov-Mart."

Listening also can be lifesaving. The Consumer Product Safety Commission's job is to protect Americans from dangerous products, provide information on product recalls, and gather reports on product-related injuries. To help its customers, the commission has reinvented its consumer hotline.

The line is open 24 hours a day, seven days a week. Information is available in English or Spanish and, during regular business hours, in other languages as well. In the first year after the upgrade, the commission received more than a quarter-million calls—nearly 80 percent more calls than before—and double the number of product complaints. And the cost per call dropped sharply.

Asking and listening is making a difference to customers—often desperate ones—of the Federal Emergency Management Agency. A survey of 1.2 million disaster assistance applicants revealed that agency representatives' compassion and willingness to listen was the most important aspect of FEMA's services for 38 percent of those surveyed.[13] That's more than twice as important as the things FEMA assumed were the most important, like the amount of assistance dollars received, the fairness of home inspections, or the length of time to apply for and receive financial assistance. So FEMA is working to balance staff members' financial skills with people skills.

And here's perhaps the most interesting thing about asking and listening to the customer: for the first time in years, public servants are doing what they have always wanted to do—serve the public. Unchained from the system, encouraged and rewarded for service by President Clinton, they have become wellsprings of ideas for making government work better and cost less.

Progress Report: Establishing Customer Service Standards

So far, 98 percent of all federal agencies have talked with their customers—something they were discouraged from doing until President Clinton made it possible—and all have developed standards in response to what their customers said.

In many cases, these service standards don't look like anything you've ever seen before from the government:[14]

- They're specific, not vague ("Lobby service in 5 minutes").
- They're personalized and aim to meet customers' expectations ("We will respond to your application within one business day").
- They make firm commitments ("You'll only have to make one stop").
- If an across-the-board commitment is impossible, they pledge to make that commitment when you contact the agency ("We will tell you if we can't give you an answer right away and tell you who will respond to your request and when").
- If customer expectations can't currently be met, they say how or when they will be ("We now process fingerprints in 21 days; by 1997 we will process them within two days of time of receipt").
- And they provide specific avenues for complaints ("If you have a problem that has not been resolved through normal processes, you may contact our Problem Resolution Office").

It isn't surprising that Americans are responding favorably to standards like these. Here's just one fan letter, from one taxpayer in San Francisco: "The Pension Benefit Guaranty Corporation has succeeded in a superior mission . . . few companies can equal...to establish and pledge service standards for customers."[15]

Progress Report: Benchmarking the Best in Business

President Clinton directed federal agencies to examine and learn from "the highest quality of service delivered to cus-

Highlights from Customer Service Standards

Social Security Administration

• If you request a new or replacement Social Security card from one of our offices, we will mail it to you within five work days of receiving all information we need. If you have an urgent need for the Social Security number, we will tell you the number within one work day.

• When you make an appointment, we'll serve you within 10 minutes of the scheduled time.

• We'll provide you with our best estimate of the time we need to complete your request, and we'll fully explain any delays.

Department of Agriculture food stamp program

• We promise to let you know if you're eligible for food stamps as soon as possible, but no later than 30 days after you file your application. You'll need to fill out your application as soon as possible, but you can start counting the days as soon as you contact the food stamp office and give us your name, address, and signature.

• If you qualify for immediate assistance, we promise to give you your food stamp benefits within five work days.

• We promise to let you know at least one month before your food stamp benefits are due to stop. If you apply to continue your food stamps by the 15th of your last month—and you still qualify—we'll make sure your benefits are not interrupted.

Consumer Product Safety Commission

• Call the CPSC Hotline at 1-800-638-2772 to report an unsafe product, report a product-related injury, receive information on product recalls and repairs/replacements, and learn what to look for in purchases. Customer service standards are:

• Answer your call 7 days a week/24 hours a day.

• Provide easy-to-follow instructions in English or Spanish, or in another language during working hours.

tomers by private organizations."This process is called "benchmarking." That's the name industry uses for the process of continuously learning—"stealing shamelessly"—from the best, not just in your own industry, but in any industry that has functions like yours.

Social Security, determined to make dramatic improvements to its "800" telephone service, helped lead a multi-agency study—the first of its kind—to examine the phone service methods of such industry leaders as American Express, AT&T Universal Card, Citibank, Bell Canada, Duke Power Company, the GE Answer Center, the Saturn Corporation, and USAA Insurance.

Sometimes the best in business isn't business at all. This year, *Business Travel News*, the newspaper of the business travel industry, looked for the best business travel management operations in the country—the "Master Tacticians," in their words—and chose four. The winners were Hewlett-Packard, Bankers Trust, Texas Instruments and...the National Security Agency.[16]

NSA, a National Performance Review "Reinvention Laboratory," had found that its travel operation took 79 days to process the paperwork for the average business trip and cost more than $8 million a year to administer. To find a better way, agency staff visited the travel offices of Allied Signal, Apple Computer, The Aerospace Corporation, Conrail, IBM,

TAX RETURNS FILED BY TELEPHONE

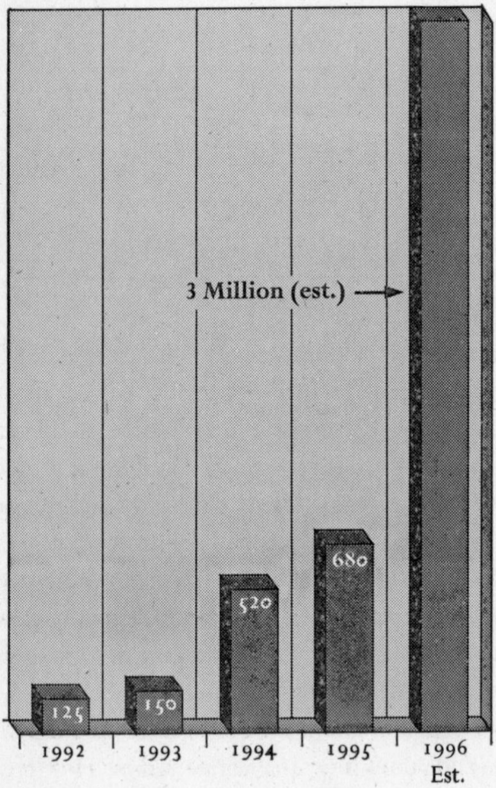

Number of Calls In Thousands
Source: Internal Revenue Service

Sun Microsystems, Texas Instruments, US West, and the World Bank. Then they sat down to design a better system than any of them.

Thanks to the benchmarking process, NSA is bringing the time required to administer the process down 93 percent, travelers' form-filing time down 74 percent, and total processing costs down 75 percent. Now, you may think $8 million isn't a lot of money to the federal government, but when hundreds of subdivisions of the federal government get the "best in the business" religion, those $8 million pots really add up.

Progress Report: Using Technology to Serve Customers Better

These days, being as good or better than the best in business—best both in quality and cost—often means making the best use of available technology. And driven by the twin incentives of reinvention and the need to economize, people have brought a lot of technology, especially information technology, to the service of the federal government's customers.

This year, for example, IRS made all of its forms and publications available to taxpayers electronically, through the Internet or simply by modem from one computer to another. What's more, the quality of IRS's presentation earned it ranking by *PC Computing* Magazine as one of the top 101 Internet sites.[17] In its first month, IRS's offerings increased the traffic on FedWorld, a government Internet information source, by 400 percent, making it the most popular service in the system—and it wasn't even April!

In addition, IRS now makes it possible for taxpayers to file electronically and for employers to submit employee tax and wage reports at one time, to one place, electronically. And employers can now deposit federal payroll taxes automatically, instead of making special trips to their bank. More than 25,000 employers signed up for this service in the first half of 1995 alone. Finally, next spring, some 5 million 1040EZ form users will have the option to file their taxes simply by using their touch-tone phone.[18] IRS estimates that 3 million will do so.

SSA has also won awards for its Internet information services and, at the same time, is testing public electronic information access kiosks, or booths, so people without computers and Internet access can still get SSA information and assistance quickly.

And in the nation's crowded airports, the Immigration folks are trying to one-up themselves. Not only do they not want you to stand in line a long time, they don't want you to stand in line at all: they've created INSPASS, a sort of "automatic teller machine" for frequent international travelers. You insert an ID card, slip your hand in a slot, are recognized by the system, and you're cleared in about 30 seconds. It's also a bargain for taxpayers. Each $35,000 inspection machine, operating 24 hours a day, seven days a week, replaces 4.2 inspectors and saves $1 million in five years. If the tests now underway at Newark and JFK airports in metropolitan New York and at the Immigration facility in Toronto are successful, the program will soon be expanded nationwide.[19]

Finally, sometimes you can improve service dramatically simply by using existing technology more efficiently. On August 30, 1995, Trans World Airlines held a ceremony in St. Louis to honor the Federal Aviation Administration's Service Improvement Team for helping restore the financially troubled carrier to profitability. By rethinking aircraft climb and descent profiles and simplifying the arrival system, the team enabled planes to land quicker than before, speeding turnaround and increasing profitability.

Progress Report: Measuring and Rewarding Service

To continuously serve customers well, you have to keep asking them what they want, assessing whether they're satisfied with what they're getting, and revising your standards and services accordingly. Businesses do this to keep from losing their customers to competitors. Government, which seldom has competitors, needs to do it too, however—because it's *right*. Because it owes it to its stockholders.

So on March 22, 1995, President Clinton issued a new directive not only reinforcing the requirement that agencies

HOW CUSTOMERS RATE THE PARK SERVICE

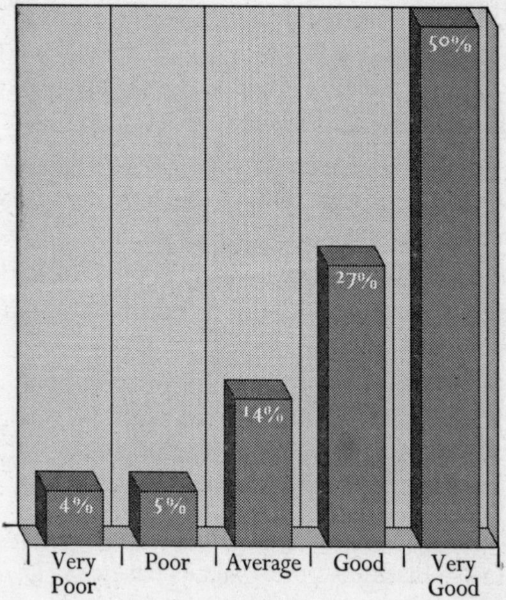

Data from 1993–94, 18 parks; 8,219 respondents
Percent is proportion of respondents
Source: NPS/University of Idaho

develop and publish customer standards, but also directing them to survey customers and their own front-line employees about how to improve service, measure customer satisfaction, integrate their customer service activities with all other performance initiatives, and identify activities that cross agency lines in order to better coordinate and deliver service. In addition, the agencies were asked to go where the need was greatest: the areas with the most customers and transactions, those that customers and employees had already suggested mattered most, and those that had suffered the most service problems.

But measurement can be tricky. For years, for example, the U.S. Postal Service has measured its efficiency, which is a good idea. And the measurements said it was efficient, which is also good. Problem is, a lot of customers didn't agree. It turns out it was measuring the wrong thing. What it was measuring was the time between when a letter is postmarked in one post office branch and delivered to another. Very useful for the agency, perhaps, but completely irrelevant to its customers, who care about what really matters: the time between when they put a letter in a mailbox and when the little devil actually is *delivered*. We don't care about the internal workings of the post office; we care about whether the letter we mailed gets where it's going.

The moral of the story: measure what matters to your customers. Now, the Postal Service does just that. And that's one reason why its customer satisfaction ratings are starting to rise.[20]

Americans don't care what goes into the process (unless it costs too much); that's the government's business. They care about what comes out the other end. They care about *outcomes*. But government agencies are used to measuring inputs:

the amount of money spent on some task or the number of people assigned, not whether customers are satisfied with the result.

But that's changing quickly. IRS, for example, measures outcomes that matter: for example, how long it takes to get your refund in the mail. A little over a year ago, IRS promised taxpayers that if we filed by mail, the agency would send our refund out in 40 days; if we filed electronically, it would respond in 21 days. Results? Ninety-eight percent of all refunds in 1995 went out on time, as promised.

Some agencies are even asking their customers to measure *them*. SSA uses "How Are We Doing?" comment cards in its field offices and teleservice center to get customer feedback on overall service, length of wait, courtesy, and whether they received the service they desired. Similarly, the National Park Service and U.S. Fish and Wildlife Service have begun a pilot project to use customer evaluation cards to collect customer comments in two national wildlife refuges.

The Office of Thrift Supervision has asked its customers—the savings and loan institutions it regulates—to evaluate OTS's examiners and exam procedures. More than 300 thrift institutions have responded, and the agency has responded in turn, reforming its own procedures. "It's a great idea," says Robert Morrison, President of Suburban Federal Savings in Landover Hills, Maryland.[21]

And the Department of Veterans Affairs has established a National Customer Feedback Center to provide customer satisfaction information to VA hospitals. Focus groups of patients and their families identify what they define as priorities for high-quality service and the employee characteristics that would embody those priorities. Their work is turned into standards, and then into questionnaires. The results are analyzed and sent to hospital administrators who, in turn, make service changes accordingly.

Finally, if all this measuring is to amount to anything, agencies have to reward individuals and programs that are truly superior. That too is underway. Nationally, more than 180 groups of federal employees who have developed pioneering reinvention innovations have been given Vice Presidential "Hammer Awards"—named, with intentional irony, after the legendary $600 Pentagon hammer purchase.

In addition, individual agencies are coming up with their own awards for creative problem-solving—like the "Giraffe Award" at SSA's Albuquerque office, given to employees who "stick out their necks" and take risks, and the VA's "Scissors Award," for employees who cut red tape and improve efficiency.

There are some monetary awards as well. Increasingly, agencies—like the Consumer Product Safety Commission—make small, symbolic on-the-spot cash awards for exceptional customer service. The Tennessee Valley Authority, which operates in a more commercial manner than traditional government agencies, provides "gain-sharing" bonuses based on customer satisfaction results.

THE ROAD AHEAD

The odd thing about finally focusing on serving customers is that it radically changes how Americans feel about and respond to their government. Frustrated, disillusioned, expecting the worst, we approach the government with trepidation and, increasingly in the last two years, come away delighted.

For example, on July 1, 1995—Saturday evening on a holiday weekend—Leah Lenox, a 16-year-old member of the U.S. National Tennis Team, was on her way to a competition in Europe. Then her purse, with her passport inside, was stolen at John F. Kennedy Airport in New York. After airport officials told her father that there was no way Leah would be permitted to leave the country, he called the State Department in Washington, D.C. He reached David Gooding, who abandoned his own weekend plans and spent the next several hours working with Leah's airline to permit her to depart while the passport issue was being resolved. She was on a flight the same night.

This winter, Tom Pajkos, claims representative in Chicago's Social Security Office, offered to pick up a Social Security application from an elderly woman at her home.[22] When he got there, he found her swathed in layers of clothes in a frigid apartment, huddled next to a small space heater. She had no water, no gas, no heat. After failing to get help from her family, he arranged for the local emergency housing department to reconnect her utilities.

Government agencies are made up of people, and people routinely go out of their way to help others in need. It's one of the things that makes us human. Nobody expected David Gooding to set aside his weekend plans, or Tom Pajkos to take an interest in a poor, elderly woman on a cold night. They just did. Just as people always have. Is it possible for a government to encourage such exceptional service? Is it possible to turn the federal government around so that Americans can come to *expect* exceptional service? Not only is it possible, but it's happening. People are actually writing their government thank-you letters—thousands of them:

> People may rant and rave about bureaucrats, but I think [Social Security] is absolutely first rate.
>
> COL. ARNOLD J. CELICK (USAF RET.)[23]
> Foresthill, California

> I want to congratulate you for another significant improvement in [the VA's] service to its policyholders. By comparison to all others, the VA insurance program is a true winner—not only because it returns significant value to its policyholders but because it truly gives excellent and accurate service.
>
> JOHN R. GRAHAM[24]
> Bellevue, Washington

> [The employees of the National Climatic Data Center] literally changed my thinking about federal employees. . . . I must confess complete (but pleasant) astonishment at the competence and efficiency exhibited by your department.
>
> MICHAEL SEIDEL[25]
> Asheville, North Carolina

> I want to take this time to thank and applaud one of your employees [at the Federal Student Aid Information Center]. . . . Never before have I had such quality help and attitude from a government office. She was patient, knowledgeable, and clear about the steps.
>
> JUDI GLENN[26]
> Cincinnati, Ohio

If talking to customers is the beginning, it's also the middle and the end. Agencies ask, respond, and survey to see if the response meets the need and whether new needs have arisen. Then they respond again, measure again, and so forth.

In the last year, this continuing process has brought about improvements to services that were already doing well. As mentioned above, the Consumer Product Safety Commission's popular consumer hotline has been upgraded to meet increased customer demands. The Labor Department's Wage and Hour Division has measured the customers' satisfaction with its new standards and found remarkable approval—in the 65 to 90 percent range.[27] Now it's working on the lower end.

Measuring what matters is crucial. The agencies are using focus groups, surveys, workshops, questionnaires, comment cards, and more to gauge customers' needs—and their customers, far from being annoyed, are responding loudly, clearly, and helpfully. And agencies are continuing to seek out businesses against whose services they can benchmark—and exceed. They're "stealing shamelessly" from the best in the private sector. They're examining complaint systems to ensure that complaints can be made by unsatisfied customers, and that the complaints will be acted upon.

The goal is to exceed customers' needs, wants, and expectations for service and, in so doing, rekindle their faith in their government. To achieve that goal with sharply limited funds, agencies—like private companies—are employing the latest technologies: online access, electronic retrieval, phone systems, access through the Internet, electronic benefits transfer, and more. As private industry already has discovered, it's the only way to keep up with change and with customer demands.

Imagine this: a recent retiree goes to a government services kiosk at his local post office to get information on his retirement benefits. After providing his Social Security number and other personal identification information, he gets a printout that summarizes his Social Security contributions as well as the benefits to which he's entitled as a veteran. His annuity distribution options appear on the printout, along with the rules governing how much additional income he can earn while collecting benefits. The kiosk also asks whether he'd like other information on retirement and on senior citizens groups.

Is this fiction? Nope: it's a pilot project called WINGS (for Web Interactive Network of Government Systems), already being tested by the Postal Service. And it's just the beginning. The plan is for WINGS to provide citizens access to a wide array of government services, from Social Security to reservations for camping space at a national park.

Turning the federal government into a world-class customer service organization won't happen overnight, but it is happening. It is both a technological challenge and a human challenge. It involves changing the culture of large organizations. The good news is that the front-line employees of those organizations, the ones who serve us every day, are enthusiastic participants.

The people's government is listening and responding at last. It will never be the same again.

4

Getting Our Money's Worth

WHO SAYS THE government isn't innovative? Now it's making money out of *thin air*! Big money. Billions. In the early days of radio, the airwaves—the portions of the electromagnetic spectrum that carry broadcast signals—were in chaos, with broadcasters jamming each other's signals in a sort of huge electronic shoving match. To bring some order out of this chaos, the Federal Communications Commission was created to parcel out frequencies. Talk about giveaways: last year alone, the industries that have gained licenses to use the airwaves had $100 billion in sales.[1]

I want to thank all those who had anything to do with...these auctions. I'd also like to thank those who won the bids... and those who bid them up!

BILL CLINTON

March 27, 1995

In the case of radio and television stations, the FCC gave licenses away based on its judgment about the applicant's proposed programming. But when cellular phones came along, the system broke down. Because there was no programming to evaluate, licenses went to all sorts of people—many of whom simply sat on them awhile, then sold them at huge profits. To reduce this crush of "air prospectors," the FCC switched to a lottery, but that solved almost nothing. Meanwhile the whole process had become incredibly complicated, and the main beneficiaries were the industry's lawyers and lobbyists.

Finally, when it came time to distribute airspace for advanced paging systems and super-light portable phones, the FCC came up with a sweepingly simple solution that perfectly embodies the spirit of reinvention: it decided to auction the airways.

The results blew away even the optimists. In 1994 alone, the first year of the auction program, industries paid $8.9 *billion* for broadcast licenses. The money went straight to the Treasury to reduce the deficit. In this case, at least, the people were getting a fair return on their assets, and the companies were paying a fair price.

WHAT AMERICANS WANT: A BUSINESSLIKE GOVERNMENT

Let's say one of the wage-earners in your family is laid off and your household income is sharply reduced. You have some savings, but they won't last long—partly because you've been living beyond your means and have built up some pretty hefty credit card debts. You get some unemployment compensation, but that won't last long, or go very far, either. Do you turn to one of your two small children and say, "Sorry, we can't afford you just now; find someplace else to live"? Hardly. Do you tear down part of your house so it won't cost as much to run? Not likely. Do you cut your family back from three meals to two? Not if you want to stay healthy, you don't. But you also don't keep right on living the way you did before.

What you do is sit down with the family, look at where the money goes, and try to live more frugally, more sensibly. You eat simpler meals, not fewer. You cut non-essential activities—like first-run movies—completely. Maybe you sell a second car, and one of you takes the bus. You might even *spend* some money to save more—say, to put plastic over your windows and cut down on heating bills. And then you have a long talk about how you got into this fix in the first place and how to make sure you never get into it again.

That's what ordinary folks do when things get tight. And that's what we expect our government to do as well. In short, to manage our money and our assets wisely.

You'd think it was just common sense—but it's been uncommon in the federal government for a long time. And it really galls us when we hear about the government wasting our money. The bipartisan Hart/Teeter poll asked Americans to name our top two complaints about the federal government. Sixty-one percent of us said that the government wastes money because it is not well managed. Fifty-six percent also said that the government spends too much on the wrong things.[2]

We understand that the government isn't a business, that it has to do a lot of things businesses don't have to do. But that doesn't mean it can't operate in a business*like* manner—efficiently, effectively, with a minimum of waste.

Since reinvention began in 1993, the federal government's been listening to what people say they want—and acting on it. Here's what people have said they want.

Stop Doing Unnecessary Things

Shortly after the turn of the century, there was an outbreak of typhoid fever at the U.S. Naval Academy in Annapolis, Maryland. It was traced to a commercial milk supplier in the area. Given the strategic importance of the Academy, Congress moved swiftly, mandating the creation of a Naval Academy Dairy to provide safe milk to midshipmen. Today, although the Centers for Disease Control and Prevention in Atlanta say there hasn't been a single case of milk-related typhoid anywhere in the United States in more than 30 years, the dairy's still there. All 856 government-owned acres of it. What's more, because the dairy's facilities are obsolete and inefficient, the Navy pays 30 cents more for every gallon of milk it buys from the dairy than it would if it shopped at the local supermarket. And it pays retail, not wholesale. In fairness, it's not like the Navy hasn't tried to unload the dairy from time to time; it has. But Congress won't do it. Holy cow.

"Clinton Outlines Cuts at 4 Agencies to Save $13 Billion"—
THE WASHINGTON POST, *March 28, 1995*

Obsolete government programs and duplication drive Americans crazy. That's not the Navy's money that's being wasted, it's *ours*. What's more, we know this isn't an isolated incident. We have 200 years' worth of government programs that have built up like sediment in a river. In places, the sediment is so thick the ship of state can't get through. And yet it's seemed almost impossible over the years to dredge a channel through this muck. Congress is quick to add programs, but powerful special interests ensure that it's slow to kill them. Federal budget expert Allen Schick has said he could identify only three major nondefense programs that had been eliminated between 1980 and 1993—an era in which the administrations in power pledged to cut government.[3]

That era is over. Since the Clinton Administration's "reinventing government" initiative began, *400 programs* have been proposed in the President's Budget for elimination—obsolete, duplicative, or just plain silly programs that waste our money.

The National Aeronautics and Space Administration has been more successful at streamlining than the Naval Academy Dairy. In 1963, President Kennedy had a simple, sweeping vision: to put an American on the moon and, in the process, make the United States the world leader in space exploration and technology. The American public thrilled to the idea, and the NASA budget continued to rise by several orders of magnitude as a result. On July 20, 1969, President Kennedy's vision became a reality: Apollo's Eagle landed on the moon.

While NASA's budget declined through the '70s and early '80s, NASA committed to several large programs toward the end of the decade, including the development of the international Space Station, several large space science programs, and the initiation of Mission to Planet Earth. For the most part, these programs followed the Apollo model, requiring large budgets and centralized management systems. With American's concern over deficits, though, NASA was out of sync with the times.

That was before Dan Goldin took over and started reinventing. Faster, better, cheaper, without compromising safety, became the new way to do business. The new NASA team worked with agency employees, field centers, and customers to find ways to streamline operations, reduce duplication and overlap, and cut costs without compromising either safety or the agency's goal of being the world leader in aerospace research and development. This past March, the results were announced. Functions duplicated across the country will be consolidated at Centers of Excellence, and programs that once belonged to the government will be privatized, commercialized, or transferred to institutes operated by universities, industry, or other team arrangements. Much work that still needs to be done by the agency will be done by contractors and not micromanaged. Says Goldin, "If we don't have to do it, we won't....If we have to do it, we'll change the way we work."

By not doing unnecessary things, the new NASA is a whole lot smaller than the old one, and a whole lot cheaper. The agency's budget has been cut by 30 percent. During the next five years, NASA will take a total of $8.7 billion out of its budget. There will be 4,000 fewer civilian personnel. Already, the average cost of launching a space shuttle has been cut by two-thirds and the time involved has been cut in half.[4] Likewise, the costs of spacecraft for NASA's space science and Mission to Planet Earth programs have been reduced by two-thirds, the development time has been cut in half, and missions are launched four times as often.

Buy Smart

When the Clinton Administration took over, the federal government was spending about $200 billion each year to buy stuff—from staples to satellites, from jeeps to jockey shorts.[5] It wasn't exactly a smart shopper. For years it tended to buy more than it needed and spend more than it should. For the most part, this wasn't because it was being ripped off by unscrupulous suppliers (though there have been a few notorious contracting scams). Most of the damage has been self-inflicted.

The government tended to spend too much because it had almost everything it bought "custom-made" to government or military specifications. For example, instead of buying Chips Ahoy cookies at wholesale—say, for the Army—it created 700 pages of procurement specifications defining for contract bakers how to make a chocolate chip cookie. The specifications, as many soldiers no doubt would tell you, don't require the cookies to taste good.

Another example: Motorola's reputation for quality is so good that its "Motorola University" now trains employees of companies from all over the world. Its products routinely outsell Japanese products—even in Japan. You'd think anything Motorola produced would be good enough for the federal government, right? Think again. For years, the government issued its own standards. In fact, every agency issued its own standards, often for the same products. So if you were Motorola or anyone else, you not only had to produce at world-class standards to sell your products around the world, you also had to meet different standards—often several different standards—to sell to your own government. Of course, if you were willing to put up with this sort of nonsense in order to make a sale, you had to charge more for the product because it was custom-made for that agency. So not only was the government getting a product that was no better than the international standard (and often worse), but it was paying extra.

Finally, some bright folks at the Defense Department and NASA, with the impetus of the reinvention initiative, took it upon themselves to persuade agencies to accept official international quality standards. It will be worth billions to taxpayers. Just one company, Raytheon, estimates that this move will save the government $30 million to $40 million annually on a single contract.[6]

Hold Government Accountable

In 1991, the General Accounting Office surveyed the 103 agencies that spent three-quarters of the $1.3 trillion in federal outlays that year. Only nine could claim they were accounting for their performance in ways that legitimately measured performance.[7]

Like the stockholders of any business, Americans expect the government's management to provide an accounting of its performance each year. And while the language of business—market share, sales levels, earnings growth, and share prices—isn't the language of government, government agencies nonetheless need mechanisms for providing that accounting.

Of course, to measure performance, organizations first need to know what they're trying to accomplish. FedEx's executive team meets every morning to review the company's performance on achieving on-time delivery. The managers collect the right data, assess it, and act on it—always with that goal in mind. In contrast, government agencies for years would have been hard-pressed to tell you what their performance goals were, never mind how well they were doing at meeting them.

Now that's changing. As part of reinventing government, this is exactly what they're doing. So far, the heads of eight major agencies have signed performance agreements with President Clinton that identify the agency's performance objectives in measurable terms and document a commitment to meet the objectives and reward employees accordingly. Perhaps not surprisingly, it turns out that the agencies with the clearest and best-communicated performance goals and most specific accountability systems have the best records in reinvention. Moreover, these agreements are no secret; they're available for public view on the Internet.[8]

THE RESULTS: A SMALLER, BETTER, FASTER, CHEAPER GOVERNMENT

Two years ago, President Clinton promised American taxpayers a government that gives us more value for our money—with fewer workers, fewer layers of management, fewer programs, and more businesslike management. Not only has the promise been kept, but progress is ahead of schedule.

The task of cutting the cost of government and managing it better involves four activities that are underway simultaneously: *downsizing* (reducing the size and number of agencies, their programs, and staff); *streamlining* (simplifying the procedures involved); *restructuring* (reforming agencies structurally to better serve their missions); and *privatizing* (spinning off functions to the private sector that are better accomplished there).

The cumulative effect of all four types of reform has been significant. President Clinton's reinvention initiative promised to reduce the size of the government by 12 percent in six years, dropping federal employment to levels that haven't been seen since the Kennedy Administration. In fact, in just two years the size of the government has been reduced 7.6 percent—that's nearly two-thirds of the way toward the goal in one-third of the time. So far, the federal workforce has slimmed down by more than 160,000 workers. In fact, civilian federal government jobs now make up a smaller share of all jobs than at any time since the eve of World War II.[9]

Perhaps more importantly, the whole point of reinventing the government is to make it work better by making it leaner, especially by reducing layers of supervisors who add relatively little value to the government enterprise and by eliminating or consolidating obsolete or duplicative programs. In just two

FEDERAL EMPLOYMENT

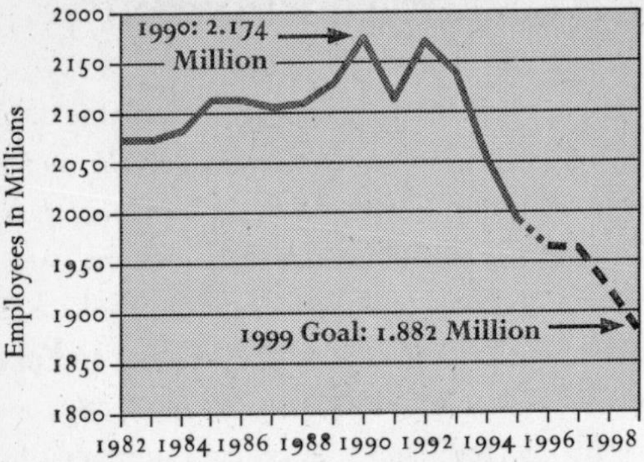

Number of executive branch employees
(Figure for 1995 is an estimate; 1996 through 1999 are targets.)

Source: Office of Management and Budget and Office of Personnel Management

years, supervisory personnel have been reduced by 30 percent. This means there is one supervisor for every ten federal workers, compared to one for every seven before reinvention began. The goal is one for every 15 by 1999.

The cost of government is dropping not just because people and programs are being reduced, but because things that do need to be done by government are being done better, with less overhead. In 1993, President Clinton promised savings of $108 billion in five years from the reinvention initiative. So far $58 billion have been saved; billions more are "in the pipeline" or awaiting congressional action.

There is still plenty of room for more streamlining, and the task of incorporating best management techniques throughout the federal government has just begun. Moreover, even with strong and persistent Presidential support, and the hard work of many federal employees, the resistance in other parts of our government to change—even necessary change—can be frustrating. Even ludicrous.

Take the tea-taster...please. In 1897, Congress passed the Import Tea Act, creating the Board of Tea Experts and an official federal tea-taster. You can picture the scene: New York harbor, the tall clipper ships at anchor, the rigging on their graceful wooden masts slapping in the breeze, the federal tea-taster prowling the docks on the lookout for poor-quality tea. We are, after all, a people who overthrew our previous government over a certain tea matter.

Now, fast-forward to 1995. We still have a federal tea-taster and a tea-tasting room in Brooklyn. Now, no one questions the extraordinary skill of the current tea-taster. The question is why the federal government is still spending $120,000 a year to support an activity that the tea industry is already supporting itself. And it's not like the tea-taster is America's foot soldier in the battle to fight back wave upon wave of shabby tea; only 1 percent of all the tea tested is rejected.

The National Performance Review featured the Federal Tea Room in its first report two years ago. The Clinton Administration proposed eliminating it last year. Some Members of Congress argued forcefully to get rid of it. It's still there. The tea industry itself has recommended that the government charge fees to cover the cost of the service.[10] Congress simply will not act on it. The tea-taster tastes on.

It's not a lot of money. It's the principle of the thing. If Congress is proposing to cut back benefits to the needy, or trim badly needed investments in education, training, and infrastructure, how can we continue to support a tea-taster? Or any other outdated or unnecessary program? The answer is, we can't.

Progress Report: Reducing, Eliminating, Spinning Off Programs

The reinvention initiative began by cutting away the most obviously obsolete programs and by trimming overhead throughout the government. These tasks continue. But there is another, more difficult task—one the reinventers will have to address repeatedly in the years to come. That task is asking the deceptively simple question: What business *should* the government be in?

Answering that question, a task that began this year, has already yielded significant organizational changes and taxpayer savings. Consider the Office of Personnel Management. OPM is, in effect, the federal government's personnel department. One of its top concerns, as you would expect, is making sure federal employees get proper training. It has done that in part by running its own 200-person Workforce Training Service. Then the people at OPM asked the crucial reinvention question: Is it our business to run a training school, or simply to ensure that employees are trained? Their answer was the latter. So, on July 1, 1995, OPM Director Jim King turned the entire operation over to the USDA Graduate School which—despite its official-sounding name, a leftover from early in this century—is a tuition-supported training school with no federal employees.

Now OPM is asking the same question about its Investigations Service—an 800-person operation that does background investigations for federal agencies. And it's arrived at the same answer: no, it doesn't need to run an investigation service. It just needs to have a way to get background checks done. This time, the solution is even more innovative: OPM is helping the employees of the Investigation Service form their own private company through an Employee Stock Ownership Plan, or ESOP. Target date for privatization? The first of the year. These and other reinvention activities at OPM will save the American taxpayers some $30 million in the next four years.[11]

Sometimes the result of applying the question "Should the government be doing this?" to a given program yields a simple answer: no. A century ago, when the U.S. Department of Agriculture had the job of increasing the productivity of America's farmers, it set up field offices throughout the young nation—a network designed so that no farmer was more than a day's horse-ride from a knowledgeable farm agent. Since then, the number of farmers has dropped to a minuscule percentage of the population, and very few of them still use horses to get around.

Two years ago, the National Performance Review and USDA promised to eliminate unnecessary field offices. This year and next, 1,200 offices representing the Farm Service Agency, the Natural Resources Conservation Service, and the Rural Economic and Community Development divisions of USDA will be eliminated or consolidated—the most sweeping field office downsizing of any federal agency, including Defense. And USDA didn't stop at field offices. Departmentwide, it has cut the number of separate agencies and offices from 43 to 29, while consolidating its administrative services.[12] Times change; government must change with them.

The Department of Energy's cutbacks may be even more dramatic. Think back to 1973. America is importing most of its oil supplies, but suddenly the international oil cartel puts the squeeze on. Gas stations draw long lines, and oil prices skyrocket. The entire energy-dependent economy is in chaos. In a version of closing the barn door after the horse is gone, the federal government tosses every government program even remotely connected with energy—including nuclear bombs—into a big box, which it calls the Department of Energy. The energy crisis passes, but DOE continues to grow. The cold war ends, but DOE still handles a huge nuclear program. This led folks to start asking what DOE does, anyway. Most people don't know. Those that do—those who have heard about nuclear waste polluting the environment at the agency's Rocky Flats or Savannah River facilities—don't like what they hear. Then, President Clinton brings in Hazel O'Leary as DOE Secretary. She starts asking a lot of very simple questions, like why the agency has so many secrets, why it's still so big even though it's mission has changed, why it owns so many things it doesn't really need and—more importantly—can't afford. To get some answers, she creates a departmentwide reinvention effort: the Strategic Alignment Initiative.

The department is off to an impressive start. DOE is shutting down 12 field offices. By September 30, 1995, it will close its Office of General Counsel field office in Dallas and fossil energy offices in Wyoming and Louisiana. By March 1996, it will close a Houston field office and merge two more fossil energy facilities. Also, it will close more offices in San Francisco, Dallas, New York, and Kansas City, and combine the Denver and Golden, Colorado, offices. In addition, the number of headquarters sites will be reduced from 16 to four. The department will sell the Naval Petroleum Reserve, created to ensure oil for World War I battleships, and the Oil Shale Reserve. It will privatize four power marketing administrations and convert a fifth to a government corporation. It will turn over much of the environmental cleanup of contaminated sites to private firms that can do the work cheaper than DOE can, and it will cut the number of private contractors it uses by 17,000 by the end of fiscal year 1996. In all, it will cut nearly 3,800 positions—2,339 from headquarters and 1,449 from field offices—and save some $1.7 billion.[13] In the next five years, DOE reinvention savings are projected to exceed $23 billion.[14] This is, in short, wholesale reinvention.

The Department of Transportation faces almost the opposite problem. Since 1967, when the agency was created by cobbling together a half-dozen different organizations, demand for its services has increased steadily, but the resources to support it are increasingly limited. Meanwhile, no one has had much success simplifying the agency or eliminating overlap and duplication—in fact, the number of agencies in DOT grew.

Until this year, that is, when Secretary Federico Peña announced the reinvention of the department. First, its ten operating administrations will be consolidated into three—an Intermodal Transportation Administration that will handle all surface and maritime transportation, a revamped Federal Aviation Administration, and the Coast Guard. Second, the department will be downsized dramatically to reduce unnecessary overhead, and the FAA's air traffic control system, given congressional approval, will be turned into a government-owned corporation to permit it to function more like a business and be supported by the airlines it serves. Third, the department will be streamlined, reducing some 30 individual grant, loan, and subsidy programs to three and providing state and local governments more discretion over how funds will be used. The results: an estimated savings to taxpayers of some $17.9 billion and a major shift of resources out of administration and into the transportation system itself.

Finally, sometimes the result of asking the basic question "Should the government be doing this?" is: yes, but differently. After a detailed review of the performance of the Department of Housing and Urban Development—a review that included studying the operations of major corporations—its Secretary, Henry Cisneros concluded, "Many aspects of this department are simply indefensible." It wasn't that its mission—ensuring the availability of decent housing for the nation's poorest fam-

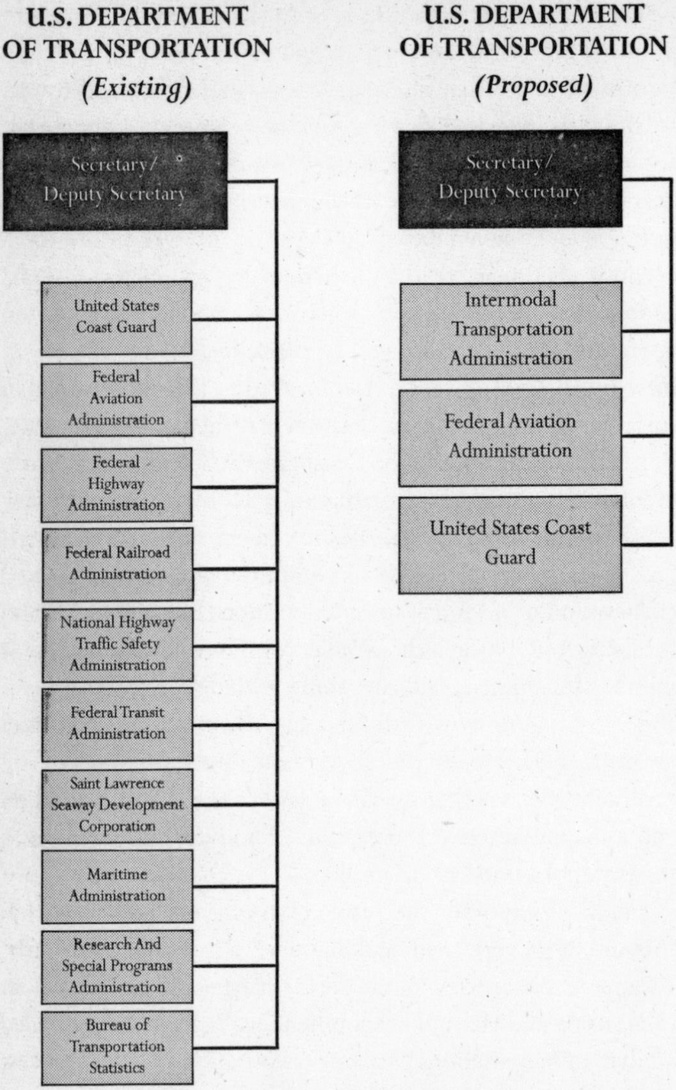

ilies—was indefensible, but that it was failing, consistently, to achieve that mission. Indeed, he concluded, it was perpetuating the problem instead of solving it: "We cannot allow landlords to keep people in slum conditions because the government provides them a check that enables them to do that."[15]

The result is a major reorientation of HUD's approach to achieving a mission which, if anything, is more urgent now than ever before. Three major legislative steps are proposed. First, HUD's 60 separate housing and urban community development programs will be consolidated to eight in 1995, and to only three performance-based programs by October 1, 1997. Second, as noted earlier, it will transform the public housing system by shifting federal dollars from funding housing authorities to providing housing vouchers to individuals who will be free to use them wherever they choose. Third, HUD will turn its Federal Housing Administration residential mortgage insurance operation into a government-owned corporation, giving it the ability to escape bureaucratic systems and personnel restrictions and "function in the marketplace as the modern, competitive insurance company that it is."[16] These changes are not simply designed to make HUD "defensible" again, but to save millions for taxpayers—a projected $825 million, to be exact, by fiscal year 2000.[17]

The foreign affairs agencies are no exception to this kind of restructuring. They are streamlining their operations and closing posts—the Agency for International Development is closing 27 posts, and the State Department has already closed 17 posts and identified an additional 19 lower priority posts for closing. These agencies are also making more fundamental changes to reduce the cost of representing U.S. interests overseas. As just one example, the United States Information Agency has consolidated overseas broadcasting and eliminated low-priority programs; by 1997, it will have saved $400 million by doing so.

The agencies have also tackled the 20-year-old system that they use to divvy up the cost for basic services like computer lines and motor pools—a system so complex and arcane that no one likes it and everyone thinks it costs them too much. Now, the agencies involved are adopting an approach called Cooperative Administrative Support Units—which involves forming interagency collectives to provide administrative support and services—that has proved successful domestically, and testing it internationally, starting at four posts. At a minimum, the new system will be more flexible for participating agencies. It will also put in place incentives to reduce costs and encourage streamlining over the long term.

This same kind of reinvention-driven major restructuring is underway throughout the federal government—in the Interior Department's Bureau of Reclamation and National Park Service, the Departments of Labor and Education, the Small Business Administration, the Federal Emergency Management Agency, the Social Security Administration, and the Internal Revenue Service, among many others.

Progress Report: Using Best Management Practices

Where programs should not be spun off either to the private sector or to state or local government—that is, where the federal government is best equipped to address the problem—Americans have a right to expect those programs to use the most effective management techniques and the most efficient technologies, just as we would expect of any business in which we owned stock. Increasingly, that is exactly what we are getting: entrepreneurial agencies using state-of-the-art techniques to do the public's business.

For entrepreneurship, you'd be hard-pressed to beat the Tennessee Valley Authority's Inspection Services Organization. TVA needed people to inspect its nuclear facilities, but couldn't keep them busy full time. So it set up ISO as a private company inside TVA, but without any government appropriation. ISO stays alive by staying competitive; it works not just on TVA projects, but also for external customers, like Duke Power and Light in North Carolina and Rochester Gas and Electric in New York. Results? A customer satisfaction rating of more than 90 percent and revenues that exceed the cost of operations by 10 percent. Says Duke Power and Light's Fred Bulgin, "They get nothing but rave reviews from me for their enthusiasm and innovation."[18]

So does the Environmental Restoration Unit of the Army Corps of Engineers. This outfit of 120 engineers and project managers primarily does environmental cleanup work for other federal agencies. But it has to compete—with the agencies themselves and with the private sector—for the work. It can only make its payroll if it prices itself competitively and does work that keeps customers satisfied, and it can only do that if it manages itself like the best in the business. And it does.

A well-managed government also ensures that it collects what's owed it, in part to reduce the need for new revenue. The Department of Housing and Urban Development's Federal Housing Administration, for example, insures residential mortgages. When a borrower defaults on the loan, the borrower's bank transfers the loan to HUD and gets an insurance reimbursement. In this way, HUD accumulated a large number of bad loans. Then someone had a reinvention idea: why not sell the bad loans to private companies and investors and let *them* work out repayment with owner/borrowers, or foreclose? HUD's estimate of the value of these loans was about $310 million. The 177 loans in the sale brought in $710 million.

In another such example, the Department of Justice has just launched a central operation to provide a single, accurate source of information on the value of debts owed by, for example, students who default on college loans and businesspeople who default on business loans. Information that used to be collected and held by 93 separate U.S. Attorneys' offices now is available, instantly, in one place. Last year, even before the new system was in place, the department was able to collect $1.83 billion in overdue debts—double the previous year's total. The new system is projected to speed the collection of such debts in the future.

What has made the widespread restructuring of the federal government under the reinvention initiative possible is, in part, a deep-seated commitment to listening to customers and using private-sector principles of quality management. Focusing on providing the highest quality service leads almost automatically to sweeping away layers of supervision and following management techniques that emphasize results over process—a very different way of thinking and being for folks in the government, and a refreshing one.

In achieving best management practices—and, in the process, seeking efficiency improvements to save taxpayers' money—technology, especially information technology, is vital. It is both a driving force of reinvention and a means of getting there. The examples are innumerable.

There's IRS's Telefile tax return filing and TAXLINK, which enables employers to deposit federal payroll taxes electronically. And there's the Defense Logistics Agency, an $8 billion-a-year buyer of supplies for the military—and others—that now awards more than 50 percent of its purchasing contracts via electronic commerce and has set up five centers around the country to train businesses in how to use the system.

In fact, electronic commerce—paperless purchasing—is going governmentwide, with projected savings of $123 million every year. The way the government is going about buying computer workstations is just one example. NASA has created an electronic commerce system, called Scientific and Engineering Workstation Procurement (SEWP, pronounced "soup") that is a recipe for simplification. An $827 million multi-contract, multi-year program connects 26 federal agencies and eight computer systems sellers, making it possible for individual offices in those agencies to acquire the computing systems and support they need quickly, without a lot of complex forms, and cheaply, at better prices than would otherwise be available to them. Orders are transmitted over the Internet, and credit card payment was just introduced. Average order time has decreased from 115 days to *five*; two days is the current target. With a credit card, the process can take as little as five minutes. Savings to date are estimated at $140 million.[19]

But perhaps the most sweeping technological advances are in electronic funds transfer. Some agencies have already made great strides in direct deposit of benefit payments to customers' bank accounts. Social Security, for example, estimates that the money it saves by not having to prepare and mail paper checks will top $70 million in postage and handling alone. As for people without bank accounts, the federal government last year announced its intention to pay a wide variety of benefits through electronic benefits transfer (EBT), which uses personal debit cards rather than checks. The use of these electronic payment systems represents a major overhaul of the way government does business.

The biggest application of EBT so far is in the food stamp program. Ten states are already issuing food stamp benefits by way of a debit card that enables customers to access their benefits at the supermarket cash register, the same way many Americans already use ATM cards. Another 35 states are in various stages of planning to do the same. Customers will no longer need to handle coupons—and neither will retailers, banks, or USDA itself. In addition, the system will make it easier to crack down on program abuse. A report last year to the Vice President describing an implementation plan for nationwide EBT estimated annual savings of $195 million once a single card delivering both cash benefits and food assistance is fully implemented.

Progress Report: Measuring and Benchmarking the Best in Business

Well-managed businesses measure. They measure their own performance and they measure themselves against the best in their business, a process called "benchmarking." For years, as described elsewhere in this report, the federal government has measured the wrong things—typically *inputs* (time, personnel, and money, among others), rather than *outcomes*. Measurement matters not simply to answer the question "How am I doing?" but also to provide regular information to the government's stockholders, the American people; to give managers the information they need to continuously improve and re-engineer what they do; and to ensure that the heads of agencies make informed "business decisions."

When the reinvention initiative began two years ago, President Clinton told government agencies to begin measuring their performance and benchmarking themselves against the best private businesses. At about the same time, performance measurement became the law of the land with the passage of the Government Performance and Results Act (discussed in Chapter II of this report).

Measuring performance is essential for guaranteeing to Americans that our government is held accountable for the work it does on our behalf. Even more, it enables government to see just how well its services stack up to the best in business. And here the news has surprised even the most optimistic reinventers. Not only have agencies—particularly those with high levels of contact with the general public—been benchmarking aggressively, but their performance has improved so markedly that they are not simply as good as business, they're often *better*. Other sections of this report describe the success of the Social Security Administration's phone service and the National Security Agency's travel system. And more examples emerge every day.

For example, when Wal-Mart—no slouch when it comes to good management—wanted to improve its pharmacies' prescription processing time, it did what quality-conscious companies throughout the nation do: it benchmarked itself against the best in the business. The "best in the business" turned out to be the Air Combat Command's pharmacy at MacDill Air Force Base, near Tampa. It's among the world's busiest pharmacies, filling between 4,000 and 6,000 prescriptions *each day*. By using a state-of-the-art inventory system and regularly measuring workload, error rate, customer waiting time, and several other factors, MacDill is able to fill 95 percent of its prescriptions within five minutes with an error rate that is half the national average. What's more, though MacDill is the star, in fact the pharmacies throughout the Air Combat Command fill 92 percent of their 60,000 prescriptions each day in less than ten minutes. Next time your local drug store chain tells you there will be a half-hour wait, you can point out that's not good enough for government work.

Progress Report: Partnering with Business

We live in a society in which it sometimes seems everyone is suing everyone else. A lot of people sue the federal government, often to block activities or projects they don't agree with. That's okay; it's their right, after all. But the cost of all those lawsuits is enormous. What if the federal government sat down with people affected by a proposed project in advance?

The idea of "alternative dispute resolution"—of negotiating settlements, rather than tying up the courts—has been around awhile. But the Army Corps of Engineers has pushed the idea to a new level. Says Lester Edelman, Chief Counsel of the Corps, "The idea was, if we're using alternative dispute resolution (ADR) to *resolve* disputes, why can't we back up a step and use it to try to *avoid* disputes." Having concluded that "nobody really wins in litigation," that's exactly what the Corps did, establishing ADR/Partnering relationships with communities, citizens, the construction and trade industry, and the legal community. It's used the technique to accelerate hazardous and toxic waste cleanup projects, resolve conflicts over the operation of multi-purpose dams, handle wetland permits, acquire real estate, even handle internal labor disputes. In all, the Corps' ADR/Partnering program has cut its legal caseload by more than 70 percent and reduced claims values from a high of nearly a half-billion dollars to $220 million. It's just good business.

Not far from New York City's famous Lincoln Center for the Performing Arts is a post office that, in 1992, was on its last legs. The building was a wreck and inaccessible to people with disabilities. Nobody much cared about the deteriorating building; the lease would run out in ten years anyway, and the post office would be history. But the neighborhood needed a post office. Enter Dennis Wamsley, a manager of U.S. Postal Service properties around the nation. Where others saw a loser, Wamsley saw a winner—indeed, a goose that could lay golden eggs. He formed a development partnership with several real estate development giants and, three years later, Lincoln Square opened: a 10-story, 400,000-square-foot urban entertainment center and shopping mall topped by 38 floors of residential housing...and space for a 50,000-square-foot permanent post office with expanded services. Wamsley had partnered with industry to leverage a lousy building and an expiring lease into a development that not only provided the neighborhood with a bigger, better post office, but also is actually generating between $1 million and $2 million in payments to the U.S. Postal Service annually.[20] Partnering pays.

Progress Report: Selling Obsolete Inventory

The government has had a habit of buying far more than it needs, in part to get a low bulk price to save taxpayers' money. But that has often created inventory storage costs that far outweighed those savings. In 1947, for example, the Central Intelligence Agency purchased bamboo snowshoes, presumably to help some agent across the Russia/Finland border to get in "out of the cold." Last year, they found the snowshoes languishing in a storage depot, along with lots of other goodies the agency didn't need. Since then, through "Project Snowshoe," it's cut its inventory by $32 million, or nearly a quarter, and will soon cut annual rent payments by $2.2 million.[21]

But the bottom line is that, in most cases, it makes very little sense to maintain big inventories anymore at all. When you buy something at a supermarket or drug store these days, the cashier scans its bar code. A computer not only tells the company it's just sold that item, it also often tells the supplier at the same time. A replacement arrives automatically. It's called "just-in-time" inventory, and it's used throughout private industry precisely to keep the cost of maintaining inventory to a minimum. Government needs to do the same thing. And it is. It's even winning awards for it.

Consider the Defense Personnel Support Center. The DPSC sits in the middle of a large, aging military base in South Philadelphia, amid acres and acres of warehouses and railroad sidings. Its job is to supply millions of troops and civilians with food, clothing, and medicine. For decades, the warehouses were stacked to the ceiling with thousands of items of everyday use stockpiled for the military. It even had its own uniform factory, a holdover from the Civil War. When the military needed to buy something, DPSC issued complex specifications, solicited and reviewed low bids, waited for the items to be manufactured to specification, then stashed them in the warehouses. And there they sat, often for years.

Today, however, the warehouses are empty, the railroad tracks rusting. And the DPSC, once King of the White Elephants, has just won one of the Ford Foundation's Innovations in American Government awards. As a result of a massive employee-led overhaul, the $3.5 billion agency is being hailed as a model of reinvention. DPSC is no longer a purchasing, billing, warehousing, and shipping agency; it's a food, clothing and medical supplies broker. The difference is profound: using the most advanced electronic ordering technologies, the agency makes it possible for its customers to buy brand-name commercial products directly from the manufacturer, through a one-stop electronic shopping catalogue, at competitive prices and with just-in-time delivery. Because of its buying power, it gets terrific prices. Because the choice of products is vast, buyers and customers are delighted. Because the entire process is electronic, delivery has gone from months to hours. Because virtually nothing is warehoused, storage costs are nil.

In fact, the effect cascades throughout the military. Walter Reed Army Medical Center used to use seven warehouses for the medical supplies it got from DPSC's warehouses. Now they use half of one. Inventory dropped 90 percent from April 1993 to February 1995. The new system saves taxpayers millions every year and is virtually invisible to its users; they just order and the goods arrive. Perhaps more important, defense readiness has actually been heightened.

How good is DPSC? When the accounting firm Price Waterhouse benchmarked electronic commerce, it looked at IBM, Motorola, Sears, J.C. Penney, Texas Instruments, and other leading companies. It also looked at the Defense Personnel Support Center. The result? DPSC's scores were well above the mean, even among this elite group of private businesses.

Under the reinvention initiative, the General Services Administration also has been slashing waste—$1.2 billion in unneeded office construction, $6 billion in inappropriate information technology purchases, and more. But in the long run, it may be the small things that mount up most. Last year, the government signed a deal with Visa for the IMPAC card—a credit card by which government workers can make small purchases easily. What's more, there are no fees, and the government will even get rebates on some purchases. No more $4 staplers that cost another $50 in paperwork. Use of the card is not as widespread as it needs to be yet, but the potential is enormous. During the 1994 fiscal year, for example, the government made more than 18 million small purchases.[22] Had they all been made with the card, savings last year would have totaled nearly $250 million.

And then there are the natural resource stockpiles the government set aside at various times in its history that have outlived their usefulness—like the Oil Shale and Naval Petroleum Reserves managed by the Energy Department, or the major power utilities it owns. Except for Bonneville Power Administration (which is proposed to become a government corporation), all are now on the block, with an estimated sale value of $5.3 billion. Also for sale are the government's excess metal and gas reserves, valued at $75 million. And the Interior Department's Bureau of Mines is in the process of privatizing the nation's helium reserve. The reserve has been strategically important for the space program, but plentiful supplies of the gas are being developed commercially.

THE ROAD AHEAD

When it comes to government's management of our money, we need to be able to "take it to the bank." We need to be sure that our government is managing professionally the work we expect it to do and, when it needs to spend our money, spending it wisely.

We're already there in some parts of the federal government, on our way in others, and only just beginning in still others. The job not only isn't done, it never will be—it will always continue.

More Measurement, More Accountability

If we want the best-managed government, then that government must be *enterprising*. And, like any good enterprise that wants to do its job well, our government needs to measure what matters. Measurement tells managers where they're succeeding and where they're not, More importantly, it tells them what levers to pull to get back on track. If the essence of enterprise is risk-taking and experimentation, measurement tells us how the experiment is going.

Measuring performance is also essential to morale. As President Clinton has said, "Most people who work for the federal government are like most people anywhere. Given a choice between being productive or unproductive, most choose being productive."[23] That means they need some way to know how they're doing. Sure, they'd like to hear they're doing a good job, but they also need to know when they're not. If they have no way of knowing whether they're succeeding—whether they're being productive—they feel irrelevant, and they may stop trying at all. The public's work is too important to permit that.

We must have a government that is accountable—not just every four years at the voting booth, but every day. But if we are going to hold agencies and individuals accountable for accomplishing certain things, we must also ensure they have the kind of flexible authority they need in order to do what needs to be done. They can't succeed with one (or both) hands behind their back.

A few years ago, Great Britain succeeded in sharply increasing performance of government agencies by striking a bargain between the political head of a department and the chief executive of each service or operational agency within that department. In exchange for maximum clarity about program objectives, annual productivity savings targets, and a clear focus on outputs and outcomes, agency heads were given significant flexibility to manage their operations. The chief executives were held personally accountable for their use of resources and for achieving results, and 20 percent of their pay was tied to performance.

We need our government to operate in a similar manner. And with the passage of the Government Management Reform Act, the Government Performance and Results Act, the Chief Financial Officers Act, and the Federal Acquisitions Streamlining Act, we have the foundation in place to do so. The 1994 Government Management Reform Act alone is a landmark—requiring 24 major federal agencies, for the first time, to provide annual audited financial statements and, by 1998, a governmentwide financial statement. We will know better where our money is going and how it is managed.

More Competition, More Privatization

If we have learned anything about economics, it is that competition increases quality and productivity and decreases cost. To the maximum extent practical, we must demand that our government operate in ways that encourage—even require—competition. Certainly we must always temper that competition—we don't want our government to be cut-throat. We still expect our government to protect us and to provide some basic level of care and protection to the least fortunate among us. We simply expect it to be done professionally.

Two years ago, the National Performance Review's first report called for the introduction of competition to reduce the monopolistic control many government agencies have over their customers. Monopolies aren't healthy, whether private or public. The government has made less progress in this area than in some others, but the objective stands. And progress is evident: some programs are competing head-to-head with one another; some are being privatized, so they can operate within the private sector themselves; still others are being reinvented as government corporations, gaining the flexibility of private companies while remaining under government supervision and control. Is the U.S. Postal Service improving, in part, because it now must compete with UPS and FedEx? Certainly. Can such competition improve the performance of other service-oriented government operations? Of course.

5
Conclusion

IF YOU WORKED in construction back before the turn of the century and someone told you your work was "good enough for government work," you'd have been pleased as punch. In those days, the government's construction standards were higher than anyone else's.

"Good enough for government work" meant the best.

But during the intervening century, that phrase has become a term of derision. A focus within government on convoluted procedures and seemingly arbitrary, often silly, and certainly costly rules drove even the best-intentioned people—government contractors and government employees alike—to work to meet the letter of the regulations, but not to excel. They didn't think excellence was appreciated by government, and they felt powerless to change the system so it would be.

Can we turn the situation around? Can "good enough" be best? Think about Japan for a moment. Only a few decades ago, "Made in Japan" meant cheap and shoddy. Now, in many product categories, it means the best there is. You can turn anything around if you work hard enough and smart enough.

You can even turn around a government.

MAKING "GOOD ENOUGH FOR GOVERNMENT WORK" MEAN "BEST"—AGAIN

It's not a theory. In the two years since President Clinton's "reinventing government" initiative began, hard evidence has emerged throughout the nation that the federal government can be fixed. It's happened already in Maine, where hassle-free partnerships of government, industry, and labor have made workers safer. It's happened in Miami, where passengers are clearing Customs and Immigration so quickly that the airline baggage systems can't keep up with them. It's happened in Seattle, where shippers know their cargo containers are cleared even before their ships dock. It's happened in New York, where veterans are getting the kind of personal service that we'd expect only from the best private insurance companies.

And in many instances, government isn't just fixed, it isn't just as good as business—it's the *best in the business*, according to private-sector evaluators. As we've seen, the National Security Agency's travel management system is the best. The Air Combat Command's pharmacy chain—one of the largest in the world—is the best. Some government services are so good that the best private industries are measuring their own performance against the government's. IBM and USAA Insurance are benchmarking themselves against Social Security. The toy manufacturing giant Mattel is benchmarking itself against the Consumer Product Safety Commission's hotline.

Has anyone noticed? *Business Week*, *Newsweek*, and *The New York Times*, among others, have begun to report on "the quiet revolution" underway to make government work better and cost less. In an open letter to President Clinton, *Financial World* magazine said of the reinvention initiative, "You've been working behind the scenes to improve government financial controls, contract oversight, performance measurement, strategic planning, training, procurement, and a host of other...procedures. ...And we think you're making real progress."[1] Says the Brookings Institution, which earlier this year released a critique of the 1993 reinvention report, "The first year of the NPR generated more progress than almost anyone—indeed, perhaps more than the reinventers themselves—imagined possible."[2] This year, for the first time, the Ford Foundation and Kennedy School of Government will award half of their prestigious Innovations in American Government awards to federal government initiatives—awards worth $100,000 each. In these and many other instances, "good enough for government work" is the best.

The power that matters in a self-governing democracy is the power we can exercise "over-the-counter" whenever we interact with our government, whenever we seek to make our needs known. Someone must be listening. Someone must act.

And Americans have noticed too. In addition to industrial workers in Maine, passengers in Miami, and veterans in New York, callers to Social Security have noticed, too, by the millions.

If you haven't felt a difference yet, you will. This year. Many of these and other initiatives have been expanded nationwide. But it's a big country, and there's still a lot to work on. As President Clinton has pointed out repeatedly, the way for government to win back the faith of the people is "one customer at a time."[3]

A MATTER OF TRUST

The essential ingredient in bringing about so great a people-led change—indeed, the essential ingredient of self-government—is trusting the people involved. In this case, that means government employees and the people they serve.

Democracy stands or falls on trust. Throughout our history, however, that trust has been tentative. Right from the start, our founding fathers made sure no single branch of government—neither executive, legislative, nor judicial—and no one group of citizens could, on its own, determine the course of the nation or, more importantly, abridge the rights of individuals. We call it our "system of checks and balances." If our federal government seems fragmented, duplicative, and inefficient, one of the reasons is that we designed it that way from the start. On purpose—because we trusted the whole of the American people more than we trusted any part that claimed to represent us. In fact, we were the first large modern republic in which dispute, disagreement, and debate were defined as hallmarks of love of country. We didn't believe—and still don't—that any system of government is perfect, but we believed fervently that any system of government is *perfectible*. And we've been perfecting ever since.

It's often said these days that the American people need to have more trust in the government. That's not all. If the reinvention initiative has taught the government anything (and it has taught it many things), it is that the government needs to have more trust in the American people—including its own employees. It needs to trust that when we say we need something, we're right. It needs to trust that when we say something needs fixing, it does. It needs to trust that when we're given a goal to reach, we'll reach it.

When we are not trusted, when nothing we say or do seems to make a difference, we feel powerless. Elections alone do not restore that power. The power that matters in a self-governing democracy is the power we can exercise "over-the-counter," on a daily basis, whenever we interact with our government, whenever we seek to make our needs known. Someone must be listening. Someone must act.

PERSONAL RESPONSIBILITY

If the American people and our government—which, after all, is simply more American people—are to build trust in one another, it can only happen through thousands, even millions, of personal interactions. Laws can't mandate it. Regulations can't require it. Executive orders won't achieve it.

We have to do it ourselves, individually and through association with one another. There are people in America who think that any individual who attempts to take responsibility for the common good is hopelessly naive. There are others who think such actions are dangerously radical. But we are a nation of hopelessly naive radicals—of people who will not give up the dream of a nation run by its own people.

We now know that the federal government cannot be the nation's caretaker. For one thing, it would cost too much. For another, it often doesn't know what needs to be taken care of. And finally, taking care of someone's every need doesn't really help them. In the end it weakens them, makes them feel helpless, and eventually resentful. If we are to redeem the promise of self-government, then we need to do it *ourselves*.

And that may be the most important lesson so far of this continuous process of reinventing our government. If it is to continue to succeed, it must never waver from its commitment to and confidence in individuals—including the American people and the government's own front-line workers.

Notes

1. A GOVERNMENT THAT MAKES SENSE

1. Daniel Franklin, "The FEMA Phoenix: How one federal agency rose from the ashes to become a symbol of what government can do," *The Washington Monthly*, July/August 1995, p. 42.
2. David Osborne, "Can This President Be Saved?" *The Washington Post Magazine*, January 8, 1995, p. 14.
3. Osborne, p. 14.
4. "Are Americans Really That Angry?" *Business Week*, January 23, 1995, p. 41.
5. Report of Peter Hart/Robert Teeter poll conducted for the Council on Excellence in Government, April 12, 1995.
6. Osborne, p. 14.
7. Hart/Teeter poll.
8. Russell M. Linden, *Seamless Government: A Practical Guide to Re-Engineering in the Public Sector* (San Francisco: Jossey-Bass Publishers, 1994), p. 29.
9. Alice M. Rivlin, Director, Office of Management and Budget, testimony before the Senate Committee on Governmental Affairs, May 17, 1995.
10. Estimate by the Office of Management and Budget in Al Gore, *From Red Tape to Results: Creating a Government That Works Better and Costs Less* (New York: Plume/Penguin Books, 1993), p. 1.
11. Michael Kelly, "Rip It Up," *The New Yorker*, January 23, 1995, p. 32.
12. Linden, p. 11.
13. Linden, p. 42.
14. Philip K. Howard, *The Death of Common Sense: How the Law is Suffocating America* (New York: Random House, 1995), p. 11.
15. Howard, p. 9.
16. Bill Clinton, remarks at Reinventing Government event, FCC Auction Office, Washington, D.C., March 27, 1995.

2. GETTING RESULTS

1. Franklin D. Roosevelt, speech at Oglethorpe University, Atlanta, Georgia, May 22, 1932.
2. Dan Margolies and Bonar Menninger, "OSHA's Obsessions Trivialize Hazards," *Kansas City Business Journal*, reprint report, December 1994, p. 13.
3. Joseph A. Dear, Application #484 for the Ford Foundation's Innovations In American Government 1995 Awards Program.
4. Bill Clinton, remarks at Regulatory Reform event, Old Executive Office Building, Washington, D.C., February 21, 1995.
5. Bill Clinton, remarks at Reinventing Government event on regulatory burden reduction, U.S. Department of the Treasury, Washington, D.C., June 9, 1995.
6. Philip K. Howard, *The Death of Common Sense: How the Law is Suffocating America* (New York: Random House, 1995), p. 7.
7. Margolies and Menninger, p. 2.
8. Howard, p. 175.
9. Howard, p. 186.
10. Arthur Levitt, Jr., speech to the Society of American Business Editors and Writers, May 1, 1995.
11. Carol Browner, Administrator, U.S. Environmental Protection Agency, press briefing on regulatory reform, May 16, 1995.
12. Unpublished National Performance Review survey, 1995.
13. Bill Clinton, remarks on reinventing worker safety at OSHA event, Stromberg Metal Works, Inc., Washington, D.C., May 16, 1995.
14. John Goshko, "To Cut Red Tape, Oregon Experiments with Federal Aid," *Washington Post*, August 6, 1995.
15. Joe Klein, "The Birth of Common Sense," *Newsweek*, March 27, 1995, p. 31.
16. Howard, p. 179.
17. Margolies and Menninger, p. 7.
18. George S. Patton, *War As I Knew It* (1947).
19. Klein, p. 31.

20. Robert Pear, "A Welfare Revolution Hits Home, But Quietly," *The New York Times*, August 13, 1995, p. 4-1.
21. Bill Clinton, remarks at Reinventing Government event, Custom Print, Arlington, Virginia, March 16, 1995.

3. PUTTING CUSTOMERS FIRST

1. "Social Security Administration Tops in Customer Service," Dalbar Financial Services, Inc., Boston, Massachusetts, press release, May 3, 1995.
2. "Stop Bashing Social Security; Its Customer Service is Tops," *Mutual Fund Market News*, May 3, 1995, p. 14.
3. National Performance Review (NPR), *Serving the American Public: Best Practices in Telephone Service*, Federal Consortium Benchmark Study Report (Washington, D.C.: U.S. Government Printing Office [GPO], February 1995), p. 2.
4. Internal Revenue Service, *Customer Service Plan,* Pub. No. 959, August 1994.
5. Teleconference between Jody Patterson, IRS Public Affairs, and Candy Kane, NPR, August 25, 1995.
6. Ted Reed, "Airport aims to cut wait at Customs," *Miami Herald*, August 1, 1995.
7. Teleconference between Olga Rodriguez, Houston Regional Office, U.S. Postal Service, and Valarie Kaplo, NPR, August 25, 1995.
8. Lisa Daniel, "Heavy Duty Answers," *Federal Times Supplement,* May 8, 1995.
9. "Post Office Licks Image Problem," *USA Today*, May 24, 1995.
10. Lawrence Magid, "The Unlikely Trailblazer," *Information Week,* October 31, 1995.
11. NPR, *Putting Customers First '95: Standards for Serving the American People* (Washington, D.C.: GPO, due for publication in 1995).
12. Henry Cisneros, Secretary of Housing and Urban Development, White House briefing, Washington, D.C., December 19, 1994.

13. The survey was a statistically valid sample of 5,000 of the 1.2 million disaster victims. See Federal Emergency Management Agency, *Customer Service Survey, Final Report* (Washington, D.C.: Human Technology, Inc., October 1994).
14. See NPR, *Putting Customers First: Standards for Serving the American People* (Washington, D.C.: GPO, 1994).
15. Letter from Walter Kordas to Insurance Operations Department, PBGC, November 3, 1994.
16. Judi Bredemeir, "Best Practitioners: 4 Who Raised the Bar," *Business Travel News*, June 19, 1995, pp. 26-30.
17. Liesl LaGrange and Neil Randall, "101 Best Net Bets," *PC Computing Magazine*, May 1995, p. 171.
18. Report of the Internal Revenue Service, U.S. Department of the Treasury, to NPR, August 1995.
19. Memo from Steve McPeak and Bob Diegelman, Department of Justice, to NPR, August 1995.
20. "Post Office Licks Image Problem," *USA Today*.
21. Joseph B. Cahill, "OTS Asking Thrifts: How Are We Doing?," *American Banker*, May 9, 1995.
22. Bob Miller, Executive Officer, Chicago Regional Office, Social Security Administration, "Public Service Anecdotes," undated. (This is an internal compilation of human interest stories for the Commissioner of Social Security. For more information, call Miller, (312) 353-1734.)
23. Letter from Colonel Arnold J. Celick, USAF Ret., to Director, Auburn Teleservice, March 4, 1995.
24. Letter from John Graham, Bellevue, Wisconsin, to Chief, Policyholder Services Division, January 14, 1995.
25. Letter from Michael Seidel, Seidel Claims Service, Glen Falls, New York, to National Climatic Data Center, Asheville, North Carolina, March 24, 1995.
26. Letter from Judi Glenn, Cincinnati, Ohio, to Federal Student Aid Information Center, February 1, 1995.
27. Report of the Wage and Hour Division, U.S. Department of Labor, to NPR, August 7, 1995.

4. GETTING OUR MONEY'S WORTH

1. Warren Cohen, "Halting the Air Raid," *The Washington Monthly*, June 1995, p. 30.
2. Report of Peter Hart/Robert Teeter poll conducted for the Council on Excellence in Government, Washington, D.C., April 12, 1995.
3. Al Gore, *From Red Tape to Results: Creating a Government That Works Better and Costs Less* (New York: Plume/Penguin Books, 1993), p. 144.
4. Daniel Goldin, Administrator, National Aeronautics and Space Administration, White House briefing, Washington, D.C., March 27, 1995.
5. U.S. General Services Administration (GSA), *FRDS Federal Procurement Report: October 1, 1993 through September 30, 1994* (Washington, D.C.: U.S. Government Printing Office [GPO], 1994), p. 2.
6. Briefing by Raytheon officials to the Department of Defense, April 1995.
7. Amy Waldman, "You Can't Fix It If You Don't Look Under the Hood," *The Washington Monthly*, July/August 1995, p. 35.
8. Information on how to find NPR materials on the Internet appears at the end of this publication.
9. "The Bureaucracy: What's Left to Shrink," *The New York Times*, June 11, 1995, p. E-1.
10. Cindy Skrzycki, "The Cup Board Isn't Bare Yet," *The Washington Post*, August 9, 1995, p. F3.
11. U.S. Office of Management and Budget (OMB), *Budget of the United States Government, Fiscal Year 1996* (Washington, D.C.: GPO, 1995), p. 144.
12. Ibid.
13. "Re-Engineering Energy," *The Washington Times*, August 4, 1995, p. A9.
14. OMB, *Budget of the U.S. Government, Fiscal Year 1996*.
15. Henry Cisneros, Secretary of Housing and Urban Development, White House briefing, Washington, D.C., December 19, 1994.

16. Cisneros, White House briefing.
17. OMB, *Budget of the U.S. Government, Fiscal Year 1996*.
18. Telephone conversation between Fred Bulgin, Duke Power and Light, and National Performance Review staff, August 11, 1995.
19. Elizabeth Sikorovsky, "NASA debuts credit card buys on the Net," *Federal Computer Week*, August 21, 1995, p. 8; and information provided by Skip Kemerer, head of NASA Goddard's ADP procurement branch.
20. Telephone conversations between Dennis Wamsley, U.S. Postal Service, and Daniel Neal of NPR, August 1995.
21. Memo from Betsy Wiley, CIA, to Pamela Johnson of NPR, August 8, 1995.
22. GSA, *FRDS Federal Procurement Report*.
23. Bill Clinton, remarks at Reinventing Government event on regulatory burden reduction, U.S. Department of the Treasury, Washington, D.C., June 9, 1995.

5. CONCLUSION

1. Katherine Barrett and Richard Green, "An Open Letter to the President," *Financial World*, October 25, 1994, p. 42.
2. Donald F. Kettl, "Building Lasting Reform: Enduring Questions, Missing Answers," in *Inside the Reinvention Machine: Appraising Governmental Reform*, Donald F. Kettl and John J. DiIulio, eds. (Washington, D.C.: Brookings Institution, 1995), p. 9.
3. Bill Clinton, remarks on release of *Standards for Serving the American People*, Washington, D.C., October 1994.

APPENDIX A

Status of Major Recommendations by Agency

THE NATIONAL PERFORMANCE Review's (NPR's) September 7, 1993, report contained 254 major recommendations affecting major government agencies. These recommendations are discussed in more detail in separate accompanying reports, which break these recommendations into 833 specific action items. Of these action items, agencies report that 32 percent are complete, and another 61 percent are in progress. Following are highlights of agency reinvention activities.

DEPARTMENT OF AGRICULTURE

NPR Recommendations

USDA01	End the Wool and Mohair Subsidy
USDA02	Eliminate Federal Support for Honey
USDA03	Reorganize the Department of Agriculture to Better Accomplish Its Mission, Streamline Its Field Structure, and Improve Service to Its Customers
USDA04	Implement a Consolidated Farm Management Plan
USDA05	Administer the Employment and Training Requirement for Food Stamp Recipients More Effectively and Efficiently
USDA06	Encourage Better Food Package Management Practices and Facilitate Multi-State Contracts for Infant Food and Formula Cost Containment in the WIC Program

USDA07 Deliver Food Stamp Benefits Via Electronic Benefits Transfer to Improve Service to Customers While Remaining Cost-Effective

Agency Progress to Date

Congress has ceased making the outdated wool and mohair subsidies and has eliminated federal support for honey from FY 1994 through the present fiscal year. Internally, the Department of Agriculture (USDA) is taking significant steps to streamline its organizational structure. It has reduced the number of agencies from 43 to 29 and is in the process of closing or consolidating 1,200 field offices. A multi-year approach is being taken to revise the department's structure to reflect its program responsibilities. Additionally, the agency has developed a more effective network of USDA Service Centers operating under a customer service plan. By 1999, the department will save $2.8 billion in personnel costs and $1.3 billion in other administrative costs as a result of streamlining and reorganizing its headquarters and field office structure. USDA has also redesigned key processes to improve customer service, empower employees, and reduce costs.

To coordinate federal agencies in assisting farm management, the department recently implemented six pilot projects on the whole farm/ranch initiative. Also, USDA is leading the governmentwide effort to assess federal field office structures.

USDA continues to provide ongoing policy guidance to Women, Infants, and Children (WIC) state agencies to maximize their formula cost-containment efforts. USDA is working with states, other agencies, and the Electronic Benefits Transfer (EBT) Task Force to implement EBT as rapidly as possible.

DEPARTMENT OF COMMERCE

NPR Recommendations

DOC01 Reinvent Federal Economic and Regional Development Efforts

DOC02	Provide Better Coordination to Refocus and Leverage Federal Export Promotion
DOC03	Reform the Federal Export Control System for Commercial Goods
DOC04	Strengthen the Tourism Policy Council
DOC05	Create Public/Private Competition for the NOAA Fleet
DOC06	Improve Marine Fisheries Management
DOC07	Provide EDA Public Works Loan Guarantees for Infrastructure Assistance
DOC08	Establish a Manufacturing Technology Data Bank
DOC09	Expand Electronic Availability of Census Data
DOC10	Amend the Omnibus Trade and Competitiveness Act to Increase the Data Quality of the National Trade Data Bank
DOC11	Eliminate Legislative Barriers to the Exchange of Business Data Among Federal Statistical Agencies
DOC12	Establish a Single Civilian Operational Environmental Polar Satellite Program
DOC13	Use Sampling to Minimize Cost of the Decennial Census
DOC14	Build a Business and Economic Information Node for the Information Highway
DOC15	Increase Access to Capital for Minority Businesses

Agency Progress to Date

The Department of Commerce (DOC) is steadily working toward making structural improvements; these include streamlining, eliminating regional offices, and creating "one-stop shops." Existing resources have been deployed to staff the newly established Advocacy Center and to open four one-stop shops with the Small Business Administration (SBA), the Export-Import Bank of the United States, and the Agency for International Development.

These shops pull the services offered by all of the agencies together into one location, enabling customers to have all their needs addressed at the same time. Eleven more are scheduled to open in 1995.

One of the major goals of DOC's streamlining effort is to flatten its hierarchical structure and increase each manager's span of control by having one less layer between employees and the Secretary by 1996.

DOC's reinvention labs have made significant progress as well. For example, the department has established a manufacturing technology data bank to expand the availability of census data and enhance the quality of the National Trade Data Bank.

Other agency accomplishments include eliminating legislative barriers to the exchange of business data among federal agencies, establishing a single civilian operational environmental polar satellite program, and rewriting export controls to make them more user-friendly for small businesses and infrequent users.

DEPARTMENT OF DEFENSE

NPR Recommendations

DOD01	Rewrite Policy Directives to Include Better Guidance and Fewer Procedures
DOD02	Establish a Unified Budget for the Department of Defense
DOD03	Purchase Best Value Common Supplies and Services
DOD04	Outsource Non-Core Department of Defense Functions
DOD05	Create Incentives for the Department of Defense to Generate Revenues
DOD06	Establish and Promote a Productivity-Enhancing Capital Investment Fund
DOD07	Create a Healthy and Safe Environment for Department of Defense Activities

DOD08	Establish a Defense Quality Workplace
DOD09	Maximize the Efficiency of DOD's Health Care Operations
DOD10	Give Department of Defense Installation Commanders More Authority and Responsibility Over Installation Management
DOD11	Reduce National Guard and Reserve Costs
DOD12	Streamline and Reorganize the U.S. Army Corps of Engineers

Agency Progress to Date

Quality training for Department of Defense (DOD) employees continues to be an important departmentwide initiative. DOD is working with the Office of Personnel Management (OPM) on a human resources management reform package and is proposing a new hiring category to replace its current temporary and term hiring authority.

DOD has significantly streamlined its operations, addressing major enhancements and cost savings while reducing its civilian workforce. It implemented policy to empower properly delegated employees to buy common supplies and nonprofessional services in an effort to purchase best value supplies and services. To create a healthy and safe environment for DOD activities, a pollution prevention program and environmental technology policy have been developed and the environmental cleanup process streamlined. In July 1995, the department completed initiatives to streamline environmental cleanup processes. Additional regional offices have been designated to form partnerships with the Environmental Protection Agency (EPA) and state offices.

More than 70 DOD reinvention labs are now under way. The Secretary of Defense endorsed a simplified waiver process that ensures that waiver requests from the labs are addressed in a timely manner. In addition, Secretary William J. Perry issued guidance to reduce business process cycle time by half by calendar year 2000.

More than 250 DOD candidates were identified for this effort; processes being streamlined include space launches, audits, material support, and maintenance. Many of these DOD reinvention initiatives have resulted in significant savings.

DOD has made great strides in streamlining its headquarters-level policy and procedural documents, and the various DOD components are well on their way to meeting planned reduction milestones. Internal regulations have been reduced 30 percent to date. In addition, all DOD directives and instructions are published on CD-ROM and are available on the World Wide Web.

DOD is accelerating deployment of currently available commercial technology in its 12 health care regions. The concept of paperless outpatient medical records is now being tested at Scott Medical Center in Belleville, Illinois. A provider workstation prototype is serving more than 90 providers in 40 clinics: 19,000-plus patient encounters have been documented to date in the workstation.

DEPARTMENT OF EDUCATION

NPR Recommendations

ED01	Redesign Chapter 1 of Elementary and Secondary Education Act
ED02	Reduce the Number of Programs the Department of Education Administers
ED03	Consolidate the Eisenhower Math and Science Education Program with Chapter 2
ED04	Consolidate National Security Education Act Programs
ED05	Streamline and Improve the Department of Education's Grant Process

ED06	Provide Incentives for the Department of Education's Debt Collection Service
ED07	Simplify and Strengthen Institutional Eligibility and Certification for Participation in Federal Student Aid
ED08	Create a Single Point of Contact for Program and Grant Information
ED09	Improve Employee Development Opportunities in Department of Education
ED10	Eliminate the Grantback Statutory Provision of the General Education Provisions Act
ED11	Build a Professional, Mission-Driven Structure for Research
ED12	Develop a Strategy for Technical Assistance and Information Dissemination

Agency Progress to Date

The Department of Education has continued to make significant progress in planning and managing systems to best meet the needs of the agency's ultimate customers, learners of all ages. NPR's 1994 status report indicated that Education had put in place a comprehensive planning process, including the establishment of desired performance outcomes. Since then, the agency has begun to use the process to develop detailed analyses to help monitor progress in its four priority areas. In addition, Education has de-layered its organization and made progress toward streamlining work and reducing numbers of people involved in personnel, budget, and other functions targeted for reduction by NPR. Plans are in place to tie the performance of each employee to the strategic plan as part of a new 360-degree system of appraisal that is now being piloted. A training strategy is being implemented to help employees carry out the strategic plan using customer-focused teams, technology, and other innovative approaches.

DEPARTMENT OF ENERGY

NPR Recommendations

DOE01	Improve Environmental Contract Management
DOE02	Incorporate Land Use Planning in Cleanup
DOE03	Make Field Facility Contracts Outcome-Oriented
DOE04	Increase Electrical Power Revenues and Study Rates
DOE05	Strengthen the Federal Energy Management Program
DOE06	Redirect Energy Laboratories to Post-Cold War Priorities
DOE07	Save Costs Through Private Power Cogeneration
DOE08	Support the Sale of the Alaska Power Administration

Agency Progress to Date

The Department of Energy (DOE) is redirecting the efforts of federal laboratories and encouraging sharing of lab assets with industry, universities, and other agencies. DOE has restructured its overall operations, including a commitment to saving $4.4 billion by restructuring the Environmental Management Program. Also, DOE is working with affected federal agencies and congressional committees that are drafting a Comprehensive Environmental Response Compensation and Liability Act reauthorization bill to ensure inclusion of future land use plans in setting contamination cleanup standards. Savings from these activities will total more than $5 billion over the next five years.

The initial NPR recommendations to increase electrical power revenues have been overtaken by a proposal to privatize the Alaska, Southeastern, Southwestern, and Western area power administrations. A study of power rates will be included in the privatization effort. Bonneville Power Administration debt restructuring congressional hearings were held in June 1995. The Senate has marked up the bill as proposed by the President; further action is expected. The Federal Energy Management Program has been strengthened by upgrading its management to a deputy assistant secretary position, and a priority status is being pursued for the program's budget requests.

A Priority Team Report on laboratory missions was sent to the Secretary, and strategic plans for FY 1995 through FY 2000 are being developed in an effort to redirect lab priorities with reference to DOE's mission areas—protecting national security and reducing the nuclear danger, weapons site cleanup and environmental management, science and technology, and enhancing energy security.

Legislation was sent to Congress in February 1995 to remove the current restriction limiting the sale or use of cogenerated electricity to federally owned facilities. No bills have been formally introduced. Also, legislation has been introduced in both houses of Congress to authorize the sale of the two Alaska Power Administration projects in accordance with previously negotiated purchase agreements.

ENVIRONMENTAL PROTECTION AGENCY

NPR Recommendations

EPA01	Improve Environmental Protection Through Increased Flexibility for Local Government
EPA02	Streamline EPA's Permit Program
EPA03	Shift EPA's Emphasis Toward Pollution Prevention and Away From Pollution Control
EPA04	Promote the Use of Economic and Market-Based Approaches to Reduce Water Pollution
EPA05	Increase Private Sector Partnerships to Accelerate Development of Innovative Technologies
EPA06	Stop the Export of Banned Pesticides

EPA07	Establish Measurable Goals, Performance Standards, and Strategic Planning Within EPA
EPA08	Reform EPA's Contract Management Process
EPA09	Establish a Blueprint for Environmental Justice Throughout EPA's Operations
EPA10	Promote Quality Science for Quality Decisions
EPA11	Reorganize EPA's Office of Enforcement

Agency Progress to Date

EPA has implemented more than 40 percent of its recommendations. It is taking steps to alleviate the burden on local governments by increasing flexibility in the regulatory process and streamlining its permit program. Through a variety of outreach efforts, EPA has developed a national strategy to promote more efficient use of pesticides and fertilizers, assisted agencies in making determinations for selecting and purchasing environmentally preferable products, and earmarked funds for environmental technology. EPA's emphasis has thus shifted from pollution control to pollution prevention.

In addition, EPA has completed an agency action plan for improving the regulatory and statutory climate for innovative technologies. It is in the process of establishing partnerships with different industries to reengineer common products and processes so as to promote pollution prevention. By establishing partnerships with, and providing technical assistance to, developing countries, EPA continues to try to prevent the export of banned pesticides.

To promote quality science for quality decisions, EPA has established guidelines for professional development and promotion of scientific and technical staff. Peer review and quality assurance programs are being expanded to promote excellence in science, and organizational effectiveness has been improved by appropriately structuring the agency's laboratories.

EXECUTIVE OFFICE OF THE PRESIDENT

NPR Recommendations

EOP01	Delegate Routine Paperwork Review to the Agencies and Redeploy OMB's Resources More Effectively
EOP02	Modify the OMB Circular System
EOP03	Strengthen the Office of U.S. Trade Representative's Coordination With State and Local Governments
EOP04	Improve Federal Advisory Committee Management
EOP05	Reinvent OMB's Management Mission
EOP06	Improve OMB's Relationship With Other Agencies
EOP07	Strengthen the Office of the U.S. Trade Representative's Trade Policy Coordination Process
EOP08	Strengthen the Office of the U.S. Trade Representative's Negotiation Process
EOP09	Establish a Customer Service Bureau in the EOP
EOP10	Conduct Qualitative Self-Reviews of Critical Administrative Processes
EOP11	Improve the Presidential Transition Process
EOP12	Improve Administrative Processes

Agency Progress to Date

The Office of Management and Budget (OMB) has continued to use its resources more effectively and improve OMB's relationship with other agencies. Internal reorganization has been designed to better integrate budget analysis, management review, and policy development functions to address cross-cutting and long-term governmental problems.

Besides improving internal processes, OMB has completed its initiatives to improve its relationships with other agencies: the office meets regularly with agencies to discuss and formulate new budget initiatives, OMB performance evaluations now include an element on maintaining good relations with agencies, and formal staff exchanges with agencies have been established.

In addition, the Executive Office of the President is in the process of reinventing its management mission. OMB 2000, OMB's internal reorganization, is paving the way toward more flexible, innovative, and effective management control programs. The plan creates linkages across government, academia, and the private sector that provide for rapid dissemination of best management practices.

FEDERAL EMERGENCY MANAGEMENT AGENCY

NPR Recommendations

FEMA01	Shift Emphasis to Preparing for and Responding to the Consequences of All Disasters
FEMA02	Develop a More Anticipatory and Customer-Driven Response to Catastrophic Disasters
FEMA03	Create Results-Oriented Incentives to Reduce the Costs of a Disaster
FEMA04	Develop a Skilled Management Team Among Political Appointees and Career Staff

Agency Progress to Date

The Federal Emergency Management Agency (FEMA) has implemented all of its recommendations; most have been completed, and some are nearing completion or are ongoing. Notably, it continues to develop innovative ways to provide quality customer service to disaster victims. It has significantly increased its teleregistration capacity to accommodate more disaster assistance applications by phone as opposed to at Disaster Application Centers (DACs); teleregistration is now also done entirely by computer. Automation of the registration process will result in a near-paperless system and has reduced the time it takes to deliver disaster assistance applications for processing by as much as one to two days. In addition, an application taken at a DAC costs more than $59, while one taken via teleregistration costs only $13.79, resulting in approximately $45 in savings per application.

Customer service standards based on the results of ongoing focus group and survey activities have been published and are distributed to disaster applicants. A telephone help line and disaster service centers have been deployed to provide applicants with up-to-date information on disaster assistance.

FEMA is working with the Red Cross and the 28 federal agencies that incorporate recovery and mitigation activities under the Federal Response Plan.

FEMA has produced a virtual electronic encyclopedia of continually updated and enhanced emergency management information. More than 850,000 inquiries have been posted to FEMA's World Wide Web site since it came on-line in November 1994. During the week after the Oklahoma City bombing incident, 80,000 Internet users accessed the FEMA site for specially produced situation reports. The latest addition to FEMA's Web site is a Global Emergency Management System that provides the user with links to dozens of other on-line databases, both domestic and international, in areas such as disaster management, disaster mitigation, risk management, natural disasters, scientific research, and search and rescue.

Also, for the first time in its history, FEMA has a strategic plan to guide policymakers toward a "Partnership for a Safer Future."

GENERAL SERVICES ADMINISTRATION

NPR Recommendations

GSA01 Separate Policymaking From Service Delivery and Make the General Services Administration a Fully Competitive, Revenue-Based Organization

Agency Progress to Date

The General Services Administration (GSA) has completed implementation of two-thirds of its recommendations. It is transforming itself into an organization with a stronger policy and oversight role in the governmentwide performance of administrative services, except personnel and financial management, by establishing a new Office of Policy, Planning, and Leadership. An internal GSA order has been drafted, to be effective October 1, 1995, which will consolidate into this new office the policy and regulatory activities formerly located in the services responsible for public buildings, federal supply, and information technology. This action will improve asset management.

In other reinvention efforts, GSA has made significant progress in eliminating mandatory sources of supply; identifying innovative procurement strategies; creating customer-focused, competitive ways of doing business; increasing the use of automation and technology; and streamlining and simplifying the organization and its operations.

DEPARTMENT OF HEALTH AND HUMAN SERVICES

NPR Recommendations

HHS01	Promote Effective Integrated Service Delivery for Customers by Increasing Collaboration Efforts
HHS02	Reengineer the HHS Process for Issuing Regulations
HHS03	Develop a National, Uniform Inspection System to Ensure a Safe Food Supply
HHS04	Reconfigure Support for Health Professions Education
HHS05	Restructure the Management of Railroad Industry Benefit Programs

HHS06	Improve Social Security Administration Disability Claims Processing to Better Serve People With Disabilities and Safeguard Trust Fund Assets
HHS07	Protect Social Security, Disability, and Medicare Trust Fund Assets by Removing Barriers to Funding Productive Oversight Activities
HHS08	Coordinate Collection and Dissemination of Social Security Administration Death Information to Protect Federal Program Assets
HHS09	Take More Aggressive Action to Collect Outstanding Debts Owed to the Social Security Trust Fund
HHS10	Institute and Collect User Fees on FDA's Inspection and Approval Process
HHS11	Redesign SSA Service Delivery and Make Better Use of Technology to Provide Improved Access and Services to Customers
HHS12	Strengthen Departmentwide Management
HHS13	Review the Field and Regional Office Structure of HHS and Develop a Plan for Shifting Resources to Match Workload Demands
HHS14	Amend the Health Care Financing Administration's Contracting Authority to Allow for Competitive Contracting

Agency Progress to Date

The Department of Health and Human Services (HHS) continues to be a leader in developing customer service plans. Moving beyond last year's efforts, which were focused on the agency's direct customers, HHS is now developing service standards governing how it will relate to its partners—the thousands of public and private grantees across the country that work with HHS to provide a vast array of programs and services to the American people.

HHS has completed its review of how the agency develops and issues regulations and is instituting a new process, one that removes layers of review by delegating authority and increases the involvement of interested staff and outside parties early in the process. The new process is expected to cut the time needed to issue final regulations in half.

In addition to reinvention labs focusing on empowering employees to improve customer service, HHS organized a reinvention lab of interested employees from all across the department to design and develop the HHS corporate presence on the Internet. As a result of this effort, a vast array of program information—including health information directed toward medical providers and the general public—is now readily available to the public. Other technology initiatives in HHS include participation on an interagency force looking to provide federal benefits electronically and expansion of the HHS e-mail system to reach 55,000 employees.

HHS included proposals to authorize the Food and Drug Administration to collect user fees in its 1996 budget submission. In addition, HHS has drafted legislation that would authorize changes in Medicare contracting that would lead to greater competition.

DEPARTMENT OF HOUSING AND URBAN DEVELOPMENT

NPR Recommendations

HUD01	Reinvent Public Housing
HUD02	Improve Multifamily Asset Management and Disposition
HUD03	Improve Single-Family Asset Management and Disposition
HUD04	Create an Assisted-Housing/Rent Subsidy Demonstration Project

HUD05	Establish a New Housing Production Program
HUD06	Streamline HUD Field Operations
HUD07	Refinance Section 235 Mortgages
HUD08	Reduce Section 8 Contract Rent Payments
HUD09	Consolidate Section 8 Certificates and Vouchers
HUD10	Reduce Operating Subsidies for Vacancies

Agency Progress to Date

The Department of Housing and Urban Development (HUD) has implemented more than 40 percent of its recommendations and continues to pursue its reinvention activities. In the past year, public housing transformation proposals to devolve control were submitted to Congress, and a department rule to decontrol public housing authorities is scheduled to be published in the fall. Other initiatives to reinvent public housing are making expected progress or have already been completed. Legislation has been introduced to establish demonstration projects to devolve control of public housing to local authorities and to authorize construction and modernization funding for models that try to provide tenants with choice.

HUD has further improved its multi- and single-family asset management and disposition. It has stimulated new multifamily housing production through a series of agreements with lenders; legislation is pending to further this objective. To reduce Section 8 contract rent payments, HUD has required owners to document and justify all operating costs and is working toward basing its annual contract rental rate increases on actual increases in costs to the owners. In July 1995, HUD published a final rule consolidating the Section 8 Certificate and Voucher programs to the extent permitted by law. It also published a proposed rule, which was developed using negotiated rulemaking, to reduce operating subsidies on vacant units.

INTELLIGENCE COMMUNITY

NPR Recommendations

INTEL01	Enhance Intelligence Community Integration
INTEL02	Enhance Community Responsiveness to Customers
INTEL03	Reassess Information Collection to Meet New Analytical Challenges
INTEL04	Integrate Intelligence Community Information Management Systems
INTEL05	Develop Integrated Personnel and Training Systems
INTEL06	Merge the President's Intelligence Oversight Board With the President's Foreign Intelligence Advisory Board
INTEL07	Improve Support to Ground Troops During Combat Operations

Agency Progress to Date

The Intelligence Community has completed implementation of almost 60 percent of its recommendations. As the Intelligence Community reorients itself in the post-Cold War world, its leadership has been meeting to chart the course ahead and is preparing a communitywide vision and action plan which include near-term initiatives and long-term priorities. The National Intelligence Needs Process is being refined to identify the essential contribution intelligence makes in accomplishing national objectives; further enhancements to this process are expected in the near future.

Intelink—the Intelligence Community's classified multimedia data exchange patterned after the Internet—is now fully operational, providing a wealth of information services to the community and its customers, as well as contributing to a better integration of the community's various elements.

In the area of human resources management—a high priority of the new Director, Central Intelligence (DCI)—a senior review panel published its findings at the end of July 1995, promising a framework of a redéfined, integrated personnel management system. Also, the DCI's Foreign Language Committee exceeded its original recommended action to spawn a number of innovative language reforms.

DEPARTMENT OF THE INTERIOR

NPR Recommendations

DOI01	Establish a Hard Rock Mine Reclamation Fund to Restore the Environment
DOI02	Redefine Federal Oversight of Coal Mine Regulation
DOI03	Establish a National Spatial Data Infrastructure
DOI04	Promote Entrepreneurial Management of the National Park Service
DOI05	Obtain a Fair Return for Federal Resources
DOI06	Rationalize Federal Land Ownership
DOI07	Improve the Land Acquisition Policies of the DOI
DOI08	Improve Minerals Management Service Royalty Collections
DOI09	Establish a System of Personnel Changes in DOI
DOI10	Consolidate Administrative and Programmatic Functions in DOI
DOI11	Streamline Management Support Systems in DOI
DOI12	Create a New Mission for the Bureau of Reclamation
DOI13	Improve the Federal Helium Program
DOI14	Enhance Environmental Management by Remediating Hazardous Material Sites

Agency Progress to Date

Mining reform legislation has been reintroduced in the current Congress. The Department of the Interior (DOI) is continuing to prioritize cleanup of abandoned mines and downsizing of the Office of Surface Mining. It is also supporting legislation to boost the federal government's return on its investment in the park system. DOI continues to play a lead role in the development of the National Spatial Data Infrastructure.

To consolidate administrative and programmatic functions within the department and reduce positions in NPR target areas, DOI is implementing its October 1994 streamlining plan. Also, DOI's human resources operation is in the midst of a major reengineering effort. Reforms include performance agreements for senior executives, an automated classification system, and a performance appraisal system. As recommended, DOI has also initiated several personnel exchange activities.

The Bureau of Reclamation has successfully implemented its new mission. Interior is working with several other federal agencies to improve environmental management of hazardous waste sites.

DEPARTMENT OF JUSTICE

NPR Recommendations

DOJ01	Improve the Coordination and Structure of Federal Law Enforcement Agencies
DOJ02	Improve Border Management
DOJ03	Redirect and Better Coordinate Resources Dedicated to the Interdiction of Drugs
DOJ04	Improve Department of Justice Debt Collection Efforts
DOJ05	Improve the Bureau of Prisons Education, Job Training, and Financial Responsibilities Programs

DOJ06	Improve the Management of Federal Assets Targeted for Disposition
DOJ07	Reduce the Duplication of Drug Intelligence Systems and Improve Computer Security
DOJ08	Reinvent the Immigration and Naturalization Service's Organization and Management
DOJ09	Make the Department of Justice Operate More Effectively as the U.S. Government Law Firm
DOJ10	Improve White Collar Fraud Civil Enforcement
DOJ11	Reduce the Duplication of Law Enforcement Training Facilities
DOJ12	Streamline Background Investigations for Federal Employees
DOJ13	Adjust Civil Monetary Penalties to the Inflation Index
DOJ14	Improve Federal Courthouse Security
DOJ15	Improve the Professionalism of the U.S. Marshals Service
DOJ16	Develop Lower Cost Solutions to Federal Prison Space Problems

Agency Progress to Date

Substantial progress has been realized in several initiatives begun during the earliest stages of NPR at the Department of Justice (DOJ). The Joint Automated Booking Station Laboratory, intended to streamline the booking process and improve access to offender information, has reduced processing times considerably. Further implementation at other sites is scheduled for later this year.

As part of a major overhaul of the Immigration and Naturalization Service (INS), increased attention has been focused on border management activities to ensure the best possible use of staff. A unified continuing training program and joint performance standards have been developed in conjunction with the U.S. Customs Service.

Also, INS is testing ways to cut through red tape in delivering services to customers at model offices in El Paso and Detroit; it is also participating in an international, multi-agency pilot effort to test ways of expediting the legal entry of low-risk border crossers.

The Bureau of Prisons continues to seek ways of reducing the expense of operating federal prisons. During 1995, about 2,800 inmates completed 151 community and public works projects. The bureau was also successful in getting Congress to approve legislation to curb the costs of confinement; this will offset inmate health care costs.

DOJ has submitted a proposed reorganization of the U.S. Marshals Service that will streamline the agency and empower its employees. It will shift approximately 100 positions from headquarters to the field, reduce the number of management layers and formal organizational units, and abolish three regional offices. The reorganization will improve delivery of services, eliminate non-value-added work and redundant processing steps, and consolidate similar business functions.

DEPARTMENT OF LABOR

NPR Recommendations

DOL01	Enhance Reemployment Programs for Occupationally Disabled Federal Employees
DOL02	Develop a Single Comprehensive Worker Adjustment Strategy
DOL03	Expand Negotiated Rulemaking and Improve Up-Front Teamwork on Regulations
DOL04	Expand the Use of Alternative Dispute Resolution by the Department of Labor
DOL05	Automate the Processing of ERISA Annual Financial Reports (Forms 5500) to Cut Costs and Delays in Obtaining Employee Benefit Plan Data

DOL06	Amend the ERISA Requirement for Summary Plan Descriptions
DOL07	Redirect the Mine Safety and Health Administration's Role in Mine Equipment Regulation
DOL08	Create One-Stop Centers for Career Management
DOL09	Create a Boundary-Spanning Workforce Development Council
DOL10	Refocus the Responsibility for Ensuring Workplace Safety and Health
DOL11	Open the Civilian Conservation Centers to Private and Public Competition
DOL12	Partially Fund Mine Safety and Health Enforcement Through Service Fees
DOL13	Integrate Enforcement Activities Within the Department of Labor
DOL14	Apply Information Technology to Expedite Wage Determinations for Federal Contracts
DOL15	Provide Research and Development Authority for the DOL's Mine Safety and Health Program
DOL16	Increase Assistance to States in Collecting Delinquent Unemployment Insurance Trust Fund Contributions
DOL17	Revise and Update the Consumer Price Index
DOL18	Improve the Delivery of Legal Services by the Office of the Solicitor in the Department of Labor
DOL19	Transfer the Veterans' Employment and Training Service to the Employment and Training Administration
DOL20	Reduce Federal Employees' Compensation Act Fraud
DOL21	Change the Focus of the Unemployment Insurance Benefits Quality Control Program to Improve Performance

Agency Progress to Date

The Department of Labor (DOL) continues to make progress in its efforts to reinvent its regulatory and enforcement activities. Several of NPR's recommendations have been completed, and almost all of the remaining recommendations are under way. In addition, 93 percent of the performance objectives in the Secretary's performance agreement with the President for FY 1994 have been accomplished. Also, more than 10 core programs or activities have been successfully reengineered in accordance with the Secretary's FY 1995 performance agreement. Reengineered activities include the Mine Safety and Health Administration regular inspection process and inspection accountability process, the Occupational Safety and Health Administration's (OSHA's) Freedom of Information Act process and OSHA's complaint processing, Federal Employees' Compensation Act claims processing, OFCCP standard investigation, and the Wage and Hour investigation process.

Substantial progress has also been made in implementing DOL's streamlining plan. Reductions in employment, headquarters positions, and senior-level positions are all ahead of target.

The department has continued to focus its reinvention activities on the customer: developing customer service standards, reengineering and improving operations to provide better customer service, and conducting widespread training on managing for results.

NATIONAL AERONAUTICS AND SPACE ADMINISTRATION

NPR Recommendations

NASA01	Improve NASA Contracting Practices
NASA02	Increase NASA Technology Transfer Efforts and Eliminate Barriers to Technology Development
NASA03	Increase NASA Coordination of Programs With the U.S. Civil Aviation Industry

NASA04	Strengthen and Restructure NASA Management
NASA05	Clarify the Objectives of the Mission to Planet Earth Program

Agency Progress to Date

The National Aeronautics and Space Administration (NASA) was already in the process of absorbing a $35 billion (31 percent) cut over five years when the President asked for an additional $8.7 billion reduction. Consequently, NASA established an internal review team to produce proposals to enable the agency to meet the funding targets set by the Administration. The review team's plan cuts infrastructure by reducing jobs, facilities, and administrative overhead, rather than terminating core science, aeronautics, and exploration programs.

The review, known as the "Zero-Based Review," proposed streamlining functions at NASA's 10 major field centers, so that each installation becomes a "center of excellence" concentrating on specific aspects of NASA's mission. At the same time, these proposed changes would reduce overlap and consolidate administrative and program functions across the agency.

Under the review team's plan, NASA's total civil service employment levels will be cut to approximately 17,500 by the year 2000. This is the lowest number of civil servants at NASA since 1961. In addition, the budget will cut an estimated 25,000 contractor personnel.

The review team proposals are being assessed as part of the agency's FY 1997 budget, due to be submitted to the Office of Management and Budget later this year.

NATIONAL SCIENCE FOUNDATION

NPR Recommendations

NSF01	Strengthen Coordination of Science Policy
NSF02	Use a Federal Demonstration Project to Increase Research Productivity

NSF03 Continue Automation of NSF Research Support Functions

Agency Progress to Date

The President strengthened the coordination of science policy by creating the National Science and Technology Council. Also, steps have been taken to formalize the Federal Demonstration Project (FDP). A certification process and certification criteria were developed by an FDP working group, and accepted by the FDP Steering Committee in 1994. The current FDP structure is being used to explore further experiments and demonstrations, particularly direct charging of facilities costs.

Through Project FastLane, the National Science Foundation (NSF) is pioneering the use of information technology to ease and streamline proposal preparation and processing and the administration of awards for research and education projects. Several pilot projects involving a cross-section of institutions that receive support from NSF are either operational or in the late stages of development. NSF is coordinating closely with other research-supporting agencies.

OFFICE OF PERSONNEL MANAGEMENT

NPR Recommendations

OPM01 Strengthen OPM's Leadership Role in Transforming Federal Human Resource Management Systems

OPM02 Redefine and Restructure OPM's Functional Responsibilities to Foster a Customer Orientation

OPM03 Change the Culture of OPM to Empower Its Staff and Increase Its Customer Orientation

Agency Progress to Date

In January 1995, OPM Director James B. King implemented a reorganization, or redesign, of the agency that has underscored

OPM's core mission as guardian of the merit system and strengthened the agency's commitment to customer service. "Whatever other roles OPM may play, there is no question that this agency must exist to guarantee to the American people that we won't slide back into the days of chaos, corruption, and discrimination in government" that existed before the institution of the career civil service, Director King told employees. OPM is now a smaller, leaner agency with 1,738 fewer full-time employees since April 1993—a decrease of more than 30 percent.

SMALL BUSINESS ADMINISTRATION

NPR Recommendations

SBA01	Allow Judicial Review of the Regulatory Flexibility Act
SBA02	Improve Assistance to Minority Small Businesses
SBA03	Reinvent the U.S. Small Business Administration's Credit Programs
SBA04	Examine Federal Guidelines for Small Business Lending Requirements
SBA05	Manage the Microloan Program to Increase Loans for Small Business
SBA06	Establish User Fees for Small Business Development Center Services
SBA07	Distribute SBA Staff Based on Workload and Administrative Efficiency
SBA08	Improve Federal Data on Small Businesses

Agency Progress to Date

The Small Business Administration (SBA) has completed implementation of more than 60 percent of its recommendations. Its reinvention activities are highlighted by continued progress under several initiatives. Specifically, by reinventing SBA's credit programs, LowDoc and FA$TRACK have been successful in trimming processing times and reducing paperwork. By relying more on the expertise and decisions of nongovernment lending partners, the agency has developed increased efficiency and garnered wide praise from borrowers and lenders alike.

SBA is also simplifying its own regulations, initiating reform as a central focus of continuing reinvention efforts. SBA will revise all of its regulations by the end of calendar year 1995, reducing their length by more then 50 percent. SBA has also redistributed its staff based on need. Regional offices have been streamlined, dropping from 336 in 1992 to 90 in 1995. Many of these employees are now working in district offices, serving small business owners directly.

DEPARTMENT OF STATE/ U.S. INFORMATION AGENCY

NPR Recommendations

DOS01	Expand the Authority of Chiefs of Mission Overseas
DOS02	Integrate the Foreign Affairs Resource Management Process
DOS03	Improve State Department Efforts to Promote U.S. Business Overseas
DOS04	Provide Leadership in the Department's Information Management
DOS05	Reduce Mission Operating Costs
DOS06	Consolidate U.S. Nonmilitary International Broadcasting
DOS07	Relocate the Mexico City Regional Administrative Management Center
DOS08	Improve the Collection of Receivables

DOS09 Change UN Administrative and Assessment Procedures

Agency Progress to Date

Under the auspices of the President's Management Council, State and other foreign affairs agencies have launched pilot projects to solve administrative cost-sharing problems overseas. Increasing the foreign affairs management authority of chiefs of mission overseas will require legislation granting them authority over non-State appropriations.

State established the Office of Resources, Plans, and Policy in 1994 to coordinate resource requirements in the Function 150 budget. This office reports directly to the Secretary.

State continues to increase its efforts to promote U.S. business overseas. Through improved coordination with other international trade agencies and shared trade information, the department is ahead of schedule in its implementation of an export promotion strategy.

The department appointed an acting chief information officer this year to guide the development of and provide oversight for information management policy. State is using private and public sector expertise in developing a department-wide strategic plan for moving to open systems.

State has made significant progress in reducing overseas operating costs; for example, it has closed several overseas posts and reduced the reporting burden on all other posts.

USIA consolidated all U.S. government nonmilitary overseas broadcasting operations into a new International Broadcasting Bureau. This will generate $400 million in savings by 1997 while still retaining the effectiveness of the various broadcast entities.

The relocation of the Mexico City Regional Administrative Management Center is under way, returning jobs to the United States, and should be completed by March 1996. State has also made significant progress in collecting accounts receivable.

Progress continues on United Nations (UN) administrative reform, with UN General Assembly agreement to establish an under secretary for inspection and a high-level working group examining the UN financial situation.

DEPARTMENT OF TRANSPORTATION

NPR Recommendations

DOT01	Measure Transportation Safety
DOT02	Streamline the Enforcement Process
DOT03	Use a Consensus-Building Approach to Expedite Transportation and Environmental Decisionmaking
DOT04	Establish a Corporation to Provide Air Traffic Control Services
DOT05	Permit States to Use Federal Aid as a Capital Reserve
DOT06	Encourage Innovations in Automotive Safety
DOT07	Examine User Fees for International Over-Flights
DOT08	Increase FAA Fees for Inspection of Foreign Repair Facilities
DOT09	Contract for Level I Air Traffic Control Towers
DOT10	Establish Aeronautical Telecommunications Network to Develop a Public-Private Consortium
DOT11	Improve Intermodal Transportation Policy Coordination and Management
DOT12	Develop an Integrated National Transportation Research and Development Plan
DOT13	Create and Evaluate Telecommuting Programs
DOT14	Improve DOT Information Technology Management
DOT15	Provide Reemployment Rights for Merchant Mariners

DOT16	Establish a Commission to Review the U.S. Maritime Industry
DOT17	Eliminate Funding for Highway Demonstration Projects
DOT18	Reduce Spending for the U.S. Merchant Marine Academy
DOT19	Rescind Unobligated Earmarks for the FTA New Starts and Bus Program
DOT20	Reduce Annual Essential Air Service Subsidies
DOT21	Terminate Grant Funding for Federal Aviation Administration Higher Education Programs
DOT22	Assign Office of Motor Carriers (OMC) Field Staff to Improve Program Effectiveness and Reduce Costs
DOT23	Automate Administrative Requirements for Federal-Aid Highway Projects

Agency Progress to Date

The Department of Transportation (DOT) has completed implementation of over half of the NPR recommendations. DOT has revamped its activities to move decisionmaking to the "front lines," provide state and local partners with more choice and flexibility, and set goals and objectives for working better and focusing on customers. The department has done extensive strategic planning, established state and local partnerships, moved to leverage federal transportation dollars, restructured its organization, established performance standards, and streamlined its regulatory process.

Through customer surveys and organizational assessments, DOT's internal and external customers identified an increasing desire for flexibility and choice, with a greater focus on results. The agency has developed several pilot programs to increase performance: these involve the U.S. Coast Guard's marine safety, security, and environmental protection program; the Federal Aviation Administration's (FAA's) Airways Facilities service delivery; the

Federal Highway Administration's Federal Lands Highway program; and all of the National Highway Traffic Safety Administration. DOT has also incorporated performance-based standards into its FY 1996 and 1997 budgets. The Federal Highway Administration Congestion Mitigation and Air Quality Improvement program has been altered to give states and localities the flexibility to use funds the way they think best. DOT is also seeking to develop a decision-making framework that uses an integrated transportation system perspective focusing on outcomes.

Transportation is currently exploring the feasibility of using cooperative agreements to incorporate promising technological innovations into its operations. FAA has joined with 11 U.S. airlines to develop a worldwide Aeronautical Telecommunication Network (ATN), a ground- and air-based system to deliver data-link communications. Planned ATN data-link information services direct controller-pilot communications, predeparture clearances, and aviation weather—all of which will greatly enhance the speed and accuracy of communications while reducing the amount of voice communication necessary. Through the use of shared networks, speed of communications, and other innovations, DOT expects to save the airline industry $600 million a year in the oceanic environment alone. Also, information technology is being developed to use the Geographic Information System and Global Positioning System to improve navigation and positioning in transportation for better safety. These information technology programs are expected to be completed in December 1995. DOT is also implementing telecommuting within the department and monitoring telecommuting in the private sector and its impacts on transportation.

The agency has been working to leverage the federal tax dollars used for operation. On May 19, 1995, FAA was given the authority to increase user fees for foreign repair station certification to current cost levels. Congress denied DOT the ability to charge tuition for the Merchant Marine Academy.

DEPARTMENT OF THE TREASURY

NPR Recommendations

TRE01	Improve the Coordination and Structure of Federal Law Enforcement Agencies
TRE02	Improve Border Management
TRE03	Redirect and Better Coordinate Resources Dedicated to the Interdiction of Drugs
TRE04	Foster Federal-State Cooperative Initiatives by the IRS
TRE05	Simplify Employer Wage Reporting
TRE06	Establish Federal Firearms License User Fees to Cover Costs
TRE07	Improve the Management of Federal Assets Targeted for Disposition
TRE08	Reduce the Duplication of Drug Intelligence Systems and Improve Computer Security
TRE09	Modernize the IRS
TRE10	Modernize the U.S. Customs Service
TRE11	Ensure the Efficient Merger of the Resolution Trust Corporation Into the FDIC
TRE12	Reduce the Duplication of Law Enforcement Training Facilities
TRE13	Streamline Background Investigations for Federal Employees
TRE14	Adjust Civil Monetary Penalties to the Inflation Index
TRE15	Increase IRS Collections Through Better Compliance Efforts
TRE16	Improve Agency Compliance With Employment Tax Reporting Requirements (Form 1099)
TRE17	Authorize Federal Tax Payments by Credit Card

TRE18	Modernize the Financial Management Service
TRE19	Repeal Section 5010 of the Internal Revenue Code to Eliminate the Tax Credits for Wine and Flavors
TRE20	Amend or Repeal Section 5121 of the Internal Revenue Code Requiring Special Occupational Taxes on Retail Alcohol Dealers

Agency Progress to Date

The Department of the Treasury is making progress on almost all of its NPR recommendations. Improvements have been made in both border management and the coordination and structure of federal law enforcement agencies. In May 1995, the Customs Service, USDA, and INS jointly formed three reinvention teams to reengineer Northern and Southern border processes and airport environments. Reorganized enforcement bureaus are now more focused on agency-specific core responsibilities; further internal restructuring is in progress.

The Internal Revenue Service is working with other federal and state agencies to develop steps to reduce employer wage and tax reporting requirements. This will eventually lead to a system of single electronic filing with state and federal governments. The agency also has published customer service standards and revised its performance measures to increase measurement of outputs directly affecting taxpayers.

A more flexible headquarters structure has been implemented as a Customs Service modernization effort, and a new field structure will be completed by this fall. Customs is proposing an electronic bulletin board to replace mailing of notices, thereby decreasing cost and modernizing service practices.

Treasury is improving governmentwide financial management systems by consolidating its operations and continuing to upgrade technology rapidly to ensure that federal agencies have the option to send payment data electronically when cost-efficient.

Legislation has been drafted to repeal the wine and flavors tax credit and Section 5121 of the tax code.

U.S. AGENCY FOR INTERNATIONAL DEVELOPMENT

NPR Recommendations

AID01	Redefine and Focus AID's Mission and Priorities
AID02	Reduce Funding, Spending, and Reporting Micro-management
AID03	Overhaul the AID Personnel System
AID04	Manage AID Employees and Consultants as a Unified Workforce
AID05	Establish an AID Innovation Capital Fund
AID06	Reengineer Management of AID Projects and Programs
AID07	Consolidate or Close AID Overseas Missions

Agency Progress to Date

In March 1994, the U.S. Agency for International Development (AID) released "Strategies for Sustainable Development," a series of reports defining the agency's long-term goals and refining the framework for foreign assistance. The reports were followed by more detailed guidelines on how to implement agency goals.

To emphasize AID's commitment to change, the entire agency was designated a "reinvention lab," and teams across the agency have reengineered major processes such as procurement and financial management. AID has developed a cross-cutting budget preparation process. It has also overhauled its personnel system to focus on more appropriate training and rotational assignments, to create a more diverse workforce, and to increase employee participation in decisionmaking. AID has reorganized and rightsized its Washington, D.C., headquarters and has begun a major realignment of field offices, with 21 missions to close by FY 1996 and six more to close by FY 1997. In addition, the agency has reduced its use of outside contractors by 20 percent. The "New AID," featuring all of its new systems and procedures, will be launched formally in FY 1996.

DEPARTMENT OF VETERANS AFFAIRS

NPR Recommendations

DVA01	Develop the Master Veteran Record and Modernize the Department's Information Infrastructure
DVA02	Modernize Benefits Claims Processing
DVA03	Eliminate Legislative Budget Constraints to Promote Management Effectiveness
DVA04	Streamline Benefits Claims Processing
DVA05	Consolidate Department of Defense and Department of Veterans Affairs Compensation and Retired Pay Programs
DVA06	Enhance VA Cost Recovery Capabilities
DVA07	Establish a Working Capital Fund
DVA08	Decentralize Decisionmaking Authority to Promote Management Effectiveness
DVA09	Establish a Comprehensive Resource Allocation Program
DVA10	Serve Veterans and Their Families as Customers
DVA11	Phase Out and Close Supply Depots
DVA12	Improve Business Practices Through Electronic Commerce
DVA13	Eliminate "Sunset" Dates in the Omnibus Budget Reconciliation Act of 1990

DVA14	Raise the Fees for Veterans Affairs' Guaranteed Home Loans
DVA15	Restructure the Veterans Affairs' Health Care System
DVA16	Recover Administrative Costs of Veterans' Insurance Program From Premiums and Dividends

Agency Progress to Date

As part of its customer service plan, the Department of Veterans Affairs (VA) has included standards for direct service; these are monitored to ensure that quality service is provided. VA has also instituted a "courtesy and caring" program to ensure that customers are treated with dignity and compassion. The department has actively sought the views and opinions of its customers in determining their needs and level of satisfaction. Customer service standards are being integrated with the Government Performance and Results Act in addition to other management and planning processes. VA's integration approach has been a model for the federal government.

VA has developed a streamlining plan to reduce overhead and management layers. The department is consolidating administration and management at VA medical centers and merging personnel, acquisition, and finance activities. The focus of streamlining is to improve the ratio of employees to supervisors to at least 15 to 1, while continuing to emphasize quality customer service. Delegations of authority in human resource management are expediting decisionmaking, reducing paperwork, and freeing scarce resources. A management framework stimulating maximum delegation of authority was approved. Largely due to the authorization for single-signature decisions, the Board of Veterans Appeals increased productivity by 27 percent.

VA and the Department of the Treasury have reached an agreement to automate many paper-driven processes, with cost savings estimated at $123 million over five years. The percentage of employees receiving their salaries by direct deposit has increased to 90 percent.

Additionally, VA has initiated several actions to better meet the needs of customers while reducing costs. It has partnered with the private sector in Houston to construct a new building on VA property in exchange for a long-term lease for a retail center. Estimated savings for the federal government exceed $16 million over the life of the partnership. The agency also helped 100,000 veterans refinance their VA-guaranteed home loans, saving each veteran an average of $14,760 over 10 years and avoiding an estimated $56 million in future foreclosure costs to the government.

The Director of OMB has accepted VA as a franchise fund pilot and has forwarded a proposal to Congress to franchise certain in-house activities. VA has presented to Congress and begun to implement a complete restructuring of the health care system that will ensure optimum quality and efficiency as well as greater access to veterans.

APPENDIX B

Status of Major Recommendations Affecting Governmental Systems

THE NATIONAL PERFORMANCE Review's (NPR's) September 7, 1993, report contains 130 major recommendations affecting governmentwide management systems such as budget, procurement, financial management, and personnel. Separate accompanying reports delineate these recommendations, breaking them into 417 specific action items. Now, two years later, agencies report that 27 percent of these action items are complete and another 63 percent are in progress. Following are highlights of these governmentwide system reinvention efforts.

CREATING QUALITY LEADERSHIP AND MANAGEMENT

NPR Recommendations

QUAL01	Provide Improved Leadership and Management of the Executive Branch
QUAL02	Improve Government Performance Through Strategic and Quality Management
QUAL03	Strengthen the Corps of Senior Leaders
QUAL04	Improve Legislative-Executive Branch Relations

Progress to Date

The President continues to provide leadership on management issues. For example, he directed the Vice President to conduct a second performance review this past year to address new issues and revisit areas first looked at two years ago. The President's Management Council, which was created two years ago as recommended by NPR, has become a pivotal and effective force in policymaking and coordination of governmentwide reform initiatives, including customer service improvement, streamlining, and civil service reform. The President has also negotiated performance agreements with eight agency heads as a way of clarifying each agency's priorities, and additional agreements are under development.

The Vice President and cabinet secretaries have made a visible commitment to leading and managing in accordance with the Baldrige Quality Award criteria; in fact, 18 of the 24 largest agencies have created top-level quality councils to help lead their efforts. Although NPR recommended that a category be created within the Malcolm Baldrige Award for federal government agencies, this has not been done. A series of quality training initiatives are being promoted across agencies, however, by the training function formerly in the Office of Personnel Management.

STREAMLINING MANAGEMENT CONTROL

NPR Recommendations

SMC01	Implement a Systems Design Approach to Management Controls
SMC02	Streamline the Internal Controls Program to Make It an Efficient and Effective Management Tool
SMC03	Change the Focus of the Inspectors General
SMC04	Increase the Effectiveness of Offices of General Counsel
SMC05	Improve the Effectiveness of the General Accounting Office Through Increased Customer Feedback
SMC06	Reduce the Burden of Congressionally Mandated Reports

SMC07 Reduce Internal Regulations by More Than 50 Percent

SMC08 Expand the Use of Waivers to Encourage Innovation

Progress to Date

The Office of Management and Budget (OMB) has taken a leadership role in streamlining management control systems by working to consolidate multiple reporting systems and integrate planning, budget, financial management, and performance reporting systems. For example, it rewrote OMB Circular A-123, "Internal Control Systems," as a succinct document—cutting it from 120 pages of process-oriented details to a 13-page set of principles that allow agencies the flexibility to best adapt them to their own environment. The revised circular has been renamed "Management Accountability and Control."

The Senate has passed S. 790, Federal Reports Elimination and Sunset Act of 1995, which will eliminate or modify more than 200 outdated or unnecessary congressionally mandated reporting requirements and place a sunset on an estimated 4,800 additional reports with an annual, semiannual, or other periodic reporting requirement four years after the bill's enactment.

The Inspectors General are, as illustrated in a recent report, making progress in implementing their January 1994 report, *Vision and Strategies to Apply Our Reinvention Principles*. Selected units in the General Accounting Office are documenting best practices, and the agency is beginning to use feedback loops more broadly.

All agencies are making progress in cutting their internal regulations in half: some continue to make significant progress. For example, the Department of Energy reduced its departmental orders from 312 to 236, with a cost avoidance of $38 million. The Community Empowerment Board is developing a process for obtaining waivers from federal regulations; it has received more than 1,000 requests from communities participating in the empowerment process.

TRANSFORMING ORGANIZATIONAL STRUCTURES

NPR Recommendations

ORG01	Reduce the Costs and Numbers of Positions Associated With Management Control Structures by Half
ORG02	Use Multi-Year Performance Agreements Between the President and Agency Heads to Guide Downsizing Strategies
ORG03	Establish a List of Specific Field Offices to Be Closed
ORG04	The President Should Request Authority to Reorganize Agencies
ORG05	Sponsor Three or More Cross-Departmental Initiatives Addressing Common Issues or Customers
ORG06	Identify and Change Legislative Barriers to Cross-Organizational Cooperation

Progress to Date

All agencies have developed plans for internal streamlining and reducing the number of positions associated with management control structures. By the end of FY 1996, agencies will have cut about 74,000 supervisory positions. Also, agencies are ahead of the statutory timetable for cutting 272,900 positions by 1999. Under the direction of the President's Management Council, a governmentwide team assessed the federal government's field office structure and in February 1995 made recommendations for additional restructuring proposals.

The Administration continues to sponsor cross-departmental initiatives addressing common issues and customers. For example, it has created an approach to improve coordination of governmental statistics and is piloting cross-agency "one-stop" offices for small businesses and other government services in several locations around the country. In addition, the Administration has also created the U.S. Business Advisor as a one-stop electronic link to government for business, so individuals can more easily search federal rules and obtain information.

The President has not asked Congress for authority to reorganize agencies, but is instead achieving the efficiencies and other results desired through streamlining and joint agency efforts, such as the Electronic Benefits Task Force. Congress has not reduced barriers to cross-organizational cooperation.

IMPROVING CUSTOMER SERVICE

NPR Recommendations

ICS01	Create Customer-Driven Programs in All Departments and Agencies That Provide Services Directly to the Public
ICS02	Customer Service Performance Standards—Internal Revenue Service
ICS03	Customer Service Performance Standards—Social Security Administration
ICS04	Customer Service Performance Standards—Postal Service
ICS05	Streamline Ways to Collect Customer Satisfaction and Other Information From the Public

Progress to Date

Last September, 150 agencies published standards telling their customers what kind of service to expect. The standards came from asking customers what they want, and are part of the agencies' response to the President's order to build a customer-driven government. In his order, the President set an overall service goal to "equal the best in business."

With the standards out, the agencies went to work to make good on their promises to be courteous, quick, accurate, and accessible. Agencies studied the best in business, running benchmarking studies on 1-800 services, complaint systems, distribution systems, and more. They also expanded training programs. For example, before the ink was dry on announcements of cuts and reorganization at the Farmers Rural Electric and Community Development Administration, all 12,500 employees had been trained in customer service skills.

Agencies also applied new information technologies to deliver better service. The Internal Revenue Service made tax forms available on the Internet—filling a huge demand as April 15 grew close. Agencies have developed new ways to serve as well. A "one-stop" U.S. General Store for Small Business opened in Houston, providing links to services offered by dozens of government agencies.

The President has directed agencies to measure their results and report them to their customers. To date, more than 1 million customers have joined in voluntary surveys of satisfaction. Agencies will publish their results this fall. In the meantime, more agencies are releasing customer service standards.

MISSION-DRIVEN, RESULTS-ORIENTED BUDGETING

NPR Recommendations

BGT01	Develop Performance Agreements With Senior Political Leadership That Reflect Organizational and Policy Goals
BGT02	Effectively Implement the Government Performance and Results Act of 1993
BGT03	Empower Managers to Perform
BGT04	Eliminate Employment Ceilings and Floors by Managing Within Budget

BGT05	Provide Line Managers With Greater Flexibility to Achieve Results
BGT06	Streamline Budget Development
BGT07	Institute Biennial Budgets and Appropriations
BGT08	Seek Enactment of Expedited Rescission Procedures

Progress to Date

As part of a shift to greater accountability for results, many federal agencies have developed performance agreements that describe their objectives and goals for the year. The Departments of Energy, Labor, and Transportation, among others, have made extensive use of performance agreements across their departments, tracking progress with innovative management information systems.

Twenty-five agencies are carrying out 71 pilot programs to define performance measures, well ahead of the schedule called for by the Government Performance and Results Act. Workgroups are developing common performance measures for such areas as research and development and public health. In Oregon, federal agencies are working with state and local government on statewide benchmarks and have signed a memorandum of understanding that grants the state greater flexibility in exchange for results.

In addition to its guidance and assistance on performance measures, requirements, and strategic planning, OMB increasingly has placed greater emphasis on integrating performance measures into budget development and presentation. OMB introduced a spring performance review to assess performance measures in every federal agency: subsequently, agencies will submit FY 1997 budgets that place a greater emphasis on the results they hope to achieve.

With an eye to empowering managers and streamlining budget development, OMB simplified the apportionment process, took steps to establish six pilot franchise funds, and initiated a review of the budget account structure as part of a broader review to improve the relationship between budget and program performance. However, with legislated employment reduction goals and, in some agencies, legislated employment floors, little progress has been made in allowing managers to manage against budget rather than against these ceilings and floors.

Legislation that includes provisions for biennial budgeting has been drafted and introduced in both houses and is awaiting congressional action (H.R. 3801, S. 1824). Both the House and Senate have passed versions of the Expedited Rescission Act.

IMPROVING FINANCIAL MANAGEMENT

NPR Recommendations

FM01	Accelerate the Issuance of Federal Accounting Standards
FM02	Clarify and Strengthen the Financial Management Roles of OMB and Treasury
FM03	Fully Integrate Budget, Financial, and Program Information
FM04	Increase the Use of Technology to Streamline Financial Services
FM05	Use the Chief Financial Officers (CFO) Act to Improve Financial Services
FM06	"Franchise" Internal Services
FM07	Create Innovation Funds
FM08	Reduce Financial Regulations and Requirements
FM09	Simplify the Financial Reporting Process
FM10	Provide an Annual Financial Report to the Public
FM11	Strengthen Debt Collection Programs
FM12	Manage Fixed Asset Investments for the Long Term
FM13	Charge Agencies for the Full Cost of Employee Benefits

Progress to date has been excellent, but much work remains to be done. A very solid infrastructure is being established. Notably, the vast majority of federal accounting standards has been issued for governmentwide implementation and a financial systems framework established. Through the Chief Financial Officers (CFO) Council, agencies and oversight organizations have developed a uniform vision, set of priorities, and program plan. FinanceNet has been institutionalized by the CFO Council and the Joint Financial Management Improvement Program as a mechanism for electronic interchange. The network's utility has been recognized across the federal government, by state and local organizations, and by other nations as well. A joint CFO Council meeting was held with members of Congress; the CFOs plan to meet with the agency Inspectors General in September.

Progress is being made in the designation of up to six pilot franchise funds authorized by the Government Management Reform Act. Also as authorized by the act, the federal financial community has proposed that agencies prepare an annual planning report each fall and an accountability report each spring to replace a plethora of financial reports throughout the year. This approach will ease agencies' reporting burden and provide *information* rather than just *data*.

A comprehensive debt collection initiative has been completed and enacting legislation introduced. Several energizing and coalescing conferences have been held on electronic commerce (EC) with contract and grant officials, and an EC Implementation Team is being designated by the CFO Council. Other targeted council priorities for the coming year include improving the state of federal financial management systems and integrating budget, program, and management information for better decisionmaking.

REINVENTING HUMAN RESOURCE MANAGEMENT

NPR Recommendations

HRM01 Create a Flexible and Responsive Hiring System

HRM02 Reform the General Schedule Classification and Basic Pay System

HRM03	Authorize Agencies to Develop Programs for Improvement of Individual and Organizational Performance
HRM04	Authorize Agencies to Develop Incentive Award and Bonus Systems to Improve Individual and Organizational Performance
HRM05	Strengthen Systems to Support Management in Dealing With Poor Performers
HRM06	Clearly Define the Objective of Training as the Improvement of Individual and Organizational Performance; Make Training More Market-Driven
HRM07	Enhance Programs to Provide Family-Friendly Workplaces
HRM08	Improve Processes and Procedures Established to Provide Workplace Due Process for Employees
HRM09	Improve Accountability for Equal Employment Opportunity Goals and Accomplishments
HRM10	Improve Interagency Collaboration and Cross-Training of Human Resource Professionals
HRM11	Strengthen the Senior Executive Service So That It Becomes a Key Element in the Governmentwide Culture Change Effort
HRM12	Eliminate Excessive Red Tape and Automate Functions and Information
HRM13	Form Labor-Management Partnerships for Success
HRM14	Provide Incentives to Encourage Voluntary Separations

Progress to Date

The Administration has drafted a legislative proposal to reform the federal government's human resource management systems. Its provisions for reforming governmentwide hiring, performance management, and classification systems are largely drawn from recommendations in the NPR and National Partnership Council (NPC) reports; its provisions for redesigning the Office of Personnel Management (OPM), alternative personnel systems, and labor law reform support NPR human resource management objectives. The draft bill also contains career transition proposals to help agencies and employees cope with further downsizing of the workforce.

OPM managed the Federal Workforce Restructuring Act of 1994, under which about 35,000 non-Department of Defense (DOD) employees accepted incentives to leave the government workforce voluntarily. This is in addition to 62,000 DOD employees who accepted separation incentives under previous legislation. Based upon its experience in helping DOD set up its separation incentive program in 1993, OPM provided other executive branch agencies with numerous resources to aid in their effective implementation of the legislation. These included best and worst practices from similar public and private sector efforts via newsletter, electronic bulletin board, and broadcast media.

Congress passed new laws and OPM issued regulations to implement family-friendly leave policies. Federal employees can now use sick leave to adopt a child, to serve as a bone-marrow or organ donor, and to care for family members or attend their funerals. The limitation on recrediting sick leave has been removed for former federal employees who return to government service. OPM also spearheaded a governmentwide leave-sharing effort related to the Oklahoma City bombing.

OPM issued final performance management regulations that provide agencies with additional flexibilities and eliminate burdensome requirements. OPM has proceeded to work on classification series consolidation, and requested public comment on proposals to consolidate approximately 450 General Schedule series to 74 and to merge or rename a number of occupational groups. The agency has made the federal personnel community a true partner in the development of personnel policy by involving the Interagency Advisory Group in several priority initiatives, including the development of a career transition business plan and the establishment of an interagency consortium to provide regularly scheduled satellite broadcasts on a broad range of human resource management issues.

OPM proposed abolishing regulations governing internal agency grievance and appeal procedures. It also issued executive core qualifications for the Senior Executive Service that simplify and strengthen the staffing process and emphasize key national and organizational priorities. OPM is sponsoring interagency working groups to identify indicators for measuring human resource management performance against merit principles, and to create a customer service survey as a new measure of human resource management performance.

Considerable progress has been made in establishing labor-management partnerships following the issuance of Executive Order 12871 in October 1993. As of July 1995, 50 percent of the bargaining units that responded to an NPC questionnaire had established partnership councils and 40 percent had partnership agreements. Partnerships are beginning to make qualitative differences in agency efficiency and worker satisfaction by addressing such issues as agency redesign and downsizing, productivity improvement, customer service, cost-savings measures, and employee working conditions.

REINVENTING FEDERAL PROCUREMENT

NPR Recommendations

PROC01	Reframe Acquisition Policy
PROC02	Build an Innovative Procurement Workforce
PROC03	Encourage More Procurement Innovation
PROC04	Establish New Simplified Acquisition Threshold and Procedures
PROC05	Reform Labor Laws and Transform the Labor Department Into an Efficient Partner for Meeting Public Policy Goals

PROC06	Amend Protest Rules
PROC07	Enhance Programs for Small Business and Small Disadvantaged Business Concerns
PROC08	Reform Information Technology Procurement
PROC09	Lower Costs and Reduce Bureaucracy in Small Purchases Through the Use of Purchase Cards
PROC10	Ensure Customer Focus in Procurement
PROC11	Improve Procurement Ethics Laws
PROC12	Allow for Expanded Choice and Cooperation in the Use of Supply Schedules
PROC13	Foster Reliance on the Commercial Marketplace
PROC14	Expand Electronic Commerce for Federal Acquisition
PROC15	Encourage Best Value Procurement
PROC16	Promote Excellence in Vendor Performance
PROC17	Authorize a Two-Phase Competitive Source Selection Process
PROC18	Authorize Multi-Year Contracts
PROC19	Conform Certain Statutory Requirements for Civilian Agencies to Those of Defense Agencies
PROC20	Streamline Buying for the Environment

Progress to Date

The Federal Acquisition Streamlining Act of 1994 contains the most important of NPR's recommended statutory changes to reinvent the federal government's $180-billion-a-year procurement system. The legislation raised the simplified acquisition threshold to $100,000, exempting procurements below this threshold from numerous statutory requirements; strongly encouraged acquiring commercial items and exempted such procurements from various statutory requirements; and lessened restrictions for micropurchases (those under $2,500). The act provides that revisions to the regulations be published and take effect by October 1, 1995. Of the

25 rulemaking cases, several have been published; the other regulations are in various stages of review, evaluation, and final revision. The simplified acquisition threshold was published as an interim final rule in July 1995, enabling its provisions to be used prior to publication of the final rule. In addition, agency-specific regulations are being developed to implement the act's requirements.

Several bills have been introduced in both houses of Congress to address most of the other key NPR-recommended statutory changes not included in the 1994 legislation. Some of the priority recommendations being proposed include bid protest reform, particularly for information technology; increased competition through a two-phase procurement process; and simplified procedures to buy commercial items.

Several related initiatives are under way to streamline the procurement process to make it more effective and efficient, foster commercial practices, reduce bureaucracy, and seize the opportunities provided by advances in information technology. A final rule to incorporate a statement of guiding principles in the Federal Acquisition Regulation was published in July 1995. *A Guide to Best Practices for Past Performance* (interim edition, May 1995) was developed and issued by the Office of Federal Procurement Policy (OFPP). A project management office was established to implement expanded use of electronic commerce for government procurement and to develop the Federal Acquisition Computer Network (FACNET). FACNET will provide "a single face to industry" by creating a single standard-based electronic commerce capability for all federal agencies.

Use of the purchase card for micropurchases under $2,500—which constitute about 85 percent of the government's procurement transactions—has risen dramatically among many agencies, cutting administrative costs and expediting purchases. NPR estimated that $180 million could be saved annually if 50 percent of the government's small purchases were made with purchase cards. In FY 1994, purchase cards were used to make nearly 2.5 million purchases with a total value of $808 million. Through June of FY 1995, purchase cards have been used to make nearly 2.9 million purchases with a total value exceeding $1 billion. Usage has nearly doubled since 1993, and has translated to an administrative cost avoidance of more than $68.5 million. The General Services Administration (GSA) is developing an electronic training package for use with the purchase card that will be available throughout the government when fully implemented.

DOD, GSA, and other agencies are aggressively working to adopt the use of commercial specifications when ordering supplies if the items are available commercially. DOD and GSA are developing acquisition workforce education and training materials and opportunities to encourage innovation among the acquisition workforce. In addition, OFPP—in a joint partnership with NPR, GSA, DOD, Lawrence Livermore National Laboratory, and the Council for Excellence in Government—has developed the Acquisition Reform Network. This on-line network provides both public and private sectors with access to federal acquisition information including a reference material toolkit, electronic conferencing forum, training packages, acquisition best practices, and acquisition opportunity links.

REINVENTING SUPPORT SERVICES

NPR Recommendations

SUP01	Authorize the Executive Branch to Establish a Printing Policy That Will Eliminate the Current Printing Monopoly
SUP02	Assure Public Access to Federal Information
SUP03	Improve Distribution Systems to Reduce Costly Inventories
SUP04	Streamline and Improve Contracting Strategies for the Multiple Award Schedule Program

SUP05 Expand Agency Authority and Eliminate Congressional Control Over Federal Vehicle Fleet Management

SUP06 Give Agencies Authority and Incentive for Personal Property Management and Disposal

SUP07 Simplify Travel and Increase Competition

SUP08 Give Customers Choices and Create Real Property Enterprises That Promote Sound Real Property Asset Management

SUP09 Simplify Procedures for Acquiring Small Blocks of Space to House Federal Agencies

SUP10 Establish New Contracting Procedures for the Continued Occupancy of Leased Office Space

SUP11 Reduce Postage Costs Through Improved Mail Management

Progress to Date

Efforts to reform government printing continue, and some progress is being made. Both houses of Congress this year have proposed legislation to address the NPR-recommended statutory changes and to streamline the process by transferring some functions away from the Government Printing Office (GPO) and eliminating others. Other efforts reflect the need for additional printing reform. For example, the legislative branch has proposed a study on the future of the Depository Library System. Also, GPO has begun an initiative to promote its reinvention, a strategic plan to streamline the agency and develop a new partnership between it and the executive branch agencies.

GSA continues to make significant progress in streamlining the distribution of federal supplies to reduce costly inventories. Efforts include direct vendor delivery, use of electronic data interchange to simplify ordering in near real-time, and development of the GSA ADVANTAGE information system for Federal Supply Service catalog ordering. In addition, regulatory changes have been made to eliminate mandatory use of supply schedules in awarding contracts, to eliminate announcement requirements for information technology acquisitions from supply schedules, and to raise information technology order limits to $500,000 for supply schedules. GSA is pilot testing the use of electronic bulletin board ordering for the Multiple Award Schedule program. It has revised the federal property management regulation to authorize agencies to dispose of their excess personal property.

For travel and relocation NPR recommendations, teams under the purview of the Chief Financial Officers Council are developing recommendations and a legislative package. GSA will submit this package to Congress and implement the regulatory changes. The agency is also pilot testing an airfare tender system and has modified related contract award criteria to emphasize service over price. GSA has published regulatory changes requiring agencies to minimize mail processing steps, increase use of automation, and streamline operations. An interagency mail management committee to lead cooperative initiatives will be in place by the end of the year.

Pending legislation would require GSA to submit a public buildings plan to Congress including a strategic asset management plan, submit a building site selection impact statement, establish a central repository for asset management information, and submit a report on the basic characteristics of court accommodations. The legislation would also require agencies to address long-term government housing needs and establish a moratorium on construction of public buildings. GSA is making progress on other NPR recommendations for real property through separate pilot projects to give agencies greater authority in choosing their sources of real property services, develop simplified procedures for small amounts of leased space, and simplify procedures for renewing leases. GSA has created real property customer-oriented centers of expertise and has implemented an asset management information system to provide real property alternatives information to agencies.

Appendix B

REENGINEERING THROUGH INFORMATION TECHNOLOGY

NPR Recommendations

IT01	Provide Clear, Strong Leadership to Integrate Information Technology Into the Business of Government
IT02	Implement Nationwide, Integrated Electronic Benefit Transfer
IT03	Develop Integrated Electronic Access to Government Information and Services
IT04	Establish a National Law Enforcement/Public Safety Network
IT05	Provide Intergovernmental Tax Filing, Reporting, and Payments Processing
IT06	Establish an International Trade Data System
IT07	Create a National Environmental Data Index
IT08	Plan, Demonstrate, and Provide Governmentwide Electronic Mail
IT09	Improve Government's Information Infrastructure
IT10	Develop Systems and Mechanisms to Ensure Privacy and Security
IT11	Improve Methods of Information Technology Acquisition
IT12	Provide Incentives for Innovation
IT13	Provide Training and Technical Assistance in Information Technology to Federal Employees

Progress to Date

Interagency teams are, under the auspices of the Government Information Technology Services Working Group, putting in place various aspects of electronic government, and the implementation of NPR recommendations is proceeding as planned. Substantial progress has been made on all recommendations. For example, the Electronic Benefits Transfer (EBT) Task Force in 1994 released its plans for distributing an estimated $111 billion in federal benefits electronically by 1999, and has partnered with several alliances of states to pilot integrated EBT. Also, in April 1995, the Customer Service Improvement Team published its plan for developing a nationwide kiosk network that will provide government services electronically to the public. The Postal Service is leading interagency efforts to pilot electronic government services based on life events such as moving or family status changes.

On June 12, 1995, at the White House Conference for Small Business, the President and Vice President announced a new way for business to work with government—the U.S. Business Advisor, an on-line service on the Internet. The U.S. Business Advisor will offer businesses a "one-stop" electronic link to all the information and services government provides. The President has formed a task force to recommend the final design, content, and services for the U.S. Business Advisor by December 15, 1995.

The Federal Law Enforcement Wireless Users Group is developing pilot projects demonstrating federal, state, and local government use of a national wireless law enforcement and public safety network. Another interagency team is piloting projects that will test integrated filing of government tax reports and payments, eliminating the need for filing duplicative reports with different agencies. The Customs Service has taken the lead in implementing an International Trade Data System that collects, consolidates, and makes available international trade data and information from across federal agencies. The first pilot project of a National Environmental Data Index consolidating environmental information from across federal agencies was successfully completed by the National Oceanic and Atmospheric Administration in May 1995.

GSA has incorporated the Information Technology Schedule into the Federal Supply Service, allowing end users to order, in one stop, everything from pencils to computers. To expedite these procurements, GSA has delegated operating authority to agencies for procurements of up to $100 million. Also, GSA formed the Information Technology Resources Board, comprising experienced information technology managers from 18 agencies; the board will be consulted on reviews of planned initiatives.

RETHINKING PROGRAM DESIGN

NPR Recommendations

DES01	Activate Program Design as a Formal Discipline
DES02	Establish Pilot Program Design Capabilities in One or Two Agencies
DES03	Encourage the Strengthening of Program Design in the Legislative Branch
DES04	Commission Program Design Courses

Progress to Date

While these specific recommendations have not been implemented, the principles involved provided the framework for the implementation of the recent agency reviews that were undertaken by the Vice President at the President's direction.

STRENGTHENING THE PARTNERSHIP IN INTERGOVERNMENTAL SERVICE DELIVERY

NPR Recommendations

FSL01	Improve the Delivery of Federal Domestic Grant Programs
FSL02	Reduce Red Tape Through Regulatory and Mandate Relief

FSL03	Simplify Reimbursement Procedures for Administrative Costs of Federal Grant Disbursement
FSL04	Eliminate Needless Paperwork by Simplifying the Compliance Certification Process
FSL05	Simplify Administration by Modifying the Common Grant Rules on Small Purchases
FSL06	Strengthen the Intergovernmental Partnership

Progress to Date

To restrict unfunded mandates by federal agencies, the President signed two executive orders: "Regulatory Planning Review" (EO 12866, signed September 30, 1993) and "Enhancing the Intergovernmental Partnership" (EO 12875, signed October 26, 1993). These orders prevent agencies from issuing any new, non-statutory unfunded regulations without strong justification. To combat statutory unfunded mandates, Congress passed the Unfunded Mandate Reform Act of 1995 (P.L. 104-4, signed by the President March 22, 1995). This law restricts Congress from imposing new mandates on state and local governments without providing funds.

In April 1995, OMB published a revised Circular A-87, to encourage federal agencies to test fee-for-service procedures for cost reimbursement to states and localities. A fee-for-service alternative would be simpler and encourage cost containment. OMB has also taken steps to eliminate needless paperwork, particularly in the representations and certifications process, as well as revise the common rules for small purchases by local governments by increasing the dollar threshold from $25,000 to $100,000.

The Administration introduced many endeavors to strengthen the intergovernmental partnership. The President's interagency Community Empowerment Board oversees a process whereby member agencies may grant waivers. Nine empowerment zones and 95 empowerment communities were designated in December 1994; each of these entities is provided with additional flexibility and funding to implement their community-developed, comprehensive, strategic plans.

To be more responsive to locally perceived needs and bottom-up planning strategies, the categorical federal grant process is being radically reformed into a system of performance partnerships. In the FY 1996 budget, President Clinton proposed six performance partnerships that would consolidate about 200 existing programs. These performance partnerships require congressional action. The consolidated plan exemplifies the replacement of a program-oriented mentality with a comprehensive approach to problem-solving.

NPR has facilitated the Oregon Option, a partnership with the state of Oregon based on results. The program focuses on bringing together community, local, state, and federal agencies to agree on desired results, how to accomplish them, how to measure them, and how to break down barriers to achieving them. Oregon now leads the West in not only moving people off welfare but in placing them in productive jobs as well. The Administration granted waivers to the state so it could operate JOBS PLUS, a unique public-private partnership designed to move even more welfare recipients into the workforce.

Four areas—metro Atlanta, metro Denver, the District of Columbia, and the state of Nebraska—have joined with the federal government in uniting their intergovernmental agencies to reduce crime and violence in a project called Pulling America's Communities Together (PACT). Through Project PACT, the federal government is vigorously fostering and supporting the development of broad-based, fully coordinated local and statewide initiatives that work strategically to secure community safety.

REINVENTING ENVIRONMENTAL MANAGEMENT

NPR Recommendations

ENV01 Improve Federal Decisionmaking Through Environmental Cost Accounting

ENV02	Develop Cross-Agency Ecosystem Planning and Management
ENV03	Increase Energy and Water Efficiency
ENV04	Increase Environmentally and Economically Beneficial Landscaping

Progress to Date

Cross-agency ecosystem management teams were formed to conduct management and budget reviews of federal programs affecting four ecosystems: South Florida, Anacostia River Watershed, Prince William Sound, and Pacific Northwest Forests. In addition, the President signed a directive requiring federal agencies to increase energy and water efficiency.

In July 1995, an interagency workgroup published guidance in the *Federal Register* to implement President Clinton's April 26, 1994, Executive Memorandum on Environmentally and Economically Beneficial Landscape Practices on Federal Landscaped Grounds. An interagency working group on environmental cost analysis has begun work and will report back to the Council on Environmental Quality in 1996.

IMPROVING REGULATORY SYSTEMS

NPR Recommendations

REG01	Create an Interagency Regulatory Coordinating Group
REG02	Encourage More Innovative Approaches to Regulation
REG03	Encourage Consensus-Based Rulemaking
REG04	Enhance Public Awareness and Participation
REG05	Streamline Agency Rulemaking Procedures
REG06	Encourage Alternative Dispute Resolution When Enforcing Regulations

REG07	Rank Risks and Engage in "Anticipatory" Regulatory Planning
REG08	Improve Regulatory Science
REG09	Improve Agency and Congressional Relationships
REG10	Provide Better Training and Incentives for Regulators

Progress to Date

In September 1993, the President signed Executive Order 12866, Regulatory Planning and Review, which articulated the Administration's regulatory principles and created an interagency Regulatory Working Group. This group has implemented many of NPR's regulatory recommendations: it has met frequently and serves as a forum to help agencies implement various provisions of the order, including those that encourage innovative approaches to regulation. The Regulatory Working Group is developing guidelines on agency use of risk assessment and cost/benefit analysis. It has also helped lead ongoing regulatory reinvention efforts (see appendix D).

Agency reliance on electronic communication and information retrieval has increased significantly. With the assistance of the Administrative Conference of the United States, agencies have begun to use direct final rulemaking for noncontroversial rulemaking. The President has issued several directives encouraging agencies to use negotiated rulemaking ("reg-neg") where feasible. He also announced that limits on the creation of new advisory committees will not apply to reg-neg committees. Training materials have been disseminated, and in response, numerous new reg-negs have been undertaken.

Federal agency use of alternative dispute resolution (ADR) techniques is increasing dramatically. The Attorney General announced a new Department of Justice initiative to increase the department's reliance on and support of ADR. The Administrative Conference reported that agencies saved more than $20 million by using ADR in the past year. Additionally, several agencies have established ombudsman offices to handle citizen complaints.

Major legislative initiatives supported by this Administration have been enacted, including the Paperwork Reduction Act of 1995 and the Unfunded Mandates Reform Act. The latter includes a small but important amendment to the Federal Advisory Committee Act that makes it easier for federal officials to meet with state, local, and tribal officials.

Work remains to be done on the recommendations to create additional science advisory boards and to establish a training program for newly appointed federal regulatory officials.

APPENDIX C

New Recommendations by Agency

IN DECEMBER 1994, President Clinton asked Vice President Gore to conduct a second review of agencies to identify opportunities for additional savings, program terminations, and privatization of selected functions. Following are more than 180 recommendations that, if adopted, would result in nearly $70 billion in savings over five years; these savings have been incorporated into the President's recent balanced budget proposal.

Each recommendation is followed by a number in parentheses that indicates the necessary avenue for effective implementation:

1. agency heads can do themselves;
2. President, Executive Office of the President, or Office of Management and Budget (OMB) can do; or
3. may require authorizing legislation.

DEPARTMENT OF AGRICULTURE

USDA2-01 Centralize Servicing of Single-Family Housing Loans (1)
Change the servicing of a $30 billion loan portfolio to a centralized system that could close additional Department of Agriculture (USDA) county offices and reduce staff by up to 1,200 full-time equivalents (FTEs).
Savings: $250 million

USDA2-02 Change Family Day Care and Child Care Rates (3)
Offer families in day care homes that are not located in low-income areas two means-testing options: one

would continue the standard per meal subsidy at a reduced rate; the other would provide full meal subsidies to children below 185 percent of the poverty level and reduced subsidies to others. Day care homes in all other areas would continue to receive full meal subsidies for all children.
Savings: $1.7 billion

USDA2-03 Allow States Greater Flexibility in Food Stamp Program (3)
Give each state the authority to change food stamp program administrative procedures to better help the needy, promote personal responsibility of parents, and help those who can work to prepare for and find work. This authority will let states extend certification periods up to 24 months and will maintain the program as a national nutrition "safety net."
Savings: $140 million

USDA2-04 Include Food Stamp Anti-Fraud Provisions for Retailers and Recipients (1)
Improve the integrity of the food stamp program by ensuring that only legitimate stores participate in the program, strengthening penalties against offenders, and accelerating the use of technology as an enforcement tool.
Savings: $40 million

USDA2-05 Terminate the Emergency Farm Loan Program Administered by the Farm Service Agency (3) The Emergency Farm Loan Program has a 41-percent delinquency rate. Also, the need for this program was reduced by the Crop Insurance Reform Act of 1994. Eliminate the program by FY 1997.
Savings: $142 million

USDA2-06 Shift USDA's Peanut Program to a No-Net-Cost Basis (3)

Change the peanut program to one that is industry-financed with no cost to U.S. taxpayers. USDA would continue to operate the program, but the costs of direct subsidy to peanut growers would be borne by the industry through increased assessments. Alternatively, eliminate the subsidy by reducing the guaranteed loan rate support price and/or by reducing the minimum quantity (quota) of peanuts supported at above-market levels.
Savings: $309 million

USDA2-07 Reform Forest Service Land Acquisition (1)
Perform a two-year review of the Forest Service's land ownership mission and land stewardship resource allocation. Review regulations and statutes affecting land ownership to determine the scope of public purposes that need to be served through continued, or expanded, Forest Service land ownership.
Savings: $105 million

USDA2-08 Consolidate Nutrition Program for the Elderly With the Administration on Aging Congregate Feeding Programs (3)
Transfer the USDA Nutrition Program for the Elderly to the Health and Human Services' Administration on Aging program.
Savings: none

USDA2-09 Streamline USDA Rural Development Programs (3)
Combine 14 rural development loan and grant programs and allow USDA state directors to work with states, localities, and other organizations to jointly set priorities. Measure results.
Savings: $68 million

By implementing these recommendations, USDA will save $2,754 million over five years.

DEPARTMENT OF COMMERCE

DOC2-01 Transform the Patent and Trademark Office into a Performance-Driven, Customer-Oriented Agency (3)
The Patent and Trademark Office (PTO) should be granted the flexibility to use commercial business practices and given waivers from selected government controls in exchange for being accountable for agreed-upon performance gains. Since PTO produces clearly identified "products" and has a basis for a measurement system, it is expected that productivity would be significantly enhanced.
Savings: none (fee-funded)

DOC2-02 Transform the National Technical Information Service into a Performance-Driven, Customer-Oriented Agency (3)
The National Technical Information Service (NTIS) receives no appropriated funds, but relies on revenues from sales to the public. Like PTO, NTIS should be given the flexibility to use commercial business practices, be granted waivers, and be accountable for agreed-upon performance gains. For example, NTIS could provide services to other federal government agencies, such as on-line services through FedWorld, production and dissemination, and technology transfers.
Savings: none (fee-funded)

DOC2-03 Transform the National Oceanic and Atmospheric Administration's Mapping and Charting Service into a Performance-Driven, Customer-Oriented Agency (3)
This function has products that are clearly identified and measured, and its customer base is well recog-

nized. Like PTO, it should be restructured to use commercial business practices, be granted waivers, and be accountable for agreed-upon performance gains. Benefits expected include improved printing quality, reduced nautical accident rates, and expanded implementation of Global Positioning Systems. Digitizing will result in reductions in overhead costs and per chart/map cost.
Savings: $2 million

DOC2-04 Privatize Portions of the Seafood Inspection Service (3)
This function is currently voluntary and fee-funded. The bulk of the program would be privatized, with federal oversight to ensure integrity and user acceptance. Benefits to be gained include continuation of valuable services to industry with substantially fewer federal employees.
Savings: none (fee-funded)

DOC2-05 Eliminate the National Oceanic and Atmospheric Administration Corps (1)
The National Oceanic and Atmospheric Administration corps is the smallest uniformed military service. It consists of about 400 officers who command a fleet of fewer than 10 obsolete ships. Reduce the current corps to 130 FTEs and eventually eliminate it.
Savings: $35.2 million

DOC2-06 Expedite Closure of National Weather Service Field Offices (3)
The weather service is in the midst of a major restructuring and modernization initiative that will deploy modern technology to improve forecasting and significantly shrink its field office structure. Therefore, P.L. 102-567, Title 7, should be amended

to expedite the closure of about 200 unneeded weather stations.
Savings: $118 million

DOC2-07 Reengineer Census 2000 (1)
The Census Bureau is reengineering the 2000 census by changing the questionnaire to an easy-to-fill-out machine-readable format, using sampling and estimation procedures to reduce the differential in the count, and using sampling and estimation to complete the enumeration. This last item is one of the most important proposed changes. Past censuses have used the very expensive method of attempting to physically locate every nonrespondent through multiple visits. Sampling is a statistically proven, cost-effective technique used extensively in the private sector. Compared to 1990, 200,000 fewer temporary employees will be hired. This recommendation expands on a similar one made in the first NPR report (DOC-13).
Savings: $780 million

DOC2-08 Increase Entrepreneurship at the Census Bureau (3)
The Census Bureau should establish a laboratory to work with the private sector to develop and market custom tabulations, with copyright protection, of decennial census data.
Revenues: $50 million

DOC2-09 Streamline Administrative Services (1)
The Department of Commerce has initiated several projects, many using business process reengineering techniques, in the areas of personnel, procurement, organizational structure, customer service, the government purchase card, budget formulation, and financial management. The broad-based initiative cuts across bureau lines. The goal is to implement

radical, breakthrough improvements in the delivery of critical administrative services.
Savings: to be determined

DOC2-10 Privatize Portions of the National Weather Service (3)
Privatize specialized weather services, thereby permitting a more active role for the commercial weather services industry which is able to provide specialized weather information for aviation, marine, and agricultural users
Savings: $47 million

By implementing these recommendations, Commerce will save $1,032 million over five years.

DEPARTMENT OF DEFENSE

[Recommendations to be announced in Fall 1995.]

DEPARTMENT OF EDUCATION

ED2-01 Restructure the Department and Reduce Personnel (3)
Through streamlining and restructuring, reduce agency personnel by 12 percent (616 FTEs) and eliminate three senior officer positions.
Savings: $100 million

ED2-02 Reduce Regulations (1)
Through simplification and elimination, cut the department regulations governing those who seek and use federal education grants by 56 percent and reinvent an additional 37 percent.
Savings: none

ED2-03 Improve Debt Collection (1)
Improve student loan debt collection by implementing a new and aggressive default management strategy. Although the savings are not scorable, the department projects savings of $900 million through increased collections.
Revenues: none

ED2-04 Terminate Low-Priority Education Programs (3)
Terminate 10 low-priority programs providing subsidies to certain colleges, and finance a number of special scholarship and fellowship programs.
Savings: $723 million

By implementing these recommendations, Education will save $823 million over the years.

DEPARTMENT OF ENERGY

DOE2-01 Terminate the Clean Coal Technology Program When Ongoing Projects Are Completed (3)
No new projects demonstrating clean coal technologies will be proposed in this program. Furthermore, if any ongoing project is canceled, its funding will be used to meet the needs of remaining ongoing projects, or rescinded if the funds are not needed by the program.

DOE2-02 Privatize the Naval Petroleum Reserves in Elk Hills, California (3)
The government established Elk Hills in the early part of this century; it no longer serves its original strategic purpose for the Navy.

DOE2-03 Sell Uranium No Longer Needed for National Defense Purposes After Rendering It Suitable for Commercial Power Reactors (3)

Sell the excess inventory of natural and enriched uranium. The enriched and natural uranium will be blended before sale to limit its use to commercial reactors.

DOE2-04 Significantly Reduce Costs in DOE's Applied Research Programs (1)
This can be accomplished by requiring more cost-sharing and through cuts in lower priority programs.

DOE2-05 Improve Program Effectiveness and Efficiencies in the Environmental Management of Nuclear Waste Cleanups (1)
Five separate improvement efforts are planned to save an estimated $4.4 billion: improving cost controls, using site-based budgeting, improving resource allocations, working closer with partners, and reauthorizing Superfund.

DOE2-06 Strategically Align Headquarters and Field Operations (1)
Realign headquarters program and administration offices with departmental goals, consolidate headquarters space, reduce headquarters support services contractors, integrate and streamline information management activities, reduce headquarters and field staffing levels, cut travel costs, sell excess inventories of metals and gases, and streamline National Environmental Policy Act processes.

By implementing these recommendations, Energy will save $23,495 million over five years.

ENVIRONMENTAL PROTECTION AGENCY

EPA2-01 Consolidate State Revolving Funds Into a Performance Partnership (3)

Consolidate the Clean Water and Drinking Water State Revolving Funds. Both of the current programs provide capitalization grants to the states, which then use the funds to provide low-interest loans to municipalities.
Savings: none

EPA2-02 Reduce EPA Oversight of States, Regions, and Federal Agencies (3)
Cut duplication of effort for a range of activities where Environmental Protection Agency (EPA) responsibilities overlap those of its federal and state partners. EPA would reduce oversight of state-delegated programs, including eliminating parallel reviews of state-issued pollution control permits.
Savings: $100 million

EPA2-03 Broaden State Participation in Superfund Program (3)
Increase the state role in the Superfund program while implementing needed reforms in the program and reducing the federal role. The previously proposed Superfund reform legislation would be enacted, including retention of retroactive liability. EPA would pursue state implementation more aggressively than under last year's proposal, providing new incentives to the states such as lower cost share and greater program implementation flexibility.
Savings: $283 million

EPA2-04 Improve Coordination of Superfund Research by National Institute of Environmental Health Science (1)
Require EPA's concurrence in the institute's annual research plan, EPA consultation on specific research projects, and an evaluation of the effectiveness of the research to address EPA's concerns that the

institute's basic research has provided little benefit to the Superfund clean-up program.
Savings: none

EPA2-05 Terminate OMB Circular A-106 (2)
Eliminate the OMB circular and, for ongoing data requirements, allow agencies to report once a year under Executive Order 12088 using their own in-house data systems.
Savings: none

EPA2-06 Create Sustainable Development Challenge Grants (3)
In the 1997 budget, include a New Sustainable Development Challenge Grant program within EPA as announced by the President as part of Reinventing Environmental Regulations.
Cost: $60 million

EPA2-07 Create Performance Partnership Grants (3)
Allow states and tribes to receive one or more consolidated grants as a substitute for several environmental categorical grants (e.g., air, water, hazardous waste). This initiative provides states and tribes an opportunity to target resources toward their most pressing environmental statutes and EPA program regulations and standards.
Savings: $103 million

By implementing these recommendations, EPA will save $426 million over five years.

FEDERAL EMERGENCY MANAGEMENT AGENCY

FEMA2-01 Sell Disaster Housing Mobile Home Inventory (1)
Terminate the Federal Emergency Management

Agency's (FEMA's) hands-on operational role in owning, storing, transporting (via contract), and refurbishing (via contract) mobile homes for disaster victims. FEMA should eliminate two permanent storage sites and sell its current inventory of about 4,000 mobile homes and 2,000 travel trailers. The agency should develop standby contracts and lease agreements to provide mobile homes, should the need arise.

FEMA2-02 Transition Federal Crime Insurance Program (3)
This program was created at a time when many American cities were experiencing riots and incidents of civil unrest, resulting in heavy losses for private insurers. Participation in the program has decreased from 80,000 policyholders in 31 states to 16,500 policyholders in 10 states, Washington, D.C., the Virgin Islands, and Puerto Rico. This proposal would begin to transition federal sponsorship of the program to the states and private sector.

FEMA2-03 Privatize Open Learning Fire Service Program (3)
Privatize the degree program for firefighters that is currently run jointly by the National Fire Academy and seven degree-granting institutions. The academy will continue to participate in the program, but will reallocate administrative resources to initiate new programs in partnership with the Emergency Management Institute.

FEMA2-04 Develop Performance Partnership Agreements With the States (3)
Integrate disparate FEMA programs and consolidates funding streams into a multi-year performance-based partnership agreement between the President and the governor of each state. The performance partnership agreement would be risk-based, tailored

to each state, focus on performance outcomes and capability development, provide incentives for increasing state capabilities in responding to disasters, establish criteria for presidential disaster declarations based on each state's unique capabilities, and reduce grant reporting requirements. FEMA would establish two funding streams: pre- and post-disaster.

FEMA2-05 Devolve State Disaster Trust Funds (3)
Encourage and provide incentives for states to establish state disaster trust funds. These funds could be used by states to enhance their existing emergency management capability. Trust fund money could be used to implement and administer state and local emergency management programs, including mitigation, for relief from nonfederally declared disasters. Revenue collection for the trust funds would have to be coordinated with the development of multi-hazard insurance to prevent duplicative reliance on the same revenue sources.

FEMA2-06 Devolve Post-Disaster Mitigation Grants (3)
Devolve administration of federal post-disaster mitigation grants to state and local jurisdictions, and eliminate FEMA's project-by-project review of mitigation activities funded by the Disaster Relief Fund. Eligible use of funds would be contingent upon federal approval of a state's adopted mitigation plan and that state's achievement of mitigation performance standards.

FEMA2-07 Franchise Mount Weather Conference Facilities (3)
Offer Mount Weather conference facilities for use by other federal agencies on a fee basis.

FEMA2-08 Franchise Mount Weather National Teleregistration Capabilities (3)

FEMA will, at a minimum, conduct a market survey within the federal government to determine interest in its providing telephonic/teleregistration services.

FEMA2-09 Expand the Use of Volunteers (1)
Use national organizations' volunteers as outreach workers to supplement disaster assistance employees during presidentially declared disasters.

FEMA2-10 Reinvent Multi-Hazard Mitigation Strategies (3)
Reinvent FEMA's mitigation efforts to focus on multi-hazard strategies that are cost-effective, contain incentives, and begin to address the economic impact of natural hazards. Under this proposal, direct federal assistance to state and local jurisdictions for new building construction could be tied to the adoption and enforcement of building codes that provide for life safety against seismic and wind hazards in new buildings. The proposal, which is consistent with the Administration's policy on disaster reform, would clearly focus FEMA on multi-hazards strategies and designate the agency as the lead for those activities.

FEMA2-11 Streamline Regional Resources (1)
Produce and implement a regional office strategic restructuring plan to advance the performance partnerships, improve program delivery and implementation, accomplish mission priorities, strengthen and revitalize FEMA's field resources, and reduce operating costs. The plan will include a comprehensive evaluation of purpose, roles, authorities, risk areas, customer needs, and mission of field offices, as well as a determination of the appropriate regional location, budget, and staff. A preliminary plan has been developed.

FEMA2-12 Streamline Staffing (1)
Develop a long-term strategic plan addressing resource utilization. This activity would include a

comprehensive review of the agency's mission and function, completion of a skills analysis for all employees, and development of criteria for determining appropriate use of contract versus staff resources. A preliminary strategic staffing plan has been developed by FEMA employees. A corresponding implementation plan is being finalized.

FEMA2-13 Streamline/Consolidate Mobile Emergency Response Support (1)
Eliminate one of five support units and consolidate the remaining four. This initiative is being reevaluated in light of the demands for such support services as a result of the Oklahoma City bombing and similar threats.

FEMA2-14 Apply a State Insurance Requirement and Fixed Cost Shares for Public Assistance (3)
Adopt the Administration policy proposal to establish a state $5 per capita insurance/self-insurance requirement for public facilities. If a presidential disaster declaration is made, a state would pay for uninsured public facilities repairs equal to $5 per capita before federal assistance would be applied to all other eligible repair costs. This requirement would be implemented over a five-year period. The proposal also implements a $75 per capita threshold below which the federal cost share is 75 percent. It provides a favorable cost share of 80 percent federal as an incentive for states that have implemented mitigation measures and developed their emergency management capabilities; the federal cost share is capped at 90 percent for disasters more than $75 per capita.

FEMA2-15 Convert the National Defense Executive Reserve Program (3)

This program has never been activated, yet FEMA spends more than $200,000 per year training and managing the National Defense Executive Reserve. This proposal integrates the reservists into the Disaster Assistance Employee program, thereby providing a mechanism by which reservists can be used on an all-hazards basis.

FEMA2-16 Streamline the National Dam Safety Program (1)
FEMA is working with dam safety organizations and the U.S. Army Corps of Engineers to ensure the most cost-effective accomplishment of the National Dam Safety Program.

FEMA2-17 Identify Options for Improving the Effectiveness of the Federal Insurance Administration (2)
The Federal Insurance Administration (FIA) provides flood insurance and supports nationally consistent floodplain management actions at the state, local, and private levels. FIA should pursue further flood insurance reforms that allow the National Flood Insurance Program to operate more in line with private insurance. It should explore how to transition the provision of flood insurance into the private sector.

FEMA2-18 Transfer Resource Preparedness to Other Agencies (1)
FEMA and other relevant agencies should jointly study the viability of transferring resource preparedness functions under the Defense Production Act to other federal agencies. The review of these resource preparedness functions is under way.

FEMA2-19 Transfer National Earthquake Hazards Reduction Program Lead Agency Responsibility (3)
FEMA's lead agency responsibilities are clearly defined in the Earthquake Hazards Reduction Act of

1977, as amended, but believes full authority to fulfill lead agency assignments is not provided. FEMA is currently working with the Office of Science and Technology Policy and other National Earthquake Hazards Reduction Program agencies to identify the optimal solution to this issue.

FEMA2-20 Franchise Operations of Mount Weather's National Emergency Coordination Center (3)
The center's operations should be franchised. Under a reimbursable agreement, the center would provide 24-hour telephone coverage for other agencies using existing technology and resources. This service would be available to all federal agencies, with emphasis on Federal Response Plan agencies.

FEMA2-21 Coordinate Hazardous Materials Emergency Preparedness (1)
EPA, the Departments of Transportation and Energy, and FEMA all have responsibilities related to hazardous materials. FEMA should study how best to coordinate the resources of these agencies, develop a unified federal hazardous materials program, and consolidate hazardous material grant programs and funding to the states. An interagency board could be formed with participating agency representatives to set technical standards and ensure that funding execution meets agencies' missions. The FEMA Director has met with the Secretaries of the Departments of Transportation and Energy and the Administrator of EPA to initiate this process.

FEMA2-22 Integrate Federal Disaster Planning (1)
Consolidate disparate, hazard-specific federal disaster planning efforts—and existing plans—into one integrated FEMA-led planning initiative for all hazards.

FEMA2-23 Coordinate Federal Disaster Assistance Activities (3)
Identify options for integrating and coordinating the appropriate disaster assistance functions of FEMA and the Small Business Administration (SBA). Activities that could be explored include post-disaster inspections.

By implementing these recommendations, FEMA will save $52.3 million over five years ($22.3 million in program and disaster relief funds, and $30 million in receipts from an asset sale).

GENERAL SERVICES ADMINISTRATION

GSA2-01 Consider Various Forms of Privatization (3)
The Business Line analyses underway in the Federal Operations Review Model (FORM) process have already begun to provide useful information regarding how GSA does business, where its strengths lie, and where it has room for improvement and for potential savings to the taxpayer. As the process continues, the agency will be able to identify ways to improve the means through which the government provides those services and products for which GSA is responsible.

GSA2-02 Encourage Agencies to Franchise These Activities to Avoid Duplication and Maximize Efficiency (3)
Provide expertise and experience in franchising support services and reducing the cost of these services for participating agencies. Through the Cooperative Administrative Support Units (CASU) program, redundant administrative services are being eliminated through centralization in lead agencies. GSA is evaluating additional opportunities to expand the

franchising of sevices to lead agencies where appropriate.

GSA2-03 Give Agencies Expanded Authority to Acquire Services and Assets (1)
GSA will delegate responsibilities to other agencies when that is the most cost-effective option for the taxpayer. This is one of several options GSA is evaluating in detail as part of the FORM review of its major business lines.

GSA2-04 Involve Employee Unions in Designing and Implemention Reinvention Details (1)
GSA's Labor-Management Partnership is based upon the understanding that involving its union partners in the pre-decisional planning and design of its reinvention activities will lead to better, more comprehensive ideas from the start of an initiative through its implementation. By including its unions from the outset, GSA is working to obtain the highest degree of cooperation, contribution, and consensus possible.

By implementing these recommendations, GSA will save $1,400 million govenmentwide over five years.

DEPARTMENT OF HEALTH AND HUMAN SERVICES

HHS2-01 Strengthen Medicare Program Integrity (3)
Provide tools to ensure that the billions—and perhaps more—currently saved continue to be saved for years to come, and that the Department of Health and Human Services (HHS) can react and adapt to the ever-changing nature of fraud in the

health care industry. The three components of this initiative are:

- Create an interdisciplinary team to target Medicare and Medicaid abuse in five key states where health care fraud is of particular concern.
- Propose new legislation for a new health care fraud fund for investigating and prosecuting illegal activities.
- Create a more stable budget mechanism to fund Medicare program integrity activities.

Savings: to be determined

HHS2-02 Create Performance Partnerships (3)
Consolidate 107 health programs into six performance partnership programs and 11 consolidated clusters of grants administered by state and local governments and private providers. These partnerships will permit greater flexibility to measure and improve program effectiveness.
Savings: $218 million

HHS2-03 Consolidate Management (1)
Eliminate an entire layer of management by consolidating into a single corporate headquarters two major department policy, leadership, and coordinating offices: the Office of the Secretary and the Office of the Assistant Secretary for Health. Many centrally provided administrative services will be franchised as internal business units that offer services competitively.
Savings: $146 million

HHS2-04 Consolidate Surveys and Coordinate Data Standards (1)
Start a thorough study to ensure that (1) policy-relevant information is available in a timely manner,

(2) gaps in existing data that inhibit analysis are eliminated, and (3) departmental data standards are coordinated and consistent from program to program.
Savings: none

HHS2-05 Improve Coordination of Programs for Older Americans (3)
Refocus and consolidate programs for the aging to improve HHS effectiveness and better focus programs on the needs of older Americans. Programs in other departments that serve the needs of the elderly may be transferred to the HHS Administration on Aging.
Savings: $20 million

HHS2-06 Privatize National Institutes of Health Clinical Center Management (3)
Privatize the management of the Clinical Center as determined by a planned analysis of the center's cost structure. The option of contracting center functions and alternative approaches to financing the construction of a new hospital of no more than 250 beds will be fully considered.
Savings: $87 million

HHS2-07 Privatize Clinical Practice Guidelines (1)
Currently, the Agency for Health Care Policy and Research develops clinical practice guidelines. Under this proposal, four private sector centers will be established to develop multiple guidelines simultaneously, and thereby achieve new efficiencies and quality improvements.
Savings: $15 million

HHS2-08 Privatize Technology Assessment (1)
Shift the function of assessing new technologies from the Agency for Health Care Policy and

Research to the private sector using collaborative arrangements with health care organizations, payers, manufacturers, clinicians, and assessors.
Savings: $3 million

HHS2-09 Reduce Food and Drug Administration and National Institutes of Health Management Control Positions (1)
Increase the proportion of FTE reductions in the department's streamlining plan that derive from management control positions at subject organizations.
Savings: $136 million

HHS2-10 Merge Two Agencies (3)
Merge the Agency for Toxic Substances and Disease Registry and the Centers for Disease Control and Prevention.
Savings: $9 million

HHS2-11 Reform the Food and Drug Administration's Regulatory Process (1)
Improve the regulatory process while maintaining critical public health and safety standards. Some of the reinvention initiatives speak directly to reduced time for review and approval. Others aim to reduce excessive regulatory burdens that cost industry unnecessary time and money, and cost the agency precious resources.
Savings: $37 million

HHS2-12 Privatize the Federal Employee Occupational Health Program (3)
Privatize this health program, which provides reimbursable health consultation and services to more than 4,000 departments, agencies, and offices. This will save 100 FTEs by FY 2000.
Savings: none

By implementing these recommendations, HHS will save $671 million over five years.

DEPARTMENT OF HOUSING AND URBAN DEVELOPMENT

HUD2-01 Consolidate 60 Programs Into Three (3)

• The Housing Certificates for Families and Individuals will consolidate HUD's rental assistance public housing programs into one fund providing rental assistance for low income tenants, especially working poor families.

• The economic development programs will be folded into a Community Opportunity Fund providing flexible resources to mayors and governors for critical economic revitalization of distressed communities.

• The Affordable Housing Fund will give mayors and governors the flexible funding they need to support the development, acquisition, and rehabilitation of affordable housing, as well as homeownership opportunities for low-income families.

HUD2-02 Transform Public Housing (3)

Under this proposal, federal assistance will no longer go to public housing projects, but will instead go directly to the people.

HUD2-03 Reinvigorate the Federal Housing Administration (3)

Make the Federal Housing Administration a government-owned corporation and give it a new entrepreneurial, private enterprise approach.

By implementing these recommendations, HUD will save $825 million in administrative costs over five years.

INTELLIGENCE COMMUNITY

INTEL2-01 Consolidate Imagery Intelligence (1)
By October 1, 1996, imagery activities will be placed under a coherent management structure to include consolidation of specific functions across the community, improving the effectiveness and efficiency of resource allocation, and providing more responsiveness to national- and tactical-level customers.

INTEL2-02 Integrate Military and Intelligence Satellite Acquisition (1)
The Intelligence Community is working with the Department of Defense (DOD) to integrate the management of Defense and Intelligence space programs and thereby reduce costs.

INTEL2-03 Reform Human Resource Management (1)
The Intelligence Community is committed to a major reform of human resource management at the Central Intelligence Agency (CIA) and throughout the community over the next decade. Already completed groundwork will pave the way for reform.

INTEL2-04 Consolidate Intelligence Collection Activities (1)
Based on changing customer priorities and reduced resources, and supported in part by new technologies, the Intelligence Community plans to reduce the number of sites used for intelligence collection efforts worldwide. This effort—which is ongoing and will be accomplished over the next several years—will result in improved effectiveness and significant cost savings.

INTEL2-05 Consolidate Office Space (1)
In an effort to reduce costs, the Intelligence Community is consolidating many of its operations in the greater Washington, D.C., area.

INTEL2-06 Consolidate Warehousing (1)
Through the use of improved inventory management techniques, large reductions of required space are possible. The National Security Agency (NSA) and CIA alone estimate eliminating 55 percent of overall warehouse space by the end of FY 1997.

INTEL2-07 Privatize Supply and Equipment Acquisition (1)
A sizable workforce and infrastructure has been established over the years to purchase, store, and distribute supplies and equipment to customers throughout the community. The Intelligence Community will develop partnerships with vendors for the direct delivery of supplies and equipment, helping ensure the timely delivery of supplies and equipment at competitive prices.

INTEL2-08 Franchise Microelectronics Production (1)
In order to fulfill its requirement for specialized computer chips, NSA currently operates its own design and manufacturing facility in partnership with the National Semiconductor Corporation. With initial coordination from the community management staff, any excess production capacity at this facility will be franchised out to other community components or possibly to other government agencies, all on a fee-for-service basis.

INTEL2-09 Reinvent Travel (1)
Under current travel policies, significant resources are expended on the administrative aspects of the travel process. Through its pilot project, NSA has already shown how reengineering and automation can streamline the travel process and reduce administrative costs by more than 70 percent. These efforts are being evaluated for application throughout the Intelligence Community.

INTEL2-10 Reinvent Community Courier Service (1)
Because each member of the Intelligence Community maintains its own courier service, significant overlap exists between the destinations and routes of the various courier services. Preliminary estimates indicate that courier costs could be reduced by at least 30 percent through cross-agency work-sharing agreements and the use of one or more common hubs.

INTEL2-11 Reinvent Training and Education (1)
At present, several members of the Intelligence Community maintain their own training components, with little cross-coordination between programs. All aspects of community training will be examined in an effort to eliminate duplication, terminate courses with marginal participation, find opportunities for privatization, and increase the use of technology.

INTEL2-12 Reinvent Excess Equipment Reutilization (1)
With the assistance of waivers from the Defense Logistics Agency, process reengineering by NSA has significantly reduced cycle time, handling costs, and storage costs for removing and disposing of excess equipment. The Intelligence Community is evaluating NSA's procedures for wider adoption within the community and is working to improve cross-agency coordination of equipment availability and acquisition.

INTEL2-13 Reinvent Security (1)
Through the work of the Security Policy Board, the Intelligence Community is reinventing its security systems to ensure that they match threats and are flexible, consistent, cost-effective, and affordable. Significant long-term savings should result for both

the Intelligence Community and its private sector partners.

INTEL2-14 Reinvent Foreign Language Activities (1)
The DCI Foreign Language Committee, as the focal point for all foreign language-related issues within the Intelligence Community, will standardize foreign language testing. It will also develop and coordinate plans for a unified language training system, explore ways to open the system to other federal agencies, create partnerships with the private sector, and market government-developed language training materials for secondary commercial use. Finally, it will explore ways to leverage the use of technology for improved training and operational use.

DEPARTMENT OF THE INTERIOR

DOI2-01 Eliminate the Office of Territorial and International Affairs (1)
Eliminate an assistant secretary position and transfer the bureau's remaining office functions to the Office of the Secretary. Create, with the concurrence of the Domestic Policy Council, an insular affairs working group to provide a focal point for resolving cross-cutting insular issues. (These activities were accomplished by a Secretarial Order signed August 4, 1995).
Savings: $5 million

DOI2-02 Accelerate the Transfer of Bureau of Indian Affairs Program Operations to Tribes (1)
This transfer reflects the Administration's commitment to the policy of self-determination and local

decisionmaking. The proposed transfer would build on an ongoing process of consultation with the tribes. The Bureau of Indian Affairs will streamline central and area offices, with savings provided to the tribes.
Savings: none

DOI2-03 Transfer Bureau of Reclamation Facilities and Terminate Five Small Reclamation Programs (3)
Implement an aggressive program of transferring title and operations/maintenance responsibilities for bureau facilities to state or local units of government or other nonfederal entities. (The program does not apply to facilities of national importance.) The bureau will also eliminate five programs no longer essential to its mission. Current commitments will be honored and completed as soon as possible.
Savings: $126 million

DOI2-04 Transfer the Baltimore-Washington, George Washington-Clara Barton, and Suitland Parkways to Maryland and Virginia (3)
Transfer these commuter parkways to the states. Interior will provide operating grants to phase out its maintenance activities over five years.
Savings: $13 million

DOI2-05 Eliminate, Reduce, or Reinvent 10 U.S. Geological Survey Programs (1)
Eliminate funding for the Water Resources Research Institute; reduce components of the Geothermal Program; commercialize aspects of its information dissemination services; privatize ship and laboratory operations of the marine, water, and mineral programs; and reinvent its scientific technical publications.

Savings: $64 million

DOI2-06 Reinvent Bureau of Land Management Energy and Road Maintenance Programs (3)
Transfer the inspection and enforcement operations in the onshore energy and minerals program to states and tribes, improve interagency coordination of road maintenance, and improve cost recovery for bureau energy/minerals management.
Savings: $31 million

DOI2-07 Divest Fish and Wildlife Service Activities (3)
Divest waterfowl protection areas (2.2 million acres) and coordination areas (0.3 million acres), as well as up to 15 fish hatcheries, to the states.
Savings: $51 million

DOI2-08 Consolidate the Activities of the National Park Service's Denver Service Center With Similar Operations (1)
Consolidate the activities of the Denver service center with those of similar Interior operations.
Savings: $17 million

DOI2-09 Reinvent the Office of the Secretary (1)
A new mission for the Assistant Secretary of Policy, Management, and Budget will focus on policy coordination and guidance. All nonpolicy activities will be transferred to a new fee-for-service support center, resulting in a streamlined and more efficient Office of the Secretary.
Savings: $10 million

DOI2-10 Allow Offshore Royalty Buy-Outs (3)
Current offshore oil and gas royalties may be acquired through buy-out alternatives to be identified and evaluated by an interagency working group with the goal of obtaining greater value for the public from royalty proceeds while reducing the public

and private costs of obtaining that value.
Savings: $3,120 million

DOI2-11 Issue a National Park Service Commemorative Coin (3)
Legislation to authorize six commemorative coins, two of which would create revenue for Interior and the National Park Service, is currently in Congress. Other fundraising methods are also being considered.
Revenues: $15 million

DOI2-12 Reinvent the Bureau of Mines (1)
Streamline bureau functions and consolidate field research centers into four "centers of excellence" and by eliminating programs that states or the private sector would more appropriately conduct.
Savings: $140 million

DOI2-13 Privatize the Helium Program (3)
Privatize this program by selling the Bureau of Mines production facility in Amarillo, Texas, or by entering a long-term lease with a private entity, and begin to liquidate its crude helium reserve through annual sales.
Savings: none

DOI2-14 Expand Lease Authority to the National Park Service (3)
Draft legislation to expand federal authority to place unused national park system facilities under long-term leases or special concessions contracts was submitted to Congress in May 1995. The proposal will allow for the productive use of unused facilities in a businesslike fashion, while maintaining the integrity of the parks.
Savings: $54 million

By implementing these recommendations, Interior will save $3,950 million over five years.

DEPARTMENT OF JUSTICE

DOJ2-01 Reinvent the Immigration and Naturalization Service Field Structure (1)
Under this proposal, the Immigration and Naturalization Service (INS) will continue its reinvention efforts. INS has selected two district offices, in Detroit and El Paso, as customer service reinvention laboratories. At these sites, employee teams will work with consultants to design and test new ways of working that put the customer first. At other sites, INS has joined with the Customs Service to conduct a series of pilot projects to test new, cooperative approaches to inspections. INS has also reengineered its naturalization process to eliminate backlogs and reduce cycle time; it will initiate a pilot project at selected district sites.

DOJ2-02 Consolidate Administrative Support Services to Bureau of Prisons' Correctional Institutions (1)
Bureau of Prisons correctional institutions traditionally have been given the authority and resources to conduct their own administrative support activities. These support activities should be consolidated at six regional offices. A 25 percent reduction in administrative personnel should result from this effort.

DOJ2-03 Consolidate U.S. Marshals Service Prisoner and INS Detainee Transportation (1)
The air fleets used by the U.S. Marshals Service and INS to transport prisoners and detainees should be consolidated to form a new Justice Prisoner and Alien Transportation System. When fully implemented, this system will improve the department's efficiency and deportation capacity.

DOJ2-04 Create "One-Stop Shopping" for Customers (1)
Collocating Justice offices with similar missions or serving the same clientele will facilitate one-stop shopping for customers. It also may improve program coordination and increase the efficiency of support activities. The department has approximately 2,000 domestic field offices, more than 55 percent of which (1,099) have 10 or fewer employees. Under this proposal, many of these small offices would be considered for possible collocation to achieve customer and staff efficiency and convenience.

DOJ2-05 Permit Nonjudicial Foreclosures (3)
Enacting legislation to create a comprehensive federal nonjudicial foreclosure act would free department attorneys from handling routine foreclosure cases. Justice attorneys, most often Assistant U.S. Attorneys, now have to apply for judicial foreclosure of a number of mortgages—thus reducing the time they can devote to the department's core mission. Therefore, the department has drafted legislation to establish a uniform, nationwide system of nonjudicial foreclosures which has been included in an omnibus debt collection legislative proposal prepared by the Department of the Treasury.

DOJ2-06 Require Hospitals to Charge Federal Prisoners Medicare Rates (3)
In a recent study, the Justice Management Division found that Bureau of Prisons, INS, and the U.S. Marshals Service each occasionally seek outside hospital care for prisoners and detainees and that hospital care rates vary widely among localities. In some locations, Justice entities have negotiated/contracted with hospitals for the federal Medicare rate

as the standard rate of reimbursement for their federal prisoners and detainees treated in hospitals that provide Medicare services. This proposal seeks legislation requiring hospitals to charge the Medicare rate in all applicable cases.

DOJ2-07 Privatize Printing, Audiovisual, and Graphics Services (1)
To the extent feasible and cost-effective, Justice will contract out for printing, audiovisual, and graphics services rather than maintain an in-house capability. The agency increasingly has been procuring these services from the private sector. Legislation should be enacted to allow Justice—as well as other agencies—to use sources other than the Government Printing Office.

DEPARTMENT OF LABOR

DOL2-01 Streamline Alien Labor Certification (3)
Streamline and speed up the Department of Labor (DOL) Alien Labor Certification process by decentralizing authority to state employment security agencies, consolidating DOL regional processing centers from 10 to four, and automating forms processing. Under this proposal, DOL will conduct spot audits of about 2 percent of its cases rather than review all state certifications. Also, states will be authorized to charge user fees to those few employers who use this service.
Savings: $223.8 million

DOL2-02 Transfer the Community Service Employment for Older Americans Program to the HHS Administration on Aging (3)

The Community Service Employment for Older Americans program finances federal project grants to public and private nonprofit national organizations and to state governments. These projects provide job training and direct services to older Americans. By transferring this program to HHS—as part of the 1995 reauthorization of the Older Americans Act—the federal government's ability to provide integrated services to older Americans will improve. This proposal also increases the state/local match requirement, thereby further leveraging federal dollars.

Savings: $326 million

DOL2-03 Privatize All DOL Penalty and Debt Collection (1)

Use private sector firms to perform its penalty and debt collection functions. Currently, penalties are collected by DOL employees, and debts are collected by DOL personnel and private sector firms. Following the Department of Education's successful collection model, this proposal will likely result in increased collections.

Savings: none

DOL2-04 Simplify Procedures of the Pension Benefit Guaranty Corporation (1)

Simplify the benefit determination process by taking advantage of the new Employee Retirement Income Security Act (ERISA) and General Agreement on Trade and Tariff Act amendments. This simplification will feature an increased reliance on employer calculations and on simplified methods of dealing with complex plan provisions.

Savings: $6 million

DOL2-05 Limit the Mine Safety and Health Administration State Grant Program to Four States (3)

This program funds training and awareness programs focusing on current accident trends and small mines. Currently, 43 states and the Navajo Nation participate in the programs, but 33 states receive less than $100,000 a year. The Mine Safety and Health Administration (MSHA) grant program should be limited to four states: Virginia, West Virginia, Pennsylvania, and Kentucky. These are the main coal mining states, and they receive the largest grants for MSHA training programs.
Savings: $16.7 million

DOL2-06 Eliminate Written Certification of Nonsegregated Facilities (1)
Successful enforcement of civil rights law has ensured that employers are aware that segregation in employee facilities is unlawful. Consequently, DOL will eliminate the requirement for federal contractors and subcontractors to provide written certification that their facilities are not segregated on the basis of race, color, religion, or national origin. DOL will continue to require that facilities be nonsegregated, and hold compliance reviews and investigate complaints to ensure this. Federal contractors will save 875,000 hours annually as a result of this initiative.
Savings: none

DOL2-07 Streamline Affirmative Action Plans for Federal Contractors (1)
The affirmative action plans submitted by contractors and subcontractors will be simplified. The factors used to determine the availability of minorities and women for employment will be reduced from 16 to four. Action-oriented plans will only be required if the participation of women and minorities does not approximate their availability for

employment. The requirement that contractors reconfigure their workforce by artificially composed job groups will be eliminated. Finally, unless selected for random audit, contractors with satisfactory plans will be exempted from further audit. This proposal will save contractors 4.5 million hours annually.
Savings: none

DOL2-08 Improve Alignment of Tasks With Office Functions (1)
Certain enforcement tasks will be realigned among DOL offices to improve efficiency and effectiveness. For example, the Occupational Safety and Health Administration (OSHA) should enforce certain environmental "whistle-blower" statutes formerly enforced by the Wage and Hour Division. The Wage and Hour Division, in turn, should enforce certain health and safety standards in areas affecting agricultural workers that were formerly enforced by OSHA. Realigning such tasks will enhance enforcement activities.
Savings: none

DOL2-09 Consolidate Regional Functions of the Wage and Hour Division (1)
Some functions of the Wage and Hour Division should be consolidated. Each of the division's eight regions now performs administrative functions related to homework certification, sheltered workshop certification, and farm labor contractor registration processing. Under this proposal, homework certification and sheltered workshop certification will each be consolidated in a single region, and farm labor contractor registration processing will be consolidated in two regions.
Savings: none

DOL2-10 Consolidate OSHA's Technical Centers and MSHA's Engineering Offices (1)
OSHA's two technical centers will be consolidated into the existing Salt Lake City center. Similarly, MSHA's engineering services will be consolidated by closing the Denver office and relocating resources and staff to its office in Bruceton, Pennsylvania.
Savings: $5.4 million

DOL2-11 Expand Private Sector Use of the MSHA Academy (1)
Use of the MSHA Academy—the central training facility for federal mine inspectors and mine safety professionals—will be more aggressively marketed to increase its use by the private sector. Increasing private sector use will improve efficiency and yield administrative savings.
Savings: $2.5 million

DOL2-12 Institute a Flexi-Place Program for MSHA Inspectors (1)
The Administration intends to equip mine inspectors to work out of their homes, as the majority of these inspectors spend most of their time on the road or in mines. This proposal will improve mine inspector morale and increase productivity.
Savings: $2.4 million

DOL2-13 Unify DOL's Adjudicative Boards (1)
Unify the Benefits Review Board, the Employee Compensation Appeals Board, the Wage Appeals Board, and the Office of Administrative Appeals within DOL. This will facilitate better sharing of resources and distribute workloads more evenly.
Savings: $5.6 million

DOL2-14 Privatize OSHA and MSHA's Accreditation Process (1)
Privatize the process for accrediting and performing gear, crane, and laboratory certifications. Private concerns should pay fees for these accreditation and certification activities.
Savings: $2.5 million

DOL2-15 Consolidate DOL's Administrative and Personnel Functions (1)
DOL's personnel and administrative functions will be substantially consolidated at the headquarters and regional levels. Duplicate functions will be eliminated, and the number of staff devoted to administrative and personnel matters will be significantly reduced.
Savings: $65 million

DOL2-16 Simplify Reporting Requirements for Federal Construction Contractors (1)
Eliminate the monthly utilization report documenting the employment hours of women and minorities in the construction trades. This proposal will save private sector contractors 400,000 hours of effort annually.
Savings: none

DOL2-17 Streamline the ERISA Summary Plan Description Filing Requirement (3)
Eliminate ERISA's statutory requirement that employee benefit plans file summary plan descriptions (SPDs) with DOL. Plans would still need to prepare and furnish SPDs to plan participants and beneficiaries, and the department could still obtain SPDs from plan administrators to respond to individual requests or to monitor compliance. Eliminat-

ing this filing requirement would substantially reduce costs and burdens for private plans and for the department.

Savings: 7 million

DOL2-18 Privatize OSHA Training Activities (1)

OSHA will expand its use of private education centers offering OSHA-approved courses on a nationwide basis.

Savings: $2 million

DOL2-19 Streamline the ERISA Annual Report (1)

The Pension and Welfare Benefits Administration, in conjunction with the Internal Revenue Service and Pension Benefit Guaranty Corporation, is streamlining the Form 5500 Series annual reporting requirements for employee benefit plans and pursuing establishment of an automated filing system for receiving and processing reports. This initiative should significantly reduce costs and burdens for the more than 750,000 employee benefit plans required to file reports.

Savings: to be determined

By implementing these recommendations, DOL will save $803 million over five years.

NATIONAL AERONAUTICS AND SPACE ADMINISTRATION

NASA2-01 Eliminate Duplication and Overlap and Consolidate Functions Between NASA Centers (1)

NASA recently completed a zero-based review of all the agency's activities and established clearly defined missions for each of its 10 field centers to reflect its role in the agency's five strategic enterprises. NASA has also established a realignment plan to eliminate overlap and duplication among the field centers. The implementation of these objectives is being incorporated in the FY 1997 budget estimates.

NASA2-02 Transfer Functions to Universities or the Private Sector (3)
NASA is moving to transition the management of some science programs to institutes located on or near NASA sites. These science institutes will be operated by a university, private industry, or a teaming arrangement.

NASA2-03 Reduce Civil Servant Involvement With and Expect More Accountability From NASA Contractors (1)
NASA will fundamentally change its relationship with the contractor community. NASA will be responsible for defining program requirements and then exercise minimal oversight. This represents a profound change from the current way of doing business.

NASA2-04 Emphasize Objective Contracting by Defining Specific Products and Deadlines (1)
NASA is moving toward performance-based contracting; this will build valuable partnerships between government and industry.

NASA2-05 Use Private Sector Capabilities Whenever Possible (1)
Consolidation of the space shuttle contracts is planned over the next several years. Outsourcing and use of commercial services will be maximized.

NASA2-06 Work to Change Regulations So NASA Can Perform Less Engineering Oversight and Reporting and More Procurement Streamlining (1)

NASA is reengineering its regulations and policies in an effort to reduce them by 50 percent. NASA has also initiated a series of procurement initiatives to improve its contracting processes.

NASA2-07 Return NASA to Its Status as a Research and Development (R&D) Agency by Focusing on High-Priority R&D and Drastically Reducing Operational Functions (1)
NASA is moving toward performing more state-of-the-art R&D and allowing the private sector to perform operational functions.

NASA2-08 Rely on the Private Sector for NASA Communication With Spacecraft (3)
The incorporation of commercial practices in the Transfer and Data Relay Satellite program will result in $200 million in savings.

By implementing these recommendations, NASA will save $8,720 million over five years.

NATIONAL SCIENCE FOUNDATION

NSF2-01 Devolve Support for Research Facilities (1)
Phase out support for modernization of academic research facilities and devolve where universities, state and local governments, and the private sector are expected to assume these responsibilities.
Savings: $1,270 million

NSF2-02 Reduce Research Projects Support (1)
Reduce support for some research projects and associated user facilities through a planning process that establishes priorities in the context of NSF and

federal programs in support of fundamental sciences.
Savings: $260 million

NSF2-03 Continue Streamlining Administrative Operations (1)
Continue internal administrative streamlining and reinventing efforts.
Savings: $80 million

By implementing these recommendations, NSF will save $1,631 million over five years.

OFFICE OF PERSONNEL MANAGEMENT

OPM2-01 Transform OPM Into an Agency That Supports a Private Sector Model for Training, Investigations, and Staffing Services to Agencies (3)
Privatize OPM's 800-person background investigations service by creating an employee-owned corporation that will ultimately compete in the private sector. OPM has already privatized its Workforce Training Service, moving 220 people off the federal payroll while providing a seamless transition for customer agencies.

OPM2-02 Allow Agencies to Perform Personnel Management Functions on Their Own, or Procure Them From the Private Sector or From Privatized OPM Business Units (1)
Working through the Interagency Advisory Group of executive branch personnel directors, OPM has made the federal personnel community a true partner in the development of personnel policy. With

OPM support, the group has played a major role in the final sunset of the Federal Personnel Manual, development of human resources management reform legislation, consolidation of the classification system, and development of a career transition business plan for federal employees facing layoff.

OPM2-03 Continue OPM Leadership and Oversight Role (1)
OPM has implemented a reorganization, or redesign, of the agency that has underscored its core mission as guardian of the merit system and strengthened the agency's commitment to customer service. As part of its redesign, OPM created a strong Office of Merit Systems Oversight and Effectiveness to oversee merit standards across government and ensure that agency human resource management programs are consistent with the merit system principles.

By implementing these recommendations, OPM will save $30 million governmentwide over five years.

SMALL BUSINESS ADMINISTRATION

SBA2-01 Reduce the Government's Cost of Financing Small Business While Serving More Customers (3)
SBA should shift the cost of its Section 7(a) and Section 504 loan guaranty programs from taxpayers to program beneficiaries—lenders and borrowers. SBA will reduce the government's cost of these loans to zero, imposing fees on lenders and borrowers and reducing the government-guaranteed portion of some loans. This proposal will allow SBA to

provide more small businesses with loan guarantees with fewer federal dollars.
Savings: $946 million

SBA2-02 Consolidate Field Operations by Making Greater Use of Public-Private Partnerships (1)
Streamline the SBA field office structure by collocating its 10 regional offices with the local district offices and consolidating its district satellite offices. As a result, SBA will work more closely with its partners—especially private lenders—and with the Small Business Development Centers that provide business counseling.
Savings: $122 million

SBA2-03 Centralize Processing to Achieve Economies of Scale and Use Current Technology (1)
Consolidate loan processing in several centers around the country and continue to centralize loan servicing.
Savings: $14 million

SBA2-04 Relocate More Headquarters Functions to Less Costly Field Locations (1)
Move SBA financial operations and the administration of several other programs to existing field offices.
Savings: $104 million

SBA2-05 Reduce the Government's Cost of Providing Surety Bond Guarantees (3)
SBA will shift some of the cost of its Surety Bond Guarantee program, which provides small contractors with bonding from private surety firms, to program beneficiaries.
Savings: $15 million

By impementing these recommendations, SBA will save $1,201 million over five years.

SOCIAL SECURITY ADMINISTRATION

SSA2-01 Provide Payment Day Cycling for New Beneficiaries (1)

Stagger payments for new beneficiaries over a number of dates throughout the month to eliminate workload spikes and allow the Social Security Administration (SSA) to provide better customer service without adding staff. Current beneficiaries and all Supplemental Security Income recipients will be unaffected by this change.

Savings: $233 million

SSA2-02 Improve 1-800 Telephone Service (1)

SSA has compared itself with some of America's top-rated telephone customer-service companies. Based on what it has learned, SSA will make improvements in its 1-800 service to help it provide world-class service to its customers, the existing and prospective beneficiaries of the social security system.

Savings: none

SSA2-03 Increase Direct Deposit/Electronic Benefit Transfer Services (3)

Increase the number of recipients paid by direct deposit in three phases over four years. In the first phase, already under way, SSA presumes the use of direct deposit by all new beneficiaries who have bank accounts. This initiative includes seeking legislation that would eventually require all government payments to be issued by direct deposit. Once legislation is enacted, phase two will mandate that all beneficiaries with bank accounts use direct deposit services. The third phase, also contingent on this

legislation, will require that all beneficiaries without bank accounts select one of the electronic benefits transfer services that will be available for them to receive their benefit payments.
Savings: $289 million

SSA2-04 Promote "One-Stop" Benefit Application (1)
Explore the development of a controlled, confidential electronic process by which employees at large companies can quickly file for retirement and/or Medicare through their company personnel office. This option would allow workers to apply for a company pension, social security, and health benefits all at one time and in one place. SSA is currently assessing the interest of companies and organizations in participating in such a process.
Savings: $8 million

SSA2-05 Stop Collecting Attorney Fees (3)
Stop being a collection and disbursement agency for attorneys and others whose clients appeal social security judgments. Under this proposal, SSA workers now involved in paying attorneys will instead be able to provide direct services to beneficiaries. There will be statutory limits on what claimant representatives may charge.
Savings: $80 million

SSA2-06 Expand Employer Electronic Wage Reporting (3)
Develop legislation to allow flexibility in developing options that would gradually increase the number of employers who file W-2 wage reports electronically. The time and effort now spent on processing and checking paperwork will be reduced, allowing SSA to focus more on better and faster service to the public.
Savings: $39 million

SSA2-07 Improve the Disability Adjudication Process (1)
Establish, with state participation, minimum performance standards and a period of time during which states will be required to meet these standards. Performance enhancement teams from the highest performing states should be made available as needed to provide on-site assistance to lower performing states. SSA will encourage the formation of labor-management partnerships to raise the level of the lowest performing states and narrow the gap between the highest and lowest performing states.
Savings: $120 million

SSA2-08 Provide "One-Stop" Service for Aliens Applying for Social Security Cards (1)
Aliens will apply for social security cards at the time they complete INS paperwork. Currently, alien applicants are required to furnish almost the same information to both SSA and INS. This one-stop service will reduce the potential for issuing social security cards based on fraudulent INS documents, and will result in efficiencies for the government.
Savings: $18 million

SSA2-09 Reduce Burden Associated With Reporting Wages (1)
Social security beneficiaries who work and earn more than the exempt amount must report their earnings to SSA by April 15th of each year. They are also required to report their wages to the Internal Revenue Service (IRS) for the previous year during the same period. SSA is developing a process that will reduce the paperwork burden associated with its current annual earnings reporting operation. A

reduction in overall wage reporting burden will result in better service to the public.
Savings: to be determined

By implementing these recomendations, SSA will save $787 million over five years.

DEPARTMENT OF STATE/ U.S. INFORMATION AGENCY

[Recommendations to be announced in the fall of 1995.]

DEPARTMENT OF TRANSPORTATION

DOT2-01 Create a Unified Transportation Infrastructure Improvement Program (3)
Highway, transit, rail, and airport capital improvement projects would be eligible for the program. Funds would be allocated by formula to states, localities, and large airports. Existing highway and aviation user charges would be the revenue sources for these programs.

DOT2-02 Capitalize State Infrastructure Banks (3)
These banks would give states flexibility to leverage federal seed money in partnership with state and local governments and private businesses for infrastructure priorities.

DOT2-03 Streamline DOT's Organizational Structure (3)
Consolidate DOT's 10 existing agencies into three—one for surface transportation programs, one for the Coast Guard, and one for aviation programs.

By implementing these recommendations, Transportation will save $17,874 million over five years (when compared to the baseline spending that would otherwise be required to maintain existing programs).

DEPARTMENT OF THE TREASURY

TRE2-01 Implement Small Business and Simplified Tax and Wage Reporting System (1)
Simplify tax compliance and payroll recordkeeping regulations, which are the most burdensome concern of businesses with 10 or fewer employees, or about 79 percent of American businesses. The initiative will eventually enable employers to file W-2 data through single returns electronically with both the federal and state governments; it also simplifies the laws, definitions, and procedures related to tax and wage reporting.

TRE2-02 Relieve Duplicate Filing Burden on Employers (1)
President Clinton presided over the signing of an agreement among the heads of the Treasury Department, the Internal Revenue Service, the Department of Labor, and the Social Security Administration that commits those agencies to work together with state agencies to eliminate duplicate tax data filing requirements on businesses and taxpayers.

TRE2-03 Streamline Treasury Field Offices (3)
Further streamline and/or consolidate field offices and improve use of space. The agency now has more than 1,700 field offices.

TRE2-04 Consolidate Administrative Functions That Yield Savings and Produce Better Service (1)
Consolidate Treasury services in personnel, pro-

curement, accounting, and budget with a goal of reducing FTEs by at least 1,500 in four years.

TRE2-05 Improve Collection of Delinquent Debt Owed the Federal Government (3)
Propose legislation to improve the government's ability to recover delinquent tax and nontax debt.
Revenues: $1 billion

TRE2-06 Assist in the Use of Smart Cards (1)
Study the feasibility of an electronic smart card to determine an appropriate role for Treasury in this emerging field.

TRE2-07 Improve Collection Systems Under the Federal Unemployment Tax Act (1)
The Department of the Treasury, in cooperation with DOL, is conducting a comprehensive analysis of the Federal Unemployment Tax Act (FUTA) to improve the 60-year-old system. The goals of the study and subsequent implementation efforts will be to reduce the employer burden imposed by both the federal and state unemployment insurance systems and to reduce government's overall cost in administering the system. All alternatives and innovations will be considered, including consolidation, devolution, and an enhanced state role in FUTA collection.
Savings: to be determined

By implementing these recommendations, Treasury will produce $1 billion in additional revenues, $400 million in cost savings, and $3 billion in reduced taxpayer burden over five years.

U.S. AGENCY FOR INTERNATIONAL DEVELOPMENT

[Recommendations to be announced in the fall of 1995.]

DEPARTMENT OF VETERANS AFFAIRS

DVA2-01 Reform VA Health Care Eligibility and Treatment (3)

Existing laws limit the ability of the Department of Veterans Affairs (VA) to provide the most appropriate care in the most appropriate setting. For example, VA doctors are presently forced to hospitalize veterans who only need such care as blood pressure treatment or crutches. The result could be an approximate 20 percent shift from inpatient to outpatient workload over two years.

Savings: none

DVA2-02 Develop Pilot Programs Allowing Use of Medicare Benefits (3)

A team of experts from VA, HHS, and OMB will develop a range of options to test the feasibility of allowing higher income veterans to use their Medicare benefits to obtain treatment at certain VA facilities.

Savings: none

DVA2-03 Allow VA to Retain a Greater Portion of Collections From Third-Party Insurers for Treating Veterans' Nonservice-Connected Conditions (3)

VA has the authority to collect from third-party insurers for the treatment of nonservice-connected conditions; however, it must return all funds in excess of the collection operating costs to the Treasury. As a result, it has little incentive to collect these funds due the government. VA should be allowed to retain 25 percent of the funds collected that exceed the budget baseline as an incentive to collect these funds. (This recommendation is related to DVA06, and revenues appear there.)

DVA2-04 Simplify Means Testing in Determining Health Care Eligibility (1)

VA is required by law to assess the financial means of veterans to pay for their health care. The existing process involves a questionnaire containing 93 questions that must be completed annually or each time a veteran seeks care at a different facility. The data in this questionnaire is then verified with IRS and the Social Security Administration after the fact. This process should be changed to allow veterans to permit immediate access to their IRS information and simply affirm that they are within allowable income ranges rather than complete the complicated questionnaire.

Savings: $46 million

DVA2-05 Study the Expansion of VA and Defense Department Health Care Sharing Agreements (1)

VA and DOD provide direct medical care to beneficiaries through 173 VA medical centers and 132 DOD hospitals. Many have cooperative arrangements, but operate independently of each other. Both serve the military retiree population. The Secretaries of VA and DOD should study and report to the Vice President on the feasibility of greatly increasing sharing and integration of the two health care systems.

Savings: to be determined

DVA2-06 Consolidate, Integrate, and Privatize Various Support Services (1)

VA should improve support services through automation, consolidation, or privatization. These

services should include laundry, housekeeping, food preparation, grounds maintenance, transportation, painting and drafting, canteens, VA police, construction management, third-party health insurance collections, and cemetery headstone application processing.
Savings: $106 million

DVA2-07 Transfer Veterans' Education Benefits Electronically (1)
Reengineer the administration of the GI Bill education program by replacing the current paper-based claims processing system with an electronic system. This will reduce costs and improve accessibility, timeliness, and quality.
Savings: $21 million

DVA2-08 Study the Privatization of VA's Insurance Activities (1)
VA directly administers seven insurance programs, including a mortgage life insurance program, covering 2.8 million veterans and amounting to $25.7 billion in coverage. These programs operate as a mutual life insurance company. VA should study the feasibility of privatizing these programs.
Savings: none

DVA2-09 Consolidate VA Insurance Operations in St. Paul With the Philadelphia Regional Office and Insurance Center (3)
VA can achieve savings by consolidating the insurance activities of its St. Paul, Minnesota, office with those of its Philadelphia, Pennsylvania, office where 86 percent of its insurance staff is currently located.
Savings: $2.2 million

DVA2-10 Terminate the Manufactured (Mobile) Home Loan Guaranty Program (3)
The number of veterans obtaining VA-guaranteed loans for mobile homes has dropped significantly; only 24 loans were guaranteed in 1994. Eliminating this program would save administrative costs. Eligible veterans could receive loans under other existing federal or VA programs.
Savings: less than $1 million

DVA2-11 Study Current Policies for Acquiring Defaulted Properties on VA-Guaranteed Loans and Issuing VA Loans to Nonveteran Buyers on These Properties (1)
VA acquires properties from mortgage lenders following foreclosure of defaulted guaranteed home loans when, following a statutory-based formula, VA determines it benefits the government. These properties are then resold to recover the government's investment, and VA provides financing. VA should study whether it would be cost-beneficial to continue doing this or to pay only the guarantee and rely on commercial lenders to provide financing.
Savings: none

DVA2-12 Contract Out the Servicing and Accounting of VA's Loans Portfolio (1)
Most loans in the VA portfolio are direct loans made to enable the department to sell foreclosed properties. VA has a mortgage service operation of approximately 29,000 loans with a value of $1.1 billion. VA should, like the private sector, contract out this operation to service its mortgages.
Savings: $34 million

By implementing these recommendations, VA will save $209 million over five years.

OTHER

OTH2-01 Terminate the Interstate Commerce Commission (3)

Eliminate the bulk of the Interstate Commerce Commission's activities, including most remaining motor carrier regulatory functions and some rail functions that have outlived their usefulness. The remaining activities would be transferred to the Departments of Transportation and Justice and the Federal Trade Commission.

Savings: $129 million

OTH2-02 Terminate the Chemical Safety and Hazard Investigation Board (3)

The board's important functions will be accomplished through increased funding for the Environmental Protection Agency and the Occupational Safety and Health Administration. Its elimination would in no way compromise emergency responses to chemical accidents, subsequent investigations, or the issuance of regulations to prevent accidents.

Savings: $1 million

OTH2-03 Modify U.S. Army Corps of Engineers Local Projects Role (1)

Phase out the Army Corps' role on beach erosion and construction and maintenance of recreational harbors that primarily provide local benefits which are best left to state and local governments. In addition, modify the Army Corps' role in local flood projects.

Savings: $960 million

OTH2-04 Mandate a State Bank Examination Fee (3)

Require the Federal Deposit Insurance Corporation and Federal Reserve to assess fees on state-chartered banks and bank holding companies, leveling the playing field among the banking regulators and eliminating an unwarranted subsidy to state banks. Banks with assets under $100 million would be exempted.

Revenues: $429 million

APPENDIX D

Regulatory Reform Efforts

IN EARLY 1995, the President and Vice President expanded on earlier National Performance Review (NPR) initiatives to reinvent agency regulatory systems to reduce burdens and make the process more open and results-oriented. To do this, they charged agencies and departments to

- conduct a page-by-page review of all their regulations in the Code of Federal Regulations (CFR), eliminating or revising those regulations that are outdated or otherwise in need of reform;
- reward results, not red tape, by changing performance measurement systems to focus on ultimate goals (e.g., cleaner air and safer workplaces) rather than the number of citations written and fines assessed;
- get out of Washington and create grassroots partnerships between the front-line regulators and the people affected by their regulations;
- negotiate, rather than dictate, by expanding opportunities for consensual rulemaking wherever possible;
- waive fines or allow them to be used to fix the problem when a small business is a first-time violator and has been acting in good faith; and
- double the amount of time that passes before a report is required to be filed (e.g., a semiannual report should now be required annually) and accept reports filed electronically whenever possible.

AGENCY EFFORTS

In June 1995, 28 agencies and departments with major regulatory responsibilities reported their progress and plans to the President.

Below are highlights of these plans and contact points for additional information.

Department of Agriculture (USDA)—USDA is eliminating or reinventing more than 81 percent of its CFR pages, and taking steps to give the public greater access to and greater involvement in the regulatory process. *For plan copies, contact Marvin Shapiro, (202) 720-1516.*

Architectural and Transportation Barriers Board—The board's regulatory reform effort has focused on increasing the involvement of the design and building industry, disability organizations, state and local governments, and other interested stakeholders in the development and review of accessibility guidelines. The board will eliminate or revise 72 percent of its CFR pages. *For plan copies, contact Clarissa Leonard, (202) 272-5434, ext. 714.*

Department of Commerce—The department's Bureau of Export Administration has published a proposed rule that would completely rework existing export regulations to make the rules more comprehensible to all customers. In addition, an interim final rule of the Economic Development Administration would delete more than 200 of its approximately 370 regulations. Departmentwide, Commerce is eliminating or revising more than 60 percent of its parts in the CFR. *For plan copies, contact Julie Rice, (202) 482-6006.*

Consumer Product Safety Commission—The commission has been successful in forging innovative partnerships with industry and consumer groups to promote greater product safety for the American public, and in encouraging industry to improve the safety of its products voluntarily in lieu of mandatory regulations. *For plan copies, contact Todd Stevenson, (301) 504-0785, ext. 1239.*

Department of Defense (DOD), U.S. Army Corps of Engineers—The Corps is taking steps to make the wetlands program fairer and more flexible for landowners and more effective in protecting aquatic resources. *For plan copies, contact Michael Davis, (202) 761-0199.*

Department of Education—The department has already eliminated more than 30 percent of its CFR parts and ultimately plans to eliminate or reinvent 93 percent. Senior department officials have held numerous meetings across the country; through these, they have developed unprecedented partnerships with states, localities, and schools, leading to customer-focused approaches to program legislation, regulations, and implementation. *For plan copies, contact Jim Bradshaw, (202) 401-2310.*

Department of Energy (DOE)—DOE is committed to abolishing or simplifying 75 percent of its regulations. *For plan copies, contact Romy Diaz, Jr., Office of Rulemaking Support, (202) 586-5575.*

Environmental Protection Agency (EPA)—EPA will delete 11 percent of existing pages of regulations and further revise another 70 percent of its CFR parts to help businesses achieve environmental protection goals faster and at less cost. *For plan copies, contact Joe Retzer, (202) 260-2472.*

Farm Credit Administration (FCA)—FCA has undertaken significant measures to ensure that its regulations are current and technically correct and that the Farm Credit System it regulates provides high value to the agricultural sector at low cost to its customers. *For plan copies, contact Robert E. Orrick, (703) 883-4455.*

Farm Credit System Insurance Corporation (FCSIC)—Although FCSIC has limited authority to issue regulations, it has reached out to Farm Credit System institutions to discuss issues relating to the insurance program and to solicit input regarding major policy issues. *For plan copies, contact Alan Glenn, (703) 883-4380.*

Federal Communications Commission (FCC)—The FCC has implemented a number of internal changes, as well as recommended regulatory changes to streamline processes and reduce burdens. Expanding payment options and delegating authority to line staff have significantly streamlined FCC processing. *For plan copies, contact Nancy Camp, (202) 418-0442.*

Federal Housing Finance Board—The Finance Board is taking steps to minimize the regulatory burden felt by federal home loan banks. Reporting requirements are being reduced, and management decisions best handled at the bank level are being delegated. *For plan copies, contact David A. Guy, (202) 408-2536.*

Federal Maritime Commission (FMC)—The commission has completely eliminated 32 percent of its CFR parts, particularly easing requirements made on common carriers by water and nonvessel-operating common carriers. FMC is simplifying and streamlining in other areas as well, particularly regarding domestic offshore trade financial filing requirements and tariff filing requirements. *For plan copies, contact Joseph Polking, (202) 523-5725.*

Federal Trade Commission (FTC)—The commission staff with day-to-day responsibilities for FTC program implementation participated in several events around the country to explain the commission's programs and regulations, to encourage voluntary compliance, and to obtain views about how well the regulations are working and what changes might be useful and appropriate to reduce regulatory burdens. *For plan copies, contact Elaine Kolish, (202) 326-3042.*

Department of Health and Human Services (HHS)—HHS is undertaking a wide range of reforms to reduce regulatory burden and promote better communication, consensus building, and a less adversarial environment while maintaining essential health and safety protections. HHS is proposing to eliminate more than 1,000 of its CFR pages by rulemaking as well as an additional 700 or so pages that will require statutory change to delete. It plans to reinvent another 2,200 pages. *For plan copies, contact HHS Press Office, (202) 690-6343.*

Department of Housing and Urban Development (HUD)—HUD is eliminating 2,800 pages of regulations, which is 65 percent of its portion of the CFR. Application and reporting processes have been consolidated for Community Development Block Grants, HOME, Emergency Shelter Grants, and Housing Opportunities for Persons With AIDS. *For plan copies, contact Mary Ellen Bergeron, (202) 708-0123.*

Department of the Interior—Interior is implementing a new plain language approach throughout its regulatory activities, to make all its regulations better organized, easier to understand, and of greater use to the public. *For plan copies, contact Julie Falkner, (202) 208-5271.*

Department of Justice—Justice is committed to having the least burdensome requirements necessary to fulfill its statutorily mandated law enforcement responsibilities. The Immigration and Naturalization Service and the Drug Enforcement Agency have eliminated or reinvented regulations to minimize costs and burdens on businesses and individuals. Also, the Office of Justice Programs has reinvented regulations relating to its grant programs to streamline, simplify, and speed the applications process for state and local governments and other entities. *For plan copies, contact Kevin R. Jones, (202) 514-4604.*

Department of Labor (DOL)—DOL agencies, particularly the Occupational Safety and Health Administration (OSHA) and the Mine Safety and Health Administration are working with their respective communities to build a set of modern workplace safety and health standards that will protect workers and that are more user-friendly for employers. *For plan copies, contact Michael Urquhart, (202) 219-7357.*

Nuclear Regulatory Commission—The commission is simplifying review requirements for writing utility applications, developing less prescriptive options for leak-rate testing of containment vessels, and taking steps to delete security requirements without compromising physical protections against radiological sabotage. *For plan copies, contact Beth Hayden, (301) 415-8200.*

Pension Benefit Guaranty Corporation—The corporation is restructuring and renumbering its regulations to make them conform to the structure and numbering system of the Employee Retirement Income Security Act (ERISA, the underlying statute), making it easier for the publication and pension professionals to find and understand the regulations. The corporation's number of CFR pages will be reduced 25 percent. *For plan copies, contact Joseph Grant, (202) 326-4080, ext. 3600.*

Securities and Exchange Commission (SEC)—SEC has several initiatives to fulfill its responsibilities to investors and markets, including streamlining review processes for self-regulatory organizations' rule filings. SEC has also increased its commitment to improve public awareness and educate investors, in part by holding town and investor education meetings. *For plan copies, contact Diane Campbell, (202) 942-4300.*

Small Business Administration (SBA)—SBA announced plans to eliminate 51 percent of its regulations by the end of 1995. The agency is also continuing its efforts to partner with the small business community and reduce burdens associated with its loan programs. *For plan copies, contact Ron Matzner, (202) 205-6642.*

Social Security Administration—The administration sought public input to its regulatory review process and has identified more than 50 percent of its CFR pages as candidates for revision or improvement. *For plan copies, contact Toni Lenane, (410) 965-7767.*

Department of State—The State Department is revising its regulations affecting consular operations; this will simplify passport operations and the issuance of visas to foreign visitors. *For plan copies, contact Mary Beth West, (202) 647-5154.*

Department of Transportation (DOT)—As a result of a recent review of regulations by all its agencies, DOT is making many changes that include actions to decrease burdens, permit electronic filing, and facilitate the use of new technology. *For plan copies, contact Neil Eisner, (202) 366-4723.*

Department of the Treasury—Treasury nontax agencies are eliminating or reinventing 57 percent of their CFR pages. The Internal Revenue Service has also examined its regulations and is eliminating 693 CFR pages and and other ruling documents and reinventing another 551 pages. *For plan copies, contact Chris Peacock, (202) 622-2930.*

Department of Veterans Affairs (VA)—VA has taken a number of actions designed to produce better and smarter regulations and to improve the way the department administers veterans' benefits. These actions include updating rating schedules used to determine payment amounts to veterans for service-related disabilities to reflect recent medical advances. *For plan copies, contact Tom Gessel, (202) 565-7625.*

CROSS-CUTTING ISSUES

The Vice President and his regulatory advisors are also addressing regulatory issues that cut across agencies. To date, seven sector-specific reports have been prepared. Following are brief descriptions of these reports and their recommendations, along with contact points to obtain additional information.

Regulatory reform work will continue over the next few months in a number of other areas, such as natural resources, education, and science and technology.

REINVENTING DRUG AND MEDICAL DEVICE REGULATIONS

Released April 5, 1995. For plan copies, contact FDA Office of Communications, (301) 443-3220.

Principles for Regulatory Reform

1. Use performance standards, rather than command and control regulations, whenever possible.
2. Expedite product review without sacrificing the health and safety of the public.
3. Eliminate unnecessary requirements that may have been appropriate once but are no longer necessary for public health.

4. Use modern automated technology as a tool in streamlining internal agency management and as an aid to industry in meeting its regulatory requirements.

Recommendations

FDA01	Reduce FDA Requirements for Companies Seeking Approval for Changes in Their Facilities or Processes for Manufacturing Drugs, Biotechnology Drugs, and Other Biologics If the Risk Is Negligible
FDA02	Allow Manufacturers of Biological Drugs to Get Licenses for Pilot Facilities Rather Than Be Forced to Build Full-Scale Plants
FDA03	Permit Greater Flexibility in the Appearance of Distributors' Names in Labeling
FDA04	Eliminate Outdated Requirements for Insulin and Antibiotics and Allow a Private Body to Establish Testing and Quality Standards
FDA05	Exclude Drug and Biologic Manufacturers From Most Environmental Assessment Requirements
FDA06	Exempt Additional Categories of Low-Risk Medical Devices From Premarket Review
FDA07	Ensure That Market Clearances of Devices Will Not Be Withheld Unless FDA Finds a Reasonable Relationship Between Current Violations and Applications Under Review
FDA08	Develop a Pilot Program for Third-Party Review of Low-Risk Medical Devices
FDA09	Speed Marketing of Medical Devices by Seeking Authority to Charge Industry User Fees to Defray the Costs of Review
FDA10	Expand Opportunities to Export Drugs and Medical Devices

FDA11 Clarify How FDA Determines the Effectiveness of New Drugs and Devices and That a Single, Multicenter Study May Support Drug Approval

FDA12 Harmonize FDA Testing Requirements With Those of Other Countries to Expedite Worldwide Marketing

FDA13 Expand and Standardize the Use of Information Technologies for Reviewing New Products and Expediting Import Entries

REINVENTING ENVIRONMENTAL REGULATIONS

Released March 17, 1995. For plan copies, contact EPA's Reinvention Team at (202) 260-7669.

Principles for Regulatory Reform

1. Protect national goals for public health and the environment and compel individuals, businesses, and government to take responsibility for the impact of their actions.
2. Design regulations to achieve environmental goals that minimize costs to individuals, businesses, and other levels of government.
3. Base environmental regulations on performance, providing maximum flexibility in the means of achieving environmental goals, but requiring accountability for the results.
4. Prevent pollution rather than just control or clean it up.
5. Use market incentives to achieve environmental goals whenever appropriate.
6. Base environmental regulation on the best science and economics, subject to expert and public scrutiny.
7. Revise government regulations so they can be understood by those affected by them.

8. Foster collaborative—not adversarial—decisionmaking, and compel decisionmakers to inform and involve those who must live with the decisions.
9. Unite federal, state, tribal, and local governments to work together to achieve common environmental goals, with non-federal partners taking the lead when appropriate.
10. Protect every citizen from unjust or disproportionate environmental impacts.

Recommendations

ENVR01	Establish Open-Market Air Emissions Trading as an Alternative Tool For Reaching Air Quality Goals
ENVR02	Establish Effluent Trading as an Alternative Tool for Achieving Water Quality Standards
ENVR03	Refocus Resource Conservation and Recovery Act on High-Risk Wastes
ENVR04	Refocus Drinking Water Treatment Requirements on Highest Health Risks
ENVR05	Expand Use of Risk Assessment in Local Communities
ENVR06	Provide Flexible Funding Mechanisms for States and Tribes
ENVR07	Develop Competitive Sustainable Development Challenge Grants
ENVR08	Expand Regulatory Negotiation and Consensus-Based Rulemaking
ENVR09	Reduce Paperwork by 25 Percent
ENVR10	Create "One-Stop" Emission Reports
ENVR11	Consolidate Federal Air Rules ("One Industry—One Rule")
ENVR12	Create a Risk-Based Enforcement Plan
ENVR13	Provide Compliance Incentives for Small Businesses and Communities

ENVR14	Establish Small Business Compliance Assistance Centers
ENVR15	Provide Incentives for Auditing, Disclosure, and Correction
ENVR16	Develop Self-Certification Programs to Reduce Reporting Burdens
ENVR17	Expand Public Electronic Access to Information
ENVR18	Establish a Center for Environmental Information and Statistics
ENVR19	Develop a Program to Give Responsible Companies the Flexibility to Develop and Test Alternative Strategies to Promote Compliance Beyond Current Requirements (Project XL)
ENVR20	Develop Alternative Strategies for Sectors to Achieve Cost-Effective Results Through Comprehensive Environmental Management Strategies
ENVR21	Conduct Pilot Projects of Community-Driven Strategies to Integrate Environmental Quality and Economic Development
ENVR22	Work With Other Federal Agencies to Demonstrate Alternative Environmental Management Strategies at Federal Facilities
ENVR23	Test Standards for Compliance Oversight Using Third-Party Audits
ENVR24	Pilot Multimedia "One-Stop" Permitting
ENVR25	Develop Design for Environment Awards for the Chemical Industry

REINVENTING FOOD SAFETY REGULATIONS

Release date: Fall 1995. For plan copies, contact Judy Riggins, (202) 720-7025.

Principles for Regulatory Reform

1. Provide consumers with safe foods and the knowledge to make informed choices in the marketplace.
2. Shift from command-and-control requirements to performance standards.
3. Adopt a common framework and approach to food safety by partnering FDA and the Food Safety and Inspection Service (FSIS) to achieve common goals.
4. Incorporate into FDA and FSIS programs a science-based system of preventive controls for food safety—the Hazard Analysis and Critical Control Points System.
5. Eliminate unnecessary burdens and requirements in food safety regulations.

Recommendations

FOOD01	Implement FSIS Science-Based Performance Standards for Meat and Poultry Plants
FOOD02	Amend FSIS Current Cooking Regulations to Incorporate Performance Standards and Flexibility
FOOD03	Eliminate FSIS's Prior Approval System for Substances Added to Meat and Poultry, for Facility Blueprints and Processing Equipment, and for Most Quality Control Plans
FOOD04	Streamline the Prior Approval System for Meat and Poultry Labels
FOOD05	Review and Revise All Remaining FSIS Prior Approval Regulations
FOOD06	Eliminate Redundant or Unnecessary Rules and Convert the Remaining Rules to Performance Standards Rather Than to Command and Control Standards
FOOD07	Amend Existing Standards to Allow Greater Flexibility and Innovation in Meat and Poultry Marketing

FOOD08	Identify Categories of Standards for Possible Elimination and Seek Comment on Reform or Elimination of the Standards Identity System
FOOD09	Restructure FSIS Meat and Poultry Inspection Regulations to Eliminate Unnecessary or Duplicative Requirements
FOOD10	Implement Performance Standards for Food Handling
FOOD11	Reform the Food Additive Petition Review Process by Establishing Performance Goals
FOOD12	Establish a Streamlined Process for Companies to Notify FDA of Their Independent Determination of Food Additives Generally Regarded as Safe
FOOD13	Promote Innovation and Efficiency by Adopting Alternatives or Eliminating Food Standards of Identity
FOOD14	Harmonize Requirements With International Partners to Facilitate Trade
FOOD15	Develop Pilot Programs to Enhance the Use of Private and State or Local Labs for Analyzing Food Imports
FOOD16	Reduce the Burden on Industry Compliance With Certain Environmental Assessments
FOOD17	Replace the Current System of Medicated Animal Feed Applications With a Licensing System for Facilities With Good Manufacturing Processes
FOOD18	Relax Restrictions on Animal Drug Exports

REINVENTING HEALTH CARE REGULATIONS

Released July 11, 1995. For plan copies, contact Victor Zonana, (202) 690-6343.

Appendix D

Principles for Regulatory Reform

1. Communicate rather than dictate—use consultation to ascertain how to best serve the customer.
2. Educate customers by developing effective educational techniques and disseminating information about how programs operate, rather than inundating them with information that is difficult to understand and that does not relate to their needs.
3. Innovate more than regulate. Rely on innovation in program operation and administration more than on regulation to improve customer service capabilities.

Recommendations

HEAL01	Eliminate the Physician Attestation Form
HEAL02	Reduce Burden and Improve the Clinical Laboratory Improvement Amendments by Rewarding Good Performance, Creating Incentives for Development of More Reliable Testing, Allowing Third-Party Accreditation of Labs, and Using Proficiency Testing to Monitor Lab Performance
HEAL03	Change Current Regulations That Focus Solely on Measuring Processes Requirements to Focus on Outcomes of Care
HEAL04	Require Federal Employee Health Benefit Plan Carriers to Use the HCFA-1500 Form (Currently Used in Medicare) for Claims to Reduce the Number of Forms
HEAL05	Eliminate Redundant Assessments of Mentally Ill and Mentally Retarded Nursing Home Residents
HEAL06	Permit States to Approve Nurse Aide Training and Competency Evaluation Programs Offered in Nursing Homes

Appendix D

REINVENTING WORKER SAFETY AND HEALTH REGULATIONS: THE NEW OSHA

Released May 16, 1995. For plan copies, contact Ann Cyr, (202) 219-8151.

Principles for Regulatory Reform

1. Save lives, prevent workplace injuries and illnesses, and protect the health of all America's workers.
2. Seek and expect implementation of hazard control strategies based upon primary prevention whenever possible.
3. Initiate strategic, public-private partnerships to identify and encourage the spread of industry best practices to solve national problems.
4. Promote employer commitment and meaningful employee participation and involvement in safety and health programs.
5. Make all safety and health services, resources, rules, and information readily accessible and understandable to employees, employers, and OSHA staff.
6. Be a performance-oriented, data-driven organization that seeks results rather than activity and process emphasis. OSHA's programs must be judged on their success at eliminating hazards and reducing injuries and illnesses.

Recommendations

OSHA01 Nationally Expand the "Maine 200" Concept of Partnering With Employers With the Most Workplace Injuries and Illnesses to Develop Effective Safety Programs

OSHA02 Conduct Focused Inspections for Employers With Strong and Effective Safety and Health Programs

OSHA03 Create Incentives for Employers With Safety and Health Programs

OSHA04 Promote Employee Participation in Safety and Health Efforts

OSHA05	Work With Stakeholders to Identify the Leading Causes of Workplace Injury and Illness to Develop a Priority Planning Process
OSHA06	Focus on Key Building Block Rules and Eliminate or Fix Confusing and Out-of-Date Standards
OSHA07	Request the Establishment of a Working Group on Hazard Communication and the Right to Know
OSHA08	Use Alternative Approaches to Address Public Concerns About Ergonomically Related Hazards in the Workplace
OSHA09	Establish Involvement in Industry Sectors With Emerging Safety and Health Needs
OSHA10	Reengineer the Structure and Operation of Field Offices to Better Serve Customers
OSHA11	Strengthen OSHA's Partnership With State Programs
OSHA12	Expand Incentives for Correcting Hazards Quickly
OSHA13	Improve OSHA's Inspection Targeting Systems
OSHA14	Provide Safety and Health Information to the Public Electronically
OSHA15	Develop a Performance Measurement System That Focuses on Results

REINVENTING PENSION REGULATIONS

Released June 11, 1995. For plan copies, contact Scott Dykema, (202) 622-2960.

Principles for Regulatory Reform

1. Simplify both the content and means of interacting with the federal government.
2. Focus on the best interests of pension beneficiaries and outcomes of a pension plan rather than on mechanical rules and processes.

3. Reduce the paperwork burden on employers to send duplicate notices or notices of plan changes that don't affect their employees.
4. Simplify the process for the smallest employers.
5. Provide family businesses with benefits equal to those for other businesses.
6. Simplify and streamline the application process.
7. Expand opportunities for pension coverage for employees of tax-exempt organizations.
8. Ensure that all participants in pension plans get the benefits they have earned.
9. Reduce the paperwork filed for each plan.
10. Exempt defined contribution plans from minimum participation rules.

Recommendations

PENS01	Create a Simple Retirement Savings Plan for Small Employers—the National Employee Savings Trust (NEST)
PENS02	Eliminate the Family Aggregation Rule Requiring Certain Highly Compensated Employees and Their Families to Be Treated as Single Employees
PENS03	Eliminate the Special Restrictions on Plans Maintained by Self-Employed Individuals
PENS04	Simplify Substantial Owner Rules Relating to Plan Terminations
PENS05	Provide Design-Based Nondiscrimination Safe Harbors That Would Give Employers the Option of Avoiding Testing of Contributions
PENS06	Facilitate Testing by Using Prior Year Data Rather than Ongoing Testing or Post-Year-End Corrections
PENS07	Improve Fairness in Correcting Distribution Rules
PENS08	Permit Tax-Exempt Organizations to Maintain 401(k) Pension Plans

PENS09	Standardize Distribution Rules for All 401(k) Pension Plans
PENS10	Eliminate Excessive Testing by Simplifying the Definition of a Highly Compensated Employee
PENS11	Exempt Defined Contribution Plans From the Requirement That at Least 50 Employees, or 40 Percent of All Employees in Smaller Companies, Be Covered
PENS12	Eliminate the Special Vesting Schedule for Multi-Employer Plans
PENS13	Allow Multi-Employer Plans to Return to Triennial, Rather than Annual, Actuarial Evaluations
PENS14	Eliminate Partial Termination Rules for Multi-Employer Plans
PENS15	Eliminate the Combined Plan Limit on Contributions and Benefits (Section 415(e))
PENS16	Exempt Government and Multi-Employer Plans From Certain Benefit and Contribution Limits
PENS17	Allow Tax-Exempt Organizations to Provide Excess Benefit Plans
PENS18	Repeal the 150-Percent Limitation on Deductible Contributions for Multi-Employer Plans
PENS19	Eliminate the Rule Requiring Employer Plans to Begin Minimum Distribution Before Retirement
PENS20	Simplify Taxation of Annuity Distributions
PENS21	Simplify Prohibited Transaction Exemption Procedures
PENS22	Simplify Prohibited Exemption Procedures for Plans With Participant-Directed Accounts (404(c) Plans)
PENS23	Streamline ERISA Annual Report (form 5500 series)
PENS24	Establish Uniform Penalties for Failure to Provide Information Reports

PENS25 Stop Requiring Employers to Provide Advance Notification of Benefit Reductions to Employees Who Are Not Affected by the Reduction

PENS26 Eliminate Mandatory Filing of Summary Plan Descriptions With the Department Of Labor and Authorize DOL to Obtain Descriptions From Plan Administrators

REINVENTING SERVICE REGULATIONS TO SMALL BUSINESSES: THE NEW SMALL BUSINESS ADMINISTRATION

Released June 12, 1995. For plan copies, contact Ron Matzner, (202) 205-6642.

Principles for Regulatory Reform

1. Promote better access to capital for small business owners.
2. Provide valuable small business education and training services.
3. Use government resources efficiently and cost-effectively.
4. Work closely with the private sector to support and assist the small business community.
5. Reduce paperwork burdens on small businesses and streamline regulations as much as possible.
6. Serve as an advocate for regulatory reform so that regulations clearly state the rights and responsibilities of small business owners and the federal government.
7. Work to ensure that affected small businesses are included at every important step in the regulatory development process.
8. Improve communications between the federal government and affected small businesses to ensure that regulations are understood and followed.

9. Promote voluntary small business compliance with regulations through flexible enforcement procedures.
10. Ensure access to government business, economic, and regulatory information by using state-of-the-art information technologies.

Recommendations and Accomplishments

SmBus01	Introduced a One-Page SBA Application and Rapid-Response, Low-Documentation Loan Program
SmBus02	Implemented a Pilot Program to Allow Selected Lenders to Use Their Own Forms, Documentation, and Procedures for Certain Loan Types (FA$TRAK Program)
SmBus03	Repealed the Opinion-Molder Rule Barring Loan Assistance to Media-Related Small Business Concerns
SmBus04	Streamlined the 504 Loan Process From Authorization to Closing, Establishing the Accredited Lenders Program and Premier Certified Lender Program
SmBus05	Implemented a Pilot Program to Increase the Number of Loans Made to Women Business Owners by Helping Them Prequalify for SBA Loan Guarantees
SmBus06	Instituted a Pilot Program to Help Small Businesses Obtain Financing for Export Purposes by Streamlining Procedures and Offering a Higher Guarantee Percentage
SmBus07	Revised Small Business Investment Company Regulations; Strengthened Oversight, Screening, and Credit Review; and Created a Class of Larger, Better Capitalized Small Business Investment Companies
SmBus08	Nationally Implemented an Enhanced Revolving Line of Credit Program for Small Businesses (CAPlines)

SmBus09	Permitted SBA Lenders and Development Companies to Use Computer-Generated Copies of SBA Forms
SmBus10	Increased Customer Access to SBA Loan Programs While Reducing the Cost to Taxpayers
SmBus11	Developed, in Cooperation With Other Agencies, a "One-Stop" Electronic Center for Small Businesses to Access Business, Economic, and Regulatory Information
SmBus12	Expanded the Business Information Centers to Provide Better Access for Small Businesses to State-of-the-Art Technologies and Information Sources
SmBus13	Streamlined Cosponsorship Program Operations and Reduced the Paperwork Burden for SBA's Private Sector Partners
SmBus14	Pursued Legislation to Streamline Administration of the Small Business Development Centers, to Reduce Costs and to Consolidate Training Programs
SmBus15	Clarified and Streamlined SBA Regulations to Revise or Eliminate Any Duplicate, Outdated, Inconsistent, or Confusing Provisions
SmBus16	Use Discretionary Enforcement Authority to Modify or Waive Penalties in Specific Instances
SmBus17	Reduce the Paperwork Burden on Small Businesses
SmBus18	Simplified the Disaster Loan Assistance Program by Reducing Filing Requirements

APPENDIX E

Summary of Savings to Date

THE NATIONAL PERFORMANCE Review's (NPR's) September 7, 1993, report estimated that approximately $108 billion would be saved over the five-year period FY 1995 through FY 1999 if its recommendations all were implemented. As of September 1, 1995, about $57.7 billion of these projected savings have been achieved, either through administrative actions or enactment by Congress. An additional $4.3 billion in savings are currently pending before Congress, awaiting approval. The remaining $46 billion in savings will be acted upon in the near future. Also, agency reinvention actions undertaken beyond those recommendations made in the original report will realize more than $10 billion in additional savings.

Recommendations from NPR's second phase, begun in December 1994, will yield additional savings of $69.6 billion.[1] The recommendations behind these savings are detailed in appendix C and are for the five-year period from FY 1996 through FY 2000. The President's June 1995 balanced budget proposal incorporates these projected savings.

Table E-1 compares NPR's September 1993 savings estimates to the savings that have accrued to date as a result of changes made and those that will occur in the future if these changes remain in place. It also identifies those savings that may occur in the near future as a result of legislative actions now well under way. Following is a brief explanation of these savings estimates and how they were derived.

STREAMLINING THE BUREAUCRACY THROUGH REENGINEERING

Agencies are making substantial progress in meeting the statutorily required reduction of civilian personnel by 272,900 by the end of

FY 1999. By law, agencies are to have reduced their staffing by 111,900 full-time equivalents (FTEs) by the end of September 1995. Our preliminary estimate is that job reductions total at least 160,000. As a result, savings for FY 1995 are projected to be $4.4 billion. Total five-year savings are estimated at $40.4 billion by the end of FY 1999.

Savings were derived by multiplying the total number of reductions by the average cost to the government for a federal employee for the year(s) following departure from federal service.[2] The reduction in the total number of federal employees is based on the Administration's baseline of 2,155,200 FTEs as of January 20, 1993.[3] The Administration estimates the FY 1995 average cost to the government of each federal employee $43,258.[4]

REINVENTING FEDERAL PROCUREMENT

The Federal Acquisition Streamlining Act of 1994 (P.L. 103-355), signed into law in October 1994, incorporates many of NPR's recommendations. The Congressional Budget Office did not estimate savings resulting from this legislation, but the Administration estimated a five-year savings of $12.3 billion. Additional legislation is now pending before Congress that could increase these savings, although the original savings estimate made in 1993 may not be achievable. The 1993 estimates were based on $200 billion in procurement spending over five years: actual procurement spending has declined from this figure. Consequently, savings from administrative efficiencies will be lower, in part because overall buying is lower.

Congress is considering additional procurement reforms that will further streamline the process. Additional savings are possible but cannot be estimated at this time.

REENGINEERING THROUGH INFORMATION TECHNOLOGY

NPR's 1993 estimated savings included decreases in federal employment due to an increased use of information technology. Because these savings are not easily separable from total savings related to overall agency streamlining, they are reflected above in item 1, "Streamlining the Bureaucracy Through Reengineering." Besides these FTE savings, the additional savings due to information technology include those from the implementation of electronic benefits transfer. The Federal Electronic Benefits Task Force estimates savings of $1.2 billion. Other information technology-related savings include the closure of several large government data processing centers. An additional $4.3 billion in estimated savings are pending in legislation before Congress.

REDUCING INTERGOVERNMENTAL ADMINISTRATIVE COSTS

NPR originally recommended modifying the Office of Management and Budget (OMB) Circular A-87, "Cost Principles for State, Local, and Indian Tribal Governments," to provide a fixed fee-for-service option in lieu of costly reimbursement procedures used to calculate the actual administrative costs of disbursing grants. It was originally estimated that half of the states and localities would adopt this approach, and that savings of up to $700 million a year could be realized. OMB revised Circular A-87 on April 19, 1995, to allow this approach. It is unclear, however, whether the projected cost savings will be realized. Estimates will be recalculated in the future based on actual experiences with this approach.

CHANGES IN INDIVIDUAL AGENCIES

Last year, President Clinton signed 34 laws affecting agency actions. Many of these included savings, such as the Department of Agriculture's reorganization bill; the Customs Modernization Act; and the appropriations bills for the Departments of Labor, Commerce, Justice, and Transportation.

Additional savings related to reinvention are being achieved by agencies beyond those savings claimed in NPR's original report. For example, the Federal Communications Commission began auctioning wireless licenses and has raised $8.9 billion so far, and the General Services Administration's time out and review of federal construction projects has resulted in savings of $1.2 billion. These savings, while included in the President's balanced budget proposal, are *not* included in the following table, which only includes savings specifically recommended in the original report.

NOTES

1. Savings are calculated using the current services baseline approach. They include mandatory as well as discretionary savings and revenue increases. For Treasury, savings include $1 billion in revenues resulting from debt collection reform.

2. This methodology does not account for severance pay, increases in annuity expenses, or the point in the year at which a person leaves federal service (obviously, savings are greater if a person leaves earlier rather than later in a year). That is why savings are not claimed until the following year. Note that the average employee cost may be lower than the actual salaries of departing personnel, since many of the people leaving are older and more highly paid than the average employee.

3. See Executive Office of the President, "Analytical Perspectives," *Budget of the U.S. Government, FY 1996* (Washington, D.C.: U.S. Government Printing Office), p. 180.

4. The Congressional Budget Office uses a different methodology to calculate employee compensation; its estimate of average employee cost is lower.

Table E-1. 1993 Estimates of Savings From NPR Recommendations Compared With Savings Estimates From Actions to Date (in billions of dollars)

	FY95	FY96	FY97	FY98	FY99	Total
1. Streamlining the Bureaucracy Through Reengineering						
Savings estimated in September 1993 report	5.0	5.8	7.4	9.5	12.7	40.4
Savings based on actions to date	5.3	7.1	7.9	9.0	11.1	40.4
2. Reinventing Federal Procurement						
Savings estimated in September 1993 report	0	5.6	5.6	5.6	5.7	22.5
Savings based on actions to date	0.7	2.8	2.8	2.9	3.1	12.3
Savings pending in legislation	0	CBE	CBE	CBE	CBE	CBE
3. Reengineering Through Information Technology						
Savings estimated in September 1993 report	0.1	0.5	1.2	1.6	2.0	5.4
Savings based on actions to date	0	0	0	0.6	1.7	2.3
Savings pending in legislation	0	0.4	0.9	1.4	1.6	4.3
4. Reducing Intergovernmental Administrative Costs						
Savings estimated in September 1993 report	0.5	0.7	0.7	0.7	0.7	3.3
Savings based on actions to date	0	CBE	CBE	CBE	CBE	CBE

5. Changes in Individual Agencies						
Savings estimated in September 1993 report	7.0*	6.2	7.0	7.3	8.9	36.4
Savings based on actions to date**	2.8*	CBE	CBE	CBE	CBE	2.8
Savings pending in legislation**	0	CBE	CBE	CBE	CBE	CBE
Total Savings for NPR Phase I						
Savings estimated in September 1993 report	12.6*	18.8	21.9	24.7	30.0	108.0
Savings based on actions to date	9.7*	8.9	10.7	12.5	15.9	57.7
Savings pending in legislation	0	0.4	0.9	1.4	1.6	4.3

CBE = Cannot be estimated at this time; estimates may be developed later.

*Figures include some FY 1994 savings.

**Outyear savings for each proposal have not been estimated at this time; however, based on both actual savings to date and anticipated implementation of additional proposals, projected savings for FY 1996 through FY 1999 are expected to be in the billions of dollars. This estimate does not consider all the impacts of subsequent changes in program levels including further reinvention activities and future congressional action.

APPENDIX F

Presidential and Congressional Actions Taken

PRESIDENTIAL DIRECTIVES

Eight presidential directives have been issued since September 1994 to implement National Performance Review (NPR) recommendations. This brings the total number of NPR-related presidential directives to 30.

Continued Commitment to Small, Small Disadvantaged, and Small Women-Owned Businesses in Federal Procurement, Presidential Memorandum, October 13, 1994

Reaffirms the federal government's policy that a fair proportion of its contracts be placed with small, small disadvantaged, and small women-owned businesses. This is in accord with the Federal Streamlining Act of 1994 which authorizes civilian agencies to use set-aside procurement for small disadvantaged businesses and—for the first time—establishes goals for contracting with small women-owned businesses. (Implements recommendation PROC07: Enhance Programs for Small Business and Small Disadvantaged Business Concerns.)

Federal Procurement Reform, Executive Order 12931, October 13, 1994

Repeals Executive Order 12352. Improves procurement effectiveness to support mission accomplishments so that, in procuring supplies and services, agency heads may reform rules and programs, improve results, and promote value over cost when selecting sources for supplies and services. Simplified acquisition procedures are implemented by expanding the use of the government purchase card and encouraging agencies to take advantage of the micropurchase authority in the new law. (Implements recommendation PROC12: Allow for Expanded Choice and Cooperation in the Use of Supply Schedules.)

Expansion of Federal Executive Boards, Executive Order 12862, December 8, 1994

Expands the leadership roles of Federal Executive Boards and Federal Executive Associations to create a government that better serves the American public. The creation of interagency forums will provide customers with the best delivery of services and overall satisfaction, cut red tape by coordinating service delivery and reporting requirements, and show citizens that federal agencies can provide services "equal to the best in business." (Implements recommendation ICS01: Create Customer-Driven Programs in All Departments and Agencies That Provide Services Directly to the Public.)

Governmentwide Reform of Regulatory System, Further Reform of Executive Order 12866, February 21, 1995

Overhauls the nation's regulatory system by June by cutting obsolete recommendations; rewarding results, not red tape; getting out of Washington and creating grassroots partnerships; and negotiating instead of dictating. (Implements recommendations REG01: Create an Interagency Regulatory Coordination Group and FSL02: Reduce Red Tape Through Regulatory and Mandate Relief.)

Improving Customer Service, Presidential Memorandum, March 22, 1995

Continues the commitment of Executive Order 12862 to improving customer service activities including benchmarking and surveying of customers and employees. The establishment and implementation of customer service standards will continue to guide the executive branch's operations. Agencies will complete the publication of their own customer service standards for public perusal by September 1, 1995. Annual reports to customers on agency progress in achieving customer service standards will be made starting no later than September 15, 1995. The development of customer service measures and standards will be integrated with other performance initiatives and related to appropriate legislative activities. In addition, agencies shall continue to communicate with their employees on ways to improve customer service and should initiate and support actions cutting across agency lines that attempt to serve shared customer groups. These improvements in customer service also apply to the independent agencies. (Implements recommendation ICS01: Create Customer-Driven Programs in All Departments and Agencies That Provide Services Directly to the Public.)

Democracy Funding Programs, Presidential Letter, May 11, 1995

Transmission by the President of a report on the democracy programs funded by the U.S. government, which—in accordance with NPR recommendations—calls on agencies to continue to seek ways in which to streamline these programs. (Helps implement AID01: Redefine and Focus AID's Mission and Priorities.)

Supporting the Role of Fathers in Families, Presidential Memorandum, June 16, 1995

Supports men in their role as fathers. Agencies are required to review all programs, policies, and initiatives that apply to families to ensure that they include fathers—especially if only mothers were previously considered. Evidence of fathers' involvement will be incorporated in measuring the success of these programs. This information will be used in accord with information gathered from the Vice President's "father-to-father" initiative and other father involvement programs. (Implements recommendation HHS01: Promote Effective, Integrated Service Delivery for Customers by Increasing Collaborative Efforts.)

Career Transition Assistance for Federal Employees, Presidential Memorandum, pending.

Requires agencies to establish programs to provide career transition assistance to all of their surplus and displaced employees. Programs shall be developed in partnership with labor and management and shall include (1) collaborating with state, local, and other federal employers, as appropriate, to make career transition services available; (2) establishing policies for retraining displaced employees for new career opportunities, either with government or in the private sector; (3) selecting well-qualified surplus or displaced internal agency employees who apply for vacant positions before selecting other candidates; and (4) selecting well-qualified displaced employees from other agencies who apply for vacant positions before selecting other candidates from outside the agency. The Director of the Office of Personnel Management will work with agency personnel directors to prescribe criteria for and monitor the effectiveness of agency programs. (Further implements recommendation HRM14: Provide Incentives to Encourage Voluntary Separations.)

PUBLIC LAWS

As of September 1, 1995, two bills containing NPR-recommended actions have been passed by the 104th Congress and signed into law by the President. This brings the total number of signed bills containing NPR-related recommendations to 36. Listed below are the two new public laws and the relevant NPR recommendations enacted by the new Congress.

Public Law 104-4, Unfunded Mandate Reform Act of 1995

FSL02	Reduce Red Tape Through Regulatory and Mandate Relief

Public Law 104-19, FY 1995 Rescissions/Disaster Assistance

ED02	Reduce the Number of Programs the Department of Education Administers
DVA03	Eliminate Legislative Budget Constraints to Promote Management Effectiveness

PENDING LEGISLATION

As of September 1, 1995, about 70 bills with NPR-related items have been introduced in the 104th Congress. Although the Administration supports the NPR-related items in these bills, some include other provisions that are objectionable. The Administration will work with Congress to satisfactorily address these objectionable provisions.

Systems Recommendations Requiring Legislation

Streamlining Management Control (SMC)

SMC06	Reduce the Burden of Congressionally Mandated Reports *S. 790,* Federal Reports Elimination and Sunset Act of 1995

Mission-Driven, Results-Oriented Budgeting (BGT)

BGT05.02	Permit Agencies to Roll Over 50 Percent of Their Unobligated Year-End Balances in Annual Operating Costs to the Next Year

	H.R. 29, Unobligated Fund Uses
	H.R. 2020, Treasury, Postal Service, and General Government Appropriations Act for FY 96
BGT07	Institute Biennial Budgets and Appropriations
	H.R. 252, Legislative Reorganization Act of 1995
	H.R. 766, Biennial Budgeting Act of 1995
BGT08	Seek Enactment of Expedited Rescission Procedures
	H.R. 2, Line-Item Veto Act
	H.R. 128, Legislative Line-Item Veto Act of 1995
	S. 14, Legislative Line-Item Veto Act

Improving Financial Management (FM)

FM09	Simplify the Financial Reporting Process
	S. 790, Federal Reports Elimination and Sunset Act of 1995
FM11	Strengthen Debt Collection Programs
	H.R. 2234, Debt Collection Improvement Act of 1995

Reinventing Federal Procurement (PROC)

PROC06	Amend Protest Rules
	H.R. 1388, Federal Acquisition Improvement Act of 1995
	H.R. 1670, Federal Acquisition Reform Act of 1995
	S. 669, Federal Acquisition Improvement Act of 1995
	S. 946, Information Technology Management Reform Act of 1995
PROC07	Enhance Programs for Small Business and Small Disadvantaged Business Concerns
	H.R. 1388, Federal Acquisition Improvement Act of 1995
	H.R. 1670, Federal Acquisition Reform Act of 1995
	S. 669, Federal Acquisition Improvement Act of 1995

PROC11 Improve Procurement Ethics Laws
H.R. 1038, Federal Acquisition Reform Act of 1995
H.R. 1388, Federal Acquisition Improvement Act of 1995
H.R. 1670, Federal Acquisition Reform Act of 1995
S. 669, Federal Acquisition Improvement Act of 1995

PROC17 Authorize a Two-Phase Competitive Source Selection Process
H.R. 1388, Federal Acquisition Improvement Act of 1995
H.R. 1670, Federal Acquisition Reform Act of 1995
S. 669, Federal Acquisition Improvement Act of 1995

Reinventing Support Services (SUP)

SUP01 Authorize the Executive Branch to Establish a Printing Policy That Will Eliminate the Current Printing Monopoly
H.R. 1024, Improve the Dissemination of Information and Printing Procedures of the Government
H. Res. 24, Government Printing Office

SUP02 Assure Public Access to Federal Information
H.R. 1854, Legislative Branch Appropriations Act for FY 96

SUP08 Give Customers Choices and Create Real Property Enterprises That Promote Sound Real Property Asset Management
S. 1005, Public Buildings Reform Act of 1995

Reengineering Through Information Technology (IT)

IT01 Provide Clear, Strong Leadership to Integrate Information Technology Into the Business of Government
S. 946, Information Technology Management Reform Act of 1995

IT09	Establish an Information Infrastructure *H.R. 1530,* National Defense Authorization Act for FY 1996
IT10	Develop Systems and Mechanisms to Ensure Privacy and Security *H.R. 184,* Individual Privacy Protection Act of 1995

Strengthening the Partnership in Intergovernmental Service Delivery (FSL)

FSL01	Improve the Delivery of Federal Domestic Grant Programs *H.R. 2086,* Local Empowerment and Flexibility Act of 1995 *S. 88,* Local Empowerment and Flexibility Act of 1995
FSL02	Reduce Red Tape Through Regulatory and Mandate Relief *H.R. 994,* Regulatory Sunset and Review Act of 1995

Reinventing Environmental Management (ENV)

ENV02	Develop Cross-Agency Ecosystem Planning and Management *S. 93,* Ecosystem Management Act of 1995
ENV03	Increase Energy and Water Efficiency *H.R. 1905,* Energy and Water Development Appropriations Act for FY 96

Agency Recommendations Requiring Legislation

Department of Agriculture (USDA)

USDA02	Eliminate Federal Support for Honey *H.R. 1235,* Terminate Price Supports for Honey

Department of Commerce (DOC)

DOC2-01 Create a Corporate Structure for the Patent and Trademark Office
H.R. 1659, Patent and Trademark Office Corporation Act of 1995

DOC2-06 Accelerate Closure of Weather Service Offices
H.R. 1815, NOAA Authorization Act of 1995

DOC06 Improve Marine Fisheries Management
H.R. 39, Fishery Conservation and Management Amendments of 1995
S. 39, Sustainable Fisheries Act

Department of Defense (DOD)

DOD09 Maximize the Efficiency of DOD Health Care Operations
S. 42, Uniformed Services University of the Health Sciences Termination and Deficit Reduction Act of 1995

Department of Energy (DOE)

DOE2-02 Privatize the Naval Petroleum Reserves
H.R. 1530, National Defense Authorization Act for FY 1996
S. 1026, National Defense Authorization Act for FY 1996

DOE04 Increase Electrical Power Reserves and Study Rates
H.R. 1801, Federal Power Asset Privatization Act of 1995
H.R. 1905, Energy and Water Development Appropriations Act for FY 96

DOE06 Redirect Energy Laboratories to Post-Cold War Priorities
H.R. 1905, Energy and Water Development Appropriations Act for FY 96

	H.R. 2142, Department of Energy Laboratory Missions Act
DOE08	Support the Sale of the Alaska Power Administration
	H.R. 310, Federal Power Administration Privatization Act of 1995
	H.R. 1122, Alaska Power Administration Sale Act of 1995
	H.R. 1801, Federal Power Asset Privatization Act of 1995
	S. 395, Alaska Power Administration Sale Act of 1995

Environmental Protection Agency (EPA)

EPA04	Promote the Use of Economic and Market-Based Approaches to Reduce Water Pollution
	H.R. 961, Clean Water Amendments of 1995

Federal Emergency Management Agency (FEMA)

FEMA03	Create Results-Oriented Incentives to Reduce the Costs of a Disaster
	H.R. 1731, Earthquake, Volcanic Eruption and Hurricane Hazard Insurance Act
	H.R. 1856, Natural Disaster Protection Act of 1995
	S. 1043, Natural Disaster Protection and Insurance Act of 1995

Department of Health and Human Services (HHS)

HHS2-02	Create Performance Partnerships
	S. 1044, Health Centers Consolidation Act of 1995
	S. 1180, SAMHSA Reauthorization, Flexibility Enhancement, and Consolidation Act of 1995
	H.R. 2206, Health Centers Consolidation Act
	H.R. 2207, Substance Abuse and Mental Health Performance Partnership Act of 1995

HHS2-05 Improve Coordination of Programs for Older Americans
H.R. 2056, Older Americans Act of 1995

HHS09 Take More Aggressive Action to Collect Outstanding Debts Owed to the Social Security Trust Fund
H.R. 2234, Debt Collection Improvement Act of 1995

Department of Housing and Urban Development (HUD)

HUD01 Reinvent Public Housing
H.R. 2099, VA, HUD and Independent Agencies Appropriations Act for FY 96

HUD04 Create an Assisted-Housing/Rent Subsidy Demonstration Project
H.R. 2099, VA, HUD and Independent Agencies Appropriations Act for FY 96

Department of the Interior (DOI)

DOI01 Establish a Hard Rock Mine Reclamation Fund to Restore the Environment
H.R. 357, Mineral Exploration and Development Act of 1995

DOI04 Promote Entrepreneurial Management of the National Park Service
H.R. 773, National Park Service Concessions Policy and Reform Act of 1995
H.R. 1580, Mining Law Reform Act of 1995
H.R. 2028, Federal Land Management Agency Concessions Reform Act of 1995
H.R. 2107, National Park Service Fee Management Act of 1995

	S. 309, National Park Service Concessions Policy and Reform Act of 1995
	S. 506, Mining Law Reform Act of 1995
DOI13	Improve the Federal Helium Program
	H.R. 846, Helium Act of 1995
	S. 45, Helium Reform and Deficit Reduction Act of 1995
	S. 898, Helium Disposal Act of 1995

Department of Justice (DOJ)

DOJ13	Adjust Civil Monetary Penalties to the Inflation Index
	H.R. 2234, Debt Collection Improvement Act of 1995

Department of Labor (DOL)

DOL08	Create One-Stop Centers for Career Management
	H.R. 1617, Consolidated and Reformed Education, Employment, and Rehabilitation Systems Act of 1995
	S. 143, Workforce Development Act of 1995
DOL11	Open the Civilian Conservation Centers to Private and Public Competition
	H.R. 2127, Department of Labor, HHS, and Education Appropriations Act for FY 96

Small Business Administration (SBA)

SBA01	Allow Judicial Review of the Regulatory Flexibility Act
	H.R. 9, Job Creation and Wage Enhancement Act of 1995
	H.R. 926, Regulatory Reform and Relief Act
	H.R. 937, Judicial Review of Regulatory Flexibility Requirements

	S. 343, Comprehensive Regulatory Reform Act of 1995
SBA06	Establish User Fees for Small Business Development Center Services
	H.R. 2076, Department of Commerce and Related Agencies Appropriations Act for FY 96

Department of Transportation (DOT)

DOT2-03	Streamline DOT's Organizational Structure
	H.R. 1440, Department of Transportation Reorganization Act of 1995
DOT2-04	Capitalize a New Network of State Infrastructure Banks
	S. 775, National Highway System Designation Act of 1995
DOT04	Establish a Corporation to Provide Air Traffic Control Services
	H.R. 589, Independent Federal Aviation Administration Act
	H.R. 1441, U.S. Air Traffic Service Corporation Act of 1995
DOT11	Improve Intermodal Transportation Policy Coordination and Management
	H.R. 1440, Department of Transportation Reorganization Act of 1995
	H.R. 2002, Department of Transportation Appropriations Act for FY 96
DOT17	Eliminate Funding for Highway Demonstration Projects
	S. 775, National Highway System Designation Act of 1995

Department of the Treasury (TRE)

TRE14	Adjust Civil Monetary Penalties to the Inflation Index

H.R. 2234, Debt Collection Improvement Act of 1995

U.S. Agency for International Development (AID)

AID02 Reduce Funding, Spending, and Reporting Micromanagement
S. 790, Federal Reports Elimination and Sunset Act of 1995

Department of Veterans Affairs (DVA)

DVA06 Enhance VA Cost Recovery Capabilities
H.R. 2234, Debt Collection Improvement Act of 1995

Additional Resources

The following National Performance Review (NPR) resources and reports are available in hard copy from the Government Printing Office (202-512-1800) or National Technical Information Service (703-487-4650). Materials can also be accessed electronically; see below for further ordering and access information.

VIDEO

"Reinventing Government . . . By the People"	S/N 040-000-00649-4

REPORTS

Creating a Government That Works Better & Costs Less: Report of the National Performance Review	S/N 040-000-00592-7
Creating a Government That Works Better & Costs Less: Executive Summary	S/N 040-000-00591-9
Creating a Government That Works Better & Costs Less: Status Report, September 1994	S/N 040-000-00646-0
Putting Customers First: Standards for Serving the American People	S/N 040-000-00647-0

Changing Internal Culture

Creating Quality Leadership and Management	S/N 040-000-00624-9
Streamlining Management Control	S/N 040-000-00623-1
Transforming Organizational Structures	S/N 040-000-00630-3
Improving Customer Service	S/N 040-000-00618-4

Reinventing Processes and Systems

Mission-Driven, Results-Oriented Budgeting	S/N 040-000-00619-2
Improving Financial Management	S/N 040-000-00619-2
Reinventing Human Resource Management	S/N 040-000-00630-3
Reinventing Support Services	S/N 040-000-00628-1
Reinventing Federal Procurement	S/N 040-000-00616-8
Reengineering Through Information Technology	S/N 040-000-00626-5
Rethinking Program Design	S/N 040-000-00629-0

Restructuring the Federal Role

Strengthening the Partnership in Intergovernmental Service Delivery	S/N 040-000-00621-4
Reinventing Environmental Management	S/N 040-000-00615-0
Improving Regulatory Systems	S/N 040-000-00620-6

Agencies and Departments

Agency for International Development	S/N 040-000-00593-5
Department of Agriculture	S/N 040-000-00594-3
Department of Commerce	S/N 040-000-00595-1
Department of Defense	S/N 040-000-00596-0
Department of Education	S/N 040-000-00597-8
Department of Energy	S/N 040-000-00598-6
Department of Housing and Urban Development	S/N 040-000-00609-5
Department of the Interior	S/N 040-000-00600-1
Department of Labor	S/N 040-000-00601-0
Department of State/U.S. Information Agency	S/N 040-000-00602-8
Department of Veterans Affairs	S/N 040-000-00614-1
Environmental Protection Agency	S/N 040-000-00605-2
Federal Emergency Management Agency	S/N 040-000-00697-9
General Services Administration	S/N 040-000-00617-6
Intelligence Community	S/N 040-000-00610-9

National Aeronautics and Space Administration	S/N 040-000-00611-7
National Science Foundation/Office of Science and Technology Policy	S/N 040-000-00612-5
Office of Personnel Management	S/N 040-000-00625-7
Small Business Administration	S/N 040-000-00613-3

CD–ROM

Creating a Government That Works Better & Costs Less, Status Report, September 1994.

Order the CD-ROM from NTIS, the National Technical Information Service at the Department of Commerce. The order number is PB94-502242. Call NTIS at (703) 487-4650 for first class mailing, (800) 553-6847 for overnight delivery, (703) 321-8547 for fax orders, and (703) 487-4639 for TTD (hearing impaired).

NPR ON-LINE LIBRARY

NPR's extensive, 800-document library can be accessed through **NetResults** by e-mail, gopher, or the World Wide Web (WWW). The library contains a wide range of information.

E-mail:	netresults@npr.gsa.gov
Gopher:	gopher:\\ace.esusda.gov then select Americans Communicating Electronically/National Performance Review Information
WWW:	http://www.npr.gov; to access reinvention documents, click on Go to Toolkit Main Menu

ORDERING INFORMATION

E-mail:	For an NPR catalog, send an e-mail to **almanac@ace.esusda.gov** with **send npr catalog** as the message text
Fax:	(202) 512-2250
Phone:	(202) 512-1800
Mail:	Superintendent of Documents, P.O. Box 371954, Pittsburgh, PA 15250-7954

ABOUT THE AUTHOR

VICE PRESIDENT AL GORE was a journalist for seven years before winning a seat in the House of Representatives in 1976. In 1984 he was elected to the Senate, and in 1992 he was chosen as Bill Clinton's running mate. The author of the bestselling *Earth in the Balance: Ecology and the Human Spirit,* the Vice President lives in Washington, D.C., and Carthage, Tennessee, with his wife, Tipper, and their four children.